CENTRALITY PRACTICED

Society of Biblical Literature

Archaeology and Biblical Studies

Andrew G. Vaughn, Editor

Number 16

CENTRALITY PRACTICED
Jerusalem in the Religious Practice of Yehud
and the Diaspora in the Persian Period

CENTRALITY PRACTICED
Jerusalem in the Religious Practice of Yehud
and the Diaspora in the Persian Period

Melody D. Knowles

Society of Biblical Literature
Atlanta

CENTRALITY PRACTICED
Jerusalem in the Religious Practice of Yehud and the Diaspora in the Persian Period

Library of Congress Cataloging-in-Publication Data

Knowles, Melody D.
  Centrality practiced : Jerusalem in the religious practice of Yehud and the diaspora during the Persian period / by Melody D. Knowles.
    p. cm. — (Archaeology and biblical studies ; no. 16)
  Includes bibliographical references and index.
  ISBN-13: 978-1-58983-175-9 (paper binding : alk. paper)
  ISBN-10: 1-58983-175-6 (paper binding : alk. paper)
  1. Temple of Jerusalem (Jerusalem)—History. 2. Jerusalem—History—To 1500. 3. Judaism—Liturgy—History—To 1500. 4. Judaism—History—Post-exilic period, 586 B.C.-210 A.D. 5. Worship in the Bible. 6. Bible. O.T.—Criticism, interpretation, etc. 7. Yehud (Persian province)—Antiquities. 8. Excavations (Archaeology)—Yehud (Persian province) I. Title. II. Series.
  BM655.K63 2005
  221.9'5—dc22

2005012573

Printed in the United States of America on acid-free, recycled paper conforming to ANSI/NISO Z39.48-1992 (R1997) and ISO 9706:1994 standards for paper permanence.

Contents

ACKNOWLEDGMENTS

This monograph is an extensively revised version of my doctoral dissertation submitted to Princeton Theological Seminary in 2001 with the title "The Centrality of the Jerusalem Temple in the Religious Practice of Yehud in the Persian Period." Since that time, many significant articles and books have been published in this area, and I have used the intervening years to incorporate some of these and reflect further upon the topic. I owe special thanks to my advisors, Choon-Leong Seow, Patrick D. Miller, Jr., Katharine Doob Sakenfeld, and Chip Dobbs-Allsopp, who taught and guided me as I began to think through this area. I would also like to thank Andrew Vaughn for accepting this work in the Archaeology and Biblical Studies series. My task of revising was aided by the helpful comments of Oded Lipschits, Edward F. Campbell, Jr., Jeffrey Zorn, Erin Kuhn, Theodore Hiebert, Esther Menn, and Timothy J. Sandoval. My research and writing was assisted by the able skills of Anette Ejsing, Meira Kensky, Karen Fitz LaBarge, Peggy Blomenberg, Jackie Pogue, and Terra Winston. Finally, and most dearly, my deep thanks goes to John A. Knight for taking time away from his own research in philosophy of religion to read and discuss my work about some of the ancient practices of religion.

Since I began teaching in 1999, I have benefited from sabbatical leave and I am grateful to President Cynthia McCall Campbell and the Trustees of McCormick Theological Seminary for the opportunity to pursue focused research outside of the classroom. In addition, support for the research in chapter 2 was given by a summer research grant from the Wabash Center for Teaching and Learning in Theology and Religion, and the generosity of the Center is gratefully acknowledged.

An earlier version of the section on pilgrimage in Ezra in chapter four was published as "Pilgrimage Imagery in the Returns in Ezra," *JBL* 123 (2004): 57–74 (used with permission).

Although it is a small gift, I dedicate this book (along with the dissertation that preceded it) to my parents, Majors John E. V. Knowles and Gertrude Schultz Knowles, whom to honor is a joy.

Melody D. Knowles
McCormick Theological Seminary, Chicago

CHAPTER 1

CENTRALITY AND RELIGIOUS PRACTICE

Although some strands of the biblical text insist that YHWH is not confined to any specific temple or region, most link YHWH and the worship of YHWH to geographic locales. Once David transferred the ark to Jerusalem, it is that city that is most often associated with YHWH's presence, seen in texts such as Ps 99:2, "YHWH-in-Zion is great!" (יהוה בציון גדול).[1] After the division of the kingdom, southern kings such as Hezekiah and Josiah emphasized the continuance of YHWH's association with Jerusalem, although there is evidence for popular worship by Judeans outside of the city (largely condemned by the biblical authors).[2]

When the Babylonians destroyed the temple, they also tampered with YHWH's link to Jerusalem, and the biblical texts reveal a variety of theological strategies generated to deal with the new situation. Deuteronomic texts emphasize that the temple houses the divine name of YHWH; God's own dwelling place was

---

1. This expression is pointed out by Michael L. Barré, *The God-List in the Treaty Between Hannibal and Philip V of Macedonia: A Study in Light of the Ancient Near Eastern Treaty Tradition* (The Johns Hopkins Near Eastern Studies; Baltimore and London: The Johns Hopkins University Press, 1983), 186 n. 473. The same construction appears in Ps 65:2: אלהים בציון, "O God-in-Zion." See also P. Kyle McCarter, Jr., "Aspects of the Religion of the Israelite Monarchy: Biblical and Epigraphic Data," in *Ancient Israelite Religion: Essays in Honor of Frank Moore Cross* (ed. Patrick D. Miller, Jr., Paul D. Hanson, and S. Dean McBride; Philadelphia: Fortress, 1987), 137–55, esp. 140–41. For the traditional history of the development of ancient Israelite worship from multiple sanctuaries to one central place, see Julius Wellhausen, *Prolegomena to the History of Israel* (New York: Meridian Books, 1957), 17–51.

2. Susan Ackerman, *Under Every Green Tree: Popular Religion in Sixth-Century Judah* (HSM 46; Atlanta: Scholars Press, 1992). Earlier evidence for extra-Jerusalem worship include the phrase "YHWH-in-Hebron" (יהוה בחברון) in 2 Sam 15:7 (McCarter, "Aspects of the Religion of the Israelite Monarchy," 140–41, and his commentary, *II Samuel* [AB 9; Garden City, N.Y.: Doubleday, 1984], 356, notes on vv. 7–8), and the eighth-century inscriptions found at Kuntillet 'Ajrud that read "YHWH of Samaria" ("YHWH šmrn") and "YHWH of Teman" ("YHWH t[y]mn"; Zeev Meshel, *Kuntillet 'Ajrud: A Religious Centre from the Time of the Judaean Monarchy on the Border of Sinai* (Israel Museum Catalogue 175; Jerusalem: Israel Museum, 1978).

Locating the divine in a specific geography was not unique to Israel, of course, and texts that link a divine name to a geographic place in a genitival relationship are found throughout the ancient Near East. For example, "Hadad of Sikan" ("הדד סכן" found in an archaic Aramaic inscription from

in heaven and thus impervious to desecration by foreign powers (1 Kgs 8:30).[3] In the book of Ezekiel, the prophet attributes to YHWH radical mobility—God can cross the Chebar in a multi-wheeled chariot (Ezek 1), God's glory can leave and return to the temple (Ezek 9:3; 10:18–19; 11:22–23; 43:1–5), and God can function as a "sanctuary for a little while" (or "to some extent;" מעט למקדש) for the people in Babylon (Ezek 11:16b).[4] In addition, religion in the exilic period also emphasized nongeographic practices such as circumcision, the keeping of the Sabbath, and the celebration of Passover in the home.[5]

In the following study, I address the choices made by the community when, after the exile, the boundaries of sacred geography were again open for renegotiation. When the exiled community was allowed to return to the land, it (along with those who remained in the land) had to discern again YHWH's geography and make decisions about how this would be reflected in and instituted by its religious practice. These decisions were negotiated in an even larger context of Yahwists who remained in Babylonia. Would YHWH's presence be centered in Jerusalem? Or, given that the exilic community in Babylonia had developed theologies and practices not centered on Jerusalem, and given that some of the community remained there,[6] would YHWH's presence remain untethered to

---

Tell Fakhariyah [Fekherye], see Ali Abou-Assaf, Pierre Bordreuil, and Alan R. Millard, *La statue de Tell Fekherye et son inscription bilingue assyro-araméenne* [Etudes Assyriologiques 7; Paris: Editions Recherche sur les civilizations, 1982]); and "Ashtart of Kition" ("'štrt kt" in a fifth-century Phoenician text [KAI 37 A.5], noted in Barré, *God-List in the Treaty*, 186 n. 473).

3. Notice that texts such as 1 Kgs 8:30 ("hear in heaven your dwelling place") and 8:17 ("My father David had it in mind to build a house for the name of YHWH . . .") contrast significantly with the poetic fragment in 8:13: "I have built you an established place for your enthronement in perpetuity." The different geographies of YHWH's dwellings reflected in this chapter seem to indicate conflated sources from different times. For summaries of attempts to untangle the dating of this chapter, see Jon D. Levenson, "From Temple to Synagogue: 1 Kings 8," in *Traditions in Transformation: Turning Points in Biblical Faith* (ed. Baruch Halpern and Jon D. Levenson; Winona Lake, Ind.: Eisenbrauns, 1981), 143–66; Marc Brettler, "Interpretation and Prayer," in *Minhah le-Nahum: Biblical and Other Studies Presented to Nahum M. Sarna in Honour of his 70th Birthday* (ed. Marc Brettler and Michael Fishbane; JSOTSupp 154; Sheffield: JSOT Press, 1993), 17–35. For a discussion of the exilic context of Deuteronomy itself, see Ronald E. Clements, "The Deuteronomic Law of Centralization and the Catastrophe of 587 B.C.E.," in *After the Exile: Essays in Honour of Rex Mason* (ed. John Barton and David J. Reimer; Macon, Ga.: Mercer University Press, 1996), 5–25.

4. For a discussion of Ezek 11:16b, see Andreas Ruwe, "Die Veränderung tempeltheologischer Konzepte in Ezechiel 8–11," in *Gemeinde ohne Tempel: Zur Substituierung und Transformation des Jerusalemer Tempels und seines Kults im Alten Testament, antiken Judentum und frühen Christentum* (ed. Beate Ego, Armin Lange, and Peter Pilhofer; Wissenschaftliche Untersuchungen zum Neuen Testament 118; Tübingen: J. C. B. Mohr [Paul Siebeck], 1999), 3–18.

5. For a discussion of aspects of religion in the exile that did not emphasize geography to a large extent, see Rainer Albertz in *A History of Israelite Religion in the Old Testament Period* (trans. John Bowden; 2 vols.; Old Testament Library; Louisville: Westminster John Knox, 1994), 407–11.

6. Evidence for Jews living in Babylon during the Achaemenid period comes partially from the names given in the business records of the Muraŝû Archive. From these texts, Ran Zadok has identified

temple or city? And how would YHWH's presence in the city be structured in the new political context of Achaemenid imperial control of the land?

This study looks at YHWH's geographical location and the role of the temple in the physical expressions of the Yahwists of the Persian period to see how the centrality of Jerusalem was practiced. Instead of considering more conceptual frameworks of the temple's centrality such as how, for example, a particular biblical book constructs Jerusalem as the source of the fructifying water of life, cosmic mountain, navel of the land, or bond between heaven and earth, the present work focuses on the physical expressions of the religious faith after (and just before) the temple was rebuilt.[7] That is to say, methodologically this work is less concerned with conceptual frameworks about the temple's centrality and more concerned with the ancient enacting of those beliefs in a landscape (although of course these are intricately related).[8] Expressions of these beliefs include the physical movements of people and the exchange of physical objects in the religious life of Yahwists, insofar as this can be constructed from the textual and archaeological records. Physical expressions of sacred geography are seen in the textual prescriptions and descriptions of practices, such as the protocols for sacrifice, pilgrimage, and tithes, that are largely tied to Jerusalem, as well practices that have less of a specified geographic context, such as the use of incense. The significance of some

---

the names of seventy Jews who lived in the region around Nippur (the seventy names represent 2.8% of the 2500 names in the archive). Ran Zadok, *The Jews in Babylonia during the Chaldean and Achaemenian Periods according to the Babylonian Sources* (Studies in the History of the Jewish People and the Land of Israel Monograph Series 3; Haifa: University of Haifa, 1979). Three earlier unprovenienced tablets (dating to the years 498, 532, and 530/29 B.C.E.) also list Yahwistic names, including one Šamaḫ-Yâma (ʾšá-ma-aḫ-iá-a-ma, l. 21; see also שמעיה in 1 Kgs 12:22 and Jer 29:31, 32). Also interesting is the town in which one of the texts was written, "Al-Yâhûdû," (uru ia-a-ḫu-du; i.e., "the town of Judah;" l. 23), probably a town in Babylonia named after the homeland. The names thus indicate ties through theophoric elements in names and geographical references. See F. Joannès and A. Lemaire, "Trois tablettes cunéiformes à onomastique ouest-sémitique (collection Sh. Moussaïeff) (Pls. I–II)," *Transeu* 17 (1999): 17–34. See also Nahman Avigad, "Seals of Exiles," *IEJ* 15 (1965): 222–32.

7. For a discussion of ancient constructions of temples as omphalos, etc. see Mircea Eliade, *The Myth of the Eternal Return* (trans. Willard R. Trask; London: Routledge & Kegan Paul, 1955), and Moshe Weinfeld, "Zion and Jerusalem as Religious and Political Capital: Ideology and Utopia," in *The Poet and the Historian: Essays in Literary and Historical Biblical Criticism* (ed. Richard Elliott Friedman; HSS 26; Chico, Ca.: Scholars Press, 1983), 75–115, esp. 104–14. For a brief critique of Eliade's phenomenology as it relates to Greek temples, see Walter Burkert, "The Meaning and Function of the Temple in Classical Greece," in *Temple in Society* (ed. Michael V. Fox; Winona Lake, Ind.: Eisenbrauns, 1988), 27–47, esp. 33–34. For a recent discussion of the history of development of Jerusalem from "navel of the world," to the "foundation stone" from which the world came into being, see Michael Tilly, *Jerusalem—Nabel der Welt: Überlieferung und Funktionen von Heiligtumstraditionen im antiken Judentum* (Stuttgart: Kohlhammer, 2002).

8. For a study that looks at another ancient practice (that of politics) in the context of landscape, see Adam T. Smith, *The Political Landscape: Constellations of Authority in Early Complex Polities* (Berkeley: University of California, 2003).

of these practices can be seen in texts such as Neh 10:32–40, where, in part of their oath "not to forget the house of our God," the people in the land swear to pay an annual tax to the temple, bring the first-fruits to the temple, and provide for the temple sacrifices.[9] Other practices of centrality also can be discerned in the archaeological record in, for example, the apparent lack of altar sites in Yehud and the disavowal of animal sacrifice at sites outside of Jerusalem by the Jewish colony at Elephantine.[10] Only religious practices that can be traced in the biblical and archaeological record are considered here, although, of course, religious life in Yehud would also have included activities that elude the historian's grasp, such as private prayer and unrecorded communal gatherings, as well as practices that have left only textual evidence, such as the development of penitential prayer.

By focusing on practice, I emphasize that insofar as the centrality of the temple was a real theological conviction of its adherents, it is reasonable to suppose that this centrality would have been enacted in their lives. If centrality was a theological reality, it should have been a physically enacted reality as well, one that had implications for the construal of attachments to Jerusalem. It may be that human activity that physically enacts protocols specific to certain spaces is just as indicative of belief as are descriptions of beliefs about spaces. Indeed, one can plausibly construe human activity as itself a description of belief. Further, lived experience, religious or otherwise, is not only expressed but also formed by words and behavior. Thoughts, aspirations, and feelings are manifested and described by physical expressions, and religious thoughts may even be constituted by this behavior.[11]

---

9. As part of their oath, the people also vow to avoid intermarriage with "the people of the land" and to keep the Sabbath. Because these practices are difficult to trace in the archaeological record, they are not discussed in this work.

10. An additional practice reflecting the centrality of Jerusalem detectable in the later textual and archaeological record is the custom of transferring Jews who had died in the Diaspora to the land of Israel for burial and reinterment, a practice dating from the early third century c.e. See Isaiah M. Gafni, *Land, Center and Diaspora: Jewish Constructs in Late Antiquity* (Journal for the Study of the Pseudepigrapha Supp 21; Sheffield: Sheffield Academic Press, 1997), 79–95; and Shumuel Safrai, "Relations between the Diaspora and the Land of Israel," in *The Jewish People in the First Century* (ed. S. Safrai and M. Stern; vol. 1 of Compendia Rerum Iudaicarum ad Novum Testamentum; Assen: Van Gorcum, 1974), 184–215, esp. 213.

11. This point labors somewhat with the distinction of Henri Lefebvre (*The Production of Space* [trans. D. Nicholson Smith; Oxford: Basil Blackwell, 1991]) and Edward W. Soja (*Postmodern Geographies: The Reassertion of Space in Critical Theory* [London: Verso, 1989] and *Thirdspace: Journeys to Los Angeles and Other Real-and-Imagined Places* [Oxford: Basil Blackwell, 1996]) between spaces that can be perceived, conceived, and lived. Although both scholars point to the essential links between the spaces, like Wesley Kort ("A Narrative-Based Theory of Human-Place Relations," paper presented in the AAR/SBL Constructions of Ancient Space Seminar at the Annual Meeting of the AAR and SBL, Nashville, Tenn., 2000, recorded in Claudia V. Camp, "Storied Space, or, Ben Sira 'Tells' a Temple," in

1.1 CENTRALITY CONSTRUCTED: MAPPING BELIEF ONTO GEOGRAPHY

What does centrality look like and how is it constructed? For Walter Christaller, a "central place" was primarily an economic structure for distribution—a place where services and goods are provided for a surrounding tributary area.[12] When these economic components are considered along with religious components such as the construction and effects of belief on geography, centrality incorporates sacrality as well: a holy place such as Jerusalem and its temple are central because God is specially related to it and expected to be revealed there. Although there is interplay between religion and economics, Jerusalem's specifically religious centrality is built on its claim of chosen-ness by God, its identity as a sacred place, and its distinction from all other profane places. This centrality has effects on the landscape even as it colors the ways in which this landscape is perceived. Oftentimes geographers want to distinguish religious geography (the ways in which religion interprets and shapes human perception of the world) and geography of religions (the social and cultural effects of religion on the landscape).[13] Although these are conceptually distinct, they cannot be separated at the level of historical research and analysis since there is a mutually forming interplay between them. For instance, designating the area between the Mediterranean and the Jordan River the "promised land" interprets that geography in ways that have implications for settlement and return after displacement. In turn, settlement and return reinforces the notion that this geography is the "promised land." Thus, in my study of the religious practice of centrality, I will consider both categories together since the landscape of Jerusalem is encoded with religious significance while at the same time affected by such encoding.

How are sacred place and centrality mapped onto geography? Mircea Eliade argued that sacred places such as Jerusalem are predominantly (though not entirely) divinely initiated, and this divine relation to geography is maintained

---

"Imagining" Biblical Worlds: Studies in Spatial, Social and Historical Constructs in Honor of James W. Flanagan [ed. David M. Gunn and Paula M. McNutt; JSOTSupp 359; London: Sheffield Academic Press (Continuum), 2002], 64–80, esp. 67), I am questioning the analytical priority of the first two spaces over lived space.

12. Walter Christaller, *Die zentralen Orte in Süddeutschland: eine ökonomisch-geographische Untersuchung über die Gesotzmässigkeit der Verbreitung und Entwicklung der Siedlungen mit städtischen Funktionen* (Jena: Gustav Fischer, 1933), English ed. translated by C. W. Baskin and published as *Central Places in Southern Germany* (Englewood Cliffs, N.J.: Prentice-Hall, 1966). For recent discussion of Christaller's work, see, among others, K. S. O. Beavon, *Central Place Theory: A Reinterpretation* (New York: Longman, 1977); Leslie J. King, *Central Place Theory* (Beverly Hills: Sage Publications, 1984); Peter Sjøholt, "Christaller Revisited: Reconsidering Christaller's Analysis of Services and Central Places," *Service Industries Journal* 21.4 (Oct. 2001): 198–200; and, most significantly for my own work, Smith, *The Political Landscape*, 38–45, 126–30.

13. See Chris C. Park, *Sacred Worlds: An Introduction to Geography and Religion* (London: Routledge, 1994), 18–19.

throughout time: "A sacred place is what it is because of the permanent nature of the hierophany that first consecrated it. . . . *There*, in *that* place, the hierophany repeats itself. . . ."[14] Yet the construction of sacred places and central places also has a human element and can be altered. Sacred places such as Jerusalem exist in the "maps" that human communities enact, within the human constructions of time and practices.[15] In the biblical texts, centrality is constructed and enacted through both divine choice and human maintenance of sacred spaces. The "altar law" in Deut 12 stipulates that YHWH shall be worshipped only in one place, the place where he will choose for his name to dwell (לשום את־שמו שם; Deut 12:5). With its cultic instructions, Deut 12 also gives the human community a critical role in centrality; since YHWH established his name in one place, all other local shrines must be demolished, and the people shall bring their sacrifices, tithes, and offerings to the central sanctuary.[16] Deuteronomy 16 subsequently gives this stipulation a chronological shape when, in repeating an earlier tradition found in Exod 23:14–17 and 34:18–24, it instructs the community to "appear before YHWH" at the chosen place three times a year at the pilgrimage festivals (חגים) of unleavened bread, weeks, and booths. It also instructs that all pilgrims "shall not appear before YHWH empty-handed" (Deut 16:16). Thus, according to Deuteronomy, centrality is based on the localized presence of YHWH (or YHWH's name) in one place, and this is enacted by maintaining only one place of worship at which sacrifices are made and to which tithes are brought at regular intervals.

Other biblical stories parse the divine and human role in constructing sacrality and centrality differently but, again, both the divine and human actors are included. In Gen 28, humans make the initial recognition of the site made sacred by God and subsequently maintain it. When YHWH appeared to Jacob in a dream as he slept in the city of Luz, the patriarch immediately marked off the site as sacred territory by renaming the site Beth-el and by erecting a pillar (Gen

---

14. Mircea Eliade, *Patterns in Comparative Religion* (trans. Rosemary Sheed; New York: Sheed & Ward, 1958), 368; emphasis in original.

15. Jonathan Z. Smith makes the point that "there is nothing that is inherently or essentially clean or unclean, sacred or profane. There are situational or relational categories, mobile boundaries which shift according to the map being employed" (*Map is Not Territory: Studies in the History of Religions* [Leiden: Brill, 1978], 291). For a survey of different approaches vis-à-vis the role of the community in the interpretation of sacred space within the study of history of religion, see Roger Friedland and Richard D. Hecht, "The Politics of Sacred Space: Jerusalem's Temple Mount/al-haram al sharif," in *Sacred Places and Profane Spaces: Essays in the Geographics of Judaism, Christianity, and Islam* (ed. Jamie Scott and Paul Simpson-Housley; Contributions to the Study of Religion 30; New York: Greenwood Press, 1991), 24–28.

16. According to Eleonore Reuter, *Kultzentralisation: Entstehung und Theologie von Dtn 12* (Athenäums Monografien: Theologie 87; Bonner Biblische Beiträge; Frankfurt am Main: Hain, 1993), the core of this text (vv. 13–14a, 15–18) was redacted already in the preexilic period and underwent two additional exilic redactions.

28:10–22). By such means, the human community was alerted to the divine presence there. In their subsequent adoption of the site's name, and in the production, writing, and canonizing of Jacob's dream, later communities also were involved in maintaining the sacred connection. In Ps 132, YHWH's declaration of his residence in Zion ("This is my resting-place for all time, here I will dwell, for I desire it," Ps 132:14) occurs only after David has vowed to find a place for YHWH to dwell (Ps 132:3–5). Although it is conceivable that the divine world is powerful and free enough to erupt in any specific location, humans also have a role in the construction of sacred geography.

As the above narratives make clear, the construction of sacred space and centrality is subject to change throughout time. Various monographs trace aspects of this change, such as the development of centrality in the various strands in D, the centralization of worship from the time of the settlement to Solomon's temple, as well as the development of centralized practices such as pilgrimage in the Hellenistic period and later.[17] This changeability is also evident in the Persian period, as this study argues. Although the religion practiced in Yehud was certainly heir to its own earlier traditions, these traditions were themselves affected by reinterpretation by various communities, as well as by the needs and concerns of their Persian colonizers.[18]

It is not only that humans have a role in the construction of sacred space and the mapping of belief onto geography, sacred space and maps also construct humankind, especially as they define themselves in groups. Intrinsic to the task of inscribing piety onto geography is the construction of community and communal boundary-making. Such practices have both a theological and a sociological dimension: although limiting the places where animal sacrifice can take place makes a claim about the locality of God's presence on earth, the enacting of such limitation permits individuals to claim their membership in a group that likewise practices such limitation. Investigating practices relating to sacred space such as pilgrimage, for instance, opens the investigation to see, as Michael Sallnow puts it in his study of Andean pilgrimage, how "social relations become spatial relations,"

---

17. Among the various studies of the changing aspects and practices of centrality, see Baruch Halpern, "The Centralization Formula in Deuteronomy," *VT* 31 (1981): 20–38; Pekka Pitkänen, *Central Sanctuary and Centralization of Worship in Ancient Israel: From the Settlement to the Building of Solomon's Temple* (Piscataway, N.J.: Gorgias, 2003); Shumuel Safrai, *Die Wallfahrt im Zeitalter des Zweiten Tempels* (trans. Dafna Mach; Forschungen zum jüdisch-christlichen Dialog 3; Neukirchen-Vluyn: Neukirchener Verlag, 1981); idem, "Relations Between the Diaspora," 191–204; Erich S. Gruen, *Diaspora: Jews amidst Greeks and Romans* (Cambridge, Mass.: Harvard University Press, 2002), 246–47; Allen Kerkeslager, "Jewish Pilgrimage and Jewish Identity in Hellenistic and Early Roman Egypt," in *Pilgrimage and Holy Space in Late Antique Egypt* (ed. David Frankfurter; Religions in the Graeco-Roman World 134; Leiden: Brill, 1998), 99–225. See also Reuter, *Kultzentralisation.*

18. For more on the impact of Persian politics on the religion of Yehud, see Jon Berquist, *Judaism in Persia's Shadow: A Social and Historical Approach* (Minneapolis: Fortress, 1995).

and how place, space, and landscape are experienced.[19] By accepting group norms regarding geography (where the pilgrimage center is located) and temporality (when one goes to the pilgrimage center), pilgrims physically define themselves as part of a larger community.[20] Various other ways of constructing social boundaries can also be discerned in the extant material, such as historical narratives and sociological subdivisions, and religious practices relating to sacred space should be seen alongside these other attempts to define and create community.[21]

The construction of community was a critical issue in the post-exilic period because, in the context of Diaspora, Yahwists were now not defined by geography. The geographic boundaries of Yahwism extended beyond the borders of Yehud, and thus adherents had to find other ways to define their relation or non-relation to each other in the context of the Persian Empire. This is precisely why the Persian period is such a significant period for centrality—enacting a map in which Jerusalem is "central" is one of the ways in which a geographically distant community can cohere as a self-identified group. The geography of habitation (dispersion) can be modified by the geography of religious practice (centrality).

Rather significant side notes in this discussion are the practical matters of the boundaries of Yehud during this period and the recognition of Yahwists within and outside the province. In a study of the means by which groups engaged in the worship of YHWH through the practice of centrality, the boundaries of Yehud should be made explicit. Yet this is an area of great debate in current studies, both in terms of the extent of the province and the time period in which the

---

19. Michael J. Sallnow, *Pilgrims of the Andes: Regional Cults in Cusco* (Washington, D.C.: Smithsonian Institution Press, 1987), 11.

20. For a study of pilgrimage and its function as an ethnic maker and marker during a later period, see the essay by Kerkeslager, "Jewish Pilgrimage and Jewish Identity," 99–223. Note though, the conclusion of John Eade and Michael J. Sallnow ("Introduction," in *Contesting The Sacred: The Anthropology of Christian Pilgrimage* [ed. John Eade and Michael J. Sallnow; London: Routledge, 1991], 1–29) that pilgrimage is a heterogeneous process (contra Turner's over-emphasis on communitas), "an arena for competing religious and secular discourses, for both the official co-optation and the non-official recovery of religious meanings, for conflict between orthodoxies, sects, and confessional groups, for drives towards consensus and communitas, *and* for counter-movements towards separateness and division" (ibid., 2).

21. For a study of identity-making in historical narratives, for instance, see Philip F. Esler, "Ezra-Nehemiah as a Narrative of (Re-Invented) Israelite Identity," *BibInt* 11 (2003): 413–26; for studies of the social unit בית אבות (father's houses) and the societal structures that they supported and/or inscribed, see H. G. M. Williamson, "The Family in Persian Period Judah: Some Textual Reflections," in *Symbiosis, Symbolism, and the Power of the Past: Canaan, Ancient Israel, and Their Neighbors from the Late Bronze Age through Roman Palaestina* (Proceedings of the Centennial Symposium W. F. Albright Institute of Archaeological Research and American Schools of Oriental Research, Jerusalem, May 29–31, 2000; ed. William G. Dever and Seymour Gitin; Winona Lake, Ind.: Eisenbrauns, 2003), 469–85. Also see John J. Collins, *Between Athens and Jerusalem: Jewish Identity in the Hellenistic Diaspora* (New York: Crossroad, 1983).

boundaries were established.[22] Although some argue about whether sites such as Bethel and Gezer should be included in Yehud, this study assumes that there is enough good evidence to do so.[23] Also, although one cannot assume that the boundaries of each Persian province strictly subdivided religious groups, this study presupposes that communities within Yehud are Yahwistic except in the face of contradictory evidence. Likewise, this study also considers groups outside of Yehud to be Yahwistic only with explicit markers such as accounts of YHWH worship or Yahwistic theophorics.[24] Of course, these stipulations are somewhat artificial, but any study of a "sacred center" involves making certain assertions and assumptions about geography and its religious claims. It is my hope that, by making these geographical assumptions explicit, those who disagree with some of them can still make use of this study.

As a caveat, I should also add that in designating communities "Yahwistic," I do not intend to indicate that all of their religious practices were identical or that there were not competing strata and definitions of these communities. The biblical texts are clear that the definition of a Yahwist was contested. For example, the book of Ezra primarily includes in the community only those who both went to Babylon and returned to the province of Yehud (the *gôlâ*), but Nehemiah's community boundaries also include those who are currently outside of Yehud.[25] The biblical texts also show differences with regard to intermarriage with "foreign" women. In Ezra and Nehemiah, foreign wives are forcibly expelled from the com-

---

22. For a discussion about the contested nature of Yehud's boundaries, see Jon Berquist, "The Shifting Frontier: The Achaemenid Empire's Treatment of Western Colonies. *Journal of World-System Research* 1 (1995). [http://jwsr.ucr.edu/archive/vol1/v1_nh.php].

23. Evidence for the boundaries of Yehud include biblical references and lists, inscriptions and the distribution of jar handles stamped with "*yhd*." The boundaries of the province assumed in my study are those mapped by Ephraim Stern in *The Assyrian, Babylonian, and Persian Periods* (vol. 2 of *Archaeology of the Land of the Bible*; Anchor Bible Reference Library; New York: Doubleday, 2001), 375, 428–31. For a set of maps showing other reconstructions of the boundaries of Yehud, see Charles E. Carter, *The Emergence of Yehud in the Persian Period: A Social and Demographic Study* (JSOTSupp 294; Sheffield: Sheffield Academic Press, 1999), 84–87. For the reconstruction of André Lemaire, see his article, "Histoire et administration de la Palestine à l'époque perse," in *La Palestine à l'époque perse* (ed. Ernest-Marie Laperrousaz and André Lemaire; Paris: Éditions du Cerf, 1994), 11–53, and the map on p. 12.

24. This evidence is not so entirely straightforward because families with Yahwistic names at Elephantine also had names that included other gods. Note, however, that in their extant texts the community referred to themselves as "יהודין" and "יהודיא" in TAD A4.7.22 and A4.8.22, A4.3.12; A4.1.1, 10. The term "יהודי" occurs in TAD B2.2.3; B2.9.2,3; B3.1.3; B3.6.2; B3.13.2; and B6.1.2 (reconstructed).

25. For more on the competing visions of the boundaries of the community and the community's "constitution," see Christiane Karrer, *Ringen um die Verfassung Judas: Eine Studie zu den theologisch-politischen Vorstellungen im Esra-Nehemia-Buch* (BZAW 308; Berlin and New York: Walter de Gruyter, 2001).

munity (Ezra 9–10; Neh 13:23–28). Yet such marriages are not condemned within the genealogies in Chronicles and, at points the author adds foreign women into Israel's family tree not known from other sources such as Judah's Canaanite wife Bath-shua (1 Chr 2:3).[26] Although his theory remains contested, Joel Weinberg has constructed a society within Yehud of property-owning בית־אבות affiliated with the priesthood and temple in distinction to the other residents of the province.[27] Others, such as Paul Hanson and Morton Smith, have detected different social groups or parties in Yehud.[28] Even such a basic tenant of communal definition as whether or when Jerusalem should have a temple was a subject of disagreement in the early part of this period.[29] This study demonstrates that the varying enactments of centrality through religious practices such as sacrifice, pilgrimage, and tithing manifest similar pluriformities and contentions.

1.2 CENTRALITY OBSERVED: HISTORY OF SCHOLARSHIP AND THE USE OF SOURCES

The assertion that the Jerusalem temple was central is itself a central tenant in much of biblical scholarship that is concerned with the Persian period, but the similarity of language camouflages distinct visions of how such centrality was enacted in the religious practice of its adherents. For instance, Martin Noth argues that the whole Jewish community of this time (including the Diaspora)

---

26. For this and other examples of the Chronicler's inclusion of foreign women, see Sara Japhet, *The Ideology of the Book of Chronicles and its Place in Biblical Thought* (Frankfurt am Main: Peter Lang, 1989), 346–51; and the discussion of the genealogies in chapters 1–9 in Gary N. Knoppers, *I Chronicles 1–9: A New Translation with Introduction and Commentary* (New York: Doubleday, 2003).

27. Joel Weinberg, *The Citizen-Temple Community* (trans. Daniel L. Smith-Christopher; JSOTSupp 151; Sheffield: JSOT Press, 1992). For a critique, see, among others, H. G. M. Williamson, "Judah and the Jews," in *Studies in Persian History: Essays in Memory of David M. Lewis* (ed. Maria Brosius and Amélie Kuhrt; Achaemenid History 11; Leiden: Nederlands Instituut voor het Nabije Oosten, 1998), 145–63.

28. Paul D. Hanson, *The Dawn of Apocalyptic: The Historical and Sociological Roots of Jewish Apocalyptic Eschatology* (Philadelphia: Fortress Press, 1979); Morton Smith, *Palestinian Parties and Politics that Shaped the Old Testament* (New York: Columbia University Press, 1971).

29. For studies that examine the contentions surrounding the reconstruction of the temple, see, among others, Sara Japhet, "The Temple in the Restoration Period: Reality and Ideology," *USQR* 44 (1991): 195–252, esp. 233–36; Peter Ross Bedford, *Temple Restoration in Early Achaemenid Judah* (JSJSupp 65; Leiden: Brill, 2001); John Kessler, "Building the Second Temple: Questions of Time, Text, and History in Haggai 1.1–15," *JSOT* 27 (2002): 243–56; Thomas Pola, *Das Priestertum bei Sacharja: Historische und traditionsgeschichtliche Untersuchungen zur frühnachexilischen Herrschererwartung* (FAT 35; Tübingen: Mohr Siebeck, 2003); James M. Trotter, "Was the Second Jerusalem Temple a Primarily Persian Project?" *SJOT* 15 (2001): 276–94; Ina Willi-Plein, "Warum musste der Zweite Tempel gebaut werden?" in *Gemeinde ohne Tempel*, 57–73.

participated in centralized worship.[30] Similarly, Gösta Ahlström considers Jerusalem to have been "the center of life for the *gôlâ* community," but only from the time of Nehemiah and after.[31] On the other hand, centrality is denied by Rainer Albertz and Robert P. Carroll, who argue that Jerusalem was not a significant focal point for the communal identity and religious life of much of the Jewish community.[32] Even those who assert Jerusalem's centrality during this time see it enacted in different ways and at different times. Ahlström dates its beginnings to the time of Nehemiah, and Noth identifies its practice in the limitation of worship areas outside of Jerusalem. Peter Ackroyd, however, sees the enacted expression of the temple's role as the "focal point" of the post-exilic community in the use of Zion psalms in corporate and private worship.[33] Loren D. Crow and Mattias Millard emphasize another aspect of centrality in the deliberate cultivation of pilgrimage to Jerusalem during this period.[34] Although this is merely a quick sketch

---

30. Martin Noth, *The History of Israel* (trans. P. R. Ackroyd; New York: Harper & Row, 1968). According to Noth, "the deuteronomic requirement of a unified place of worship appears to have been strictly adhered to [throughout the Diaspora]; and, so far as we know, no other sanctuaries, such as had flourished a generation previously, emerged again, even in the period when the sanctuary in Jerusalem was in ruins. After its restoration, however, the Temple of Jerusalem was regarded all the more as the only legitimate shrine" (Noth, *History of Israel*, 317).

31. Gösta W. Ahlström, *The History of Ancient Palestine* (ed. Diana Edelman; Sheffield: Sheffield Academic Press, 1993), 881. Ahlström claims that at the beginning of Nehemiah's time, "even if the temple was rebuilt, it had not yet gained the status of a 'national' center in the eyes of the people. Probably Mizpah was still the administrative center" (ibid., 851).

32. Because of the geographical separation of the Diaspora groups and the critiques of temple theology made by prophetic and Deuteronomic/Deuteronomistic circles, Albertz argues that the centralized cult was not a sufficiently vital symbol around which to unify the community, claiming that the identity of the community was found not in the temple but in the law: the people put "not the temple but a book at the centre of official Yahweh religion. . . ." (Albertz, *A History of Israelite Religion*, 2:466).

Adopting a different line of argument, Carroll claims that, although the temple plays a major role in most biblical texts, this emphasis reflects only the ideological interests of those responsible for the canon: "I would tend to say that the Hebrew Bible is propaganda for the temple cult/guild based on Palestinian territory. . . ." Robert P. Carroll, "Madonna of Silences: Clio and the Bible," in *Can a 'History of Israel' Be Written?* (ed. Lester L. Grabbe; JSOTSupp 245; Sheffield: Sheffield Academic Press, 1997), 83–103, esp. 101. See also his article, "So What Do We *Know* about the Temple? The Temple in the Prophets," in *Second Temple Studies: 2. Temple Community in the Persian Period* (ed. Tamara C. Eskenazi and Kent H. Richards; JSOTSupp 175; Sheffield: JSOT Press, 1994), 34–51.

33. Peter R. Ackroyd, *Exile and Restoration: A Study of Hebrew Thought of the Sixth Century BC* (London: SCM Press, 1968), 248–49.

34. According to Loren D. Crow, Pss 120–134 were redacted in the Persian period to "convince Israelites from outlying areas to make pilgrimage to Jerusalem." See his book, *The Songs of Ascents (Psalms 120–134): Their Place in Israelite History and Religion* (SBLDS 148; Atlanta: Scholars Press, 1996), 187. According to Mattias Millard (*Die Komposition des Psalters: Ein formgeschichtlicher Ansatz* [FAT 9; Tübingen: J. C. B. Mohr (Paul Siebeck), 1994]), the Psalter in the Persian time was an "Ersatz für die Wallfahrt . . . [und] ein Propagandabuch der Wallfahrt" (p. 209; see also p. 195).

of current scholarship (and influences of past scholarship), it is clear that general affirmations of "the centrality of the Jerusalem temple" comprise various delineations of how and to what extent this centrality was practiced.

As sources for mapping the role of the temple in religious practice, I use the biblical text and archaeological record. The specific biblical texts are those dated to the Persian period by current scholarly consensus, namely Haggai, Zechariah, Malachi, Trito-Isaiah, Ezra, Nehemiah, Chronicles, and Psalms 120–134 in their edited form.[35] (Second-Isaiah is not part of the core components of my study because of its early date and perspective. Since it was probably written during the time of Cyrus, the book is more reflective of the dreams and anxieties of the exilic period than of the post-exilic period, and, since it was written before any exiles returned and before the temple was rebuilt, it does not fully comprehend a situation in which centrality of the temple is self-consciously enacted or ignored. Although the decision not to include Second-Isaiah is somewhat arbitrary, it allows me to concentrate on the situation a bit later in the Persian period during which the self-understanding expressed in the biblical texts posits a restored community in the Jerusalem center, as well as a persistent periphery outside of the land that relates to or ignores this restored center). Although these texts certainly do not contain the whole strata of Persian period texts woven throughout the Hebrew Bible, and although they are themselves mixed with earlier sources and later redactions, they nevertheless comprise a reliable picture of the textual

---

35. For discussions of the dates of the various books, refer to the following sources (this list does not pretend to be comprehensive but contains some of the most recent and widely available texts that include an argument for a Persian period date of the specific text and an overview of other proposals). For Haggai, see Janet E. Tollington, *Tradition and Innovation in Haggai and Zechariah 1–8* (JSOTSupp 150; Sheffield: JSOT Press, 1993); and Michael H. Floyd, "The Nature of the Narrative and the Evidence of Redaction in Haggai," *VT* 45 (1995): 470–90. For Zechariah 1–8, see Tollington, *Tradition and Innovation*, 23–47. For Malachi, see the overview by Eugene H. Merrill in *Haggai, Zechariah, Malachi: An Exegetical Commentary* (Chicago: Moody Press, 1994), 371–78, and Andrew E. Hill, "Dating the Book of Malachi: A Linguistic Reexamination," in *The Word of the Lord Shall Go Forth* (ed. Carol L. Meyers and M. O'Connor; Winona Lake, Ind.: Eisenbrauns, 1983), 77–89. For Trito-Isaiah, see Joseph Blenkinsopp, *Isaiah 56–66* (AB 19; New York: Doubleday, 2003), 51–60. For an overview of the dates assigned to Ezra and Nehemiah, see H. G. M. Williamson, *Ezra, Nehemiah* (WBC 16; Waco: Word Books, 1985), xxxv–xxxvi; Aaron Demsky, "Who Came First, Ezra or Nehemiah? The Synchronistic Approach," *HUCA* 65 (1994): 1–19; and for a proposal for the book's several literary stages, see Jacob L. Wright, *Rebuilding Identity: The Nehemiah-Memoir and its Earliest Readers* (BZAW 348; Berlin: Walter de Gruyter). For discussion of the date of Chronicles, see H. G. M. Williamson, *1 and 2 Chronicles* (NCB; Grand Rapids: Eerdmans, 1982), 15–16; Sara Japhet, *I & II Chronicles: A Commentary* (OTL; Louisville: Westminster John Knox, 1993), 3–7; John W. Kleinig, "Recent Research in Chronicles," *CurBS* 2 (1994): 43–76, esp. 46–47; J. E. Dyck, *The Theocratic Ideology of the Chronicler* (Biblical Interpretation Series 33; Leiden: Brill, 1998), 30–35; and Knoppers, *I Chronicles 1–9*, 101–17. For the date of Psalms 120–134, see Millard, *Komposition* and Crow, *Songs of Ascents*. The standard work on this topic is by Avi Hurvitz, בין לשון ללשון: לתולדות לשון המקרא בימי בית שני (Jerusalem: Bialik Institute, 1972).

traditions of this time period.[36] Given that individuals date these texts differently and may wish to add to or excise from the above list, I examine each book individually in terms of its treatment of specific practices of religion. This should allow readers to disregard the discussion of some texts or choose to consider the same practices in other texts not considered here.

Aside from the issues of dating, the biblical texts must be read carefully for the task of historical reconstruction because, as literary creations, they can sacrifice factuality for the sake of a coherent and satisfying narrative or literary schema. Yet this skewing is itself descriptive of the aims and hopes of the author and the author's community and, as such, can be part of the historical narrative. Take, for example, the letter of Artaxerxes incorporated into Ezra 7:12–26. If the letter is inauthentic,[37] the document is a piece of literary fiction to support the author's literary vision of a wished-for reality. These wishes themselves form part of the historical picture—at some point, an author (and the community that read and transmitted the work) wanted to demonstrate that Ezra was sent at the direct command of the emperor and was charged to provide funding for the temple from the king's treasury. If the letter is authentic, or at least reliable, the document poses other problems for historical reconstruction, because putting such documents into a narrative entails authorial choices about periodization, chronology, character development, and, as in Ezra 3, plot lines and literary trajectories. In the context of the larger narrative of Ezra 1–7, Artaxerxes' letter is part of the author's point that the construction of the temple was the defining project of the early returnees with the special encouragement and patronage of the Persian emperors. Authentic or inauthentic, the text of the letter in its literary context witnesses to a historical desire that the temple be central in the life of the early returnees and had the support of the empire.

Besides the literary nature of biblical texts, one also has to deal with their tendentiousness. Because the texts are products of one or several social groups, there is no reason to assume in advance that the world they present is anything other than "the ideological positions favoured and propagated by the dominant

---

36. Thus I do not use texts such as J, considered postexilic by Thomas L. Thompson, *The Historicity of the Patriarchal Narratives: The Quest for the Historical Abraham* (New York: de Gruyter, 1974), John Van Seters, *Abraham in History and Tradition* (New Haven, Conn.: Yale, 1975), and Hans Heinrich Schmid, *Der sogenannte Jahwist: Beobachtungen und Fragen zur Pentateuchforschung* (Zurich: Theologischer Verlag, 1976).

37. Those who consider the letter not to be authentic include Charles C. Torrey, *Ezra Studies* (New York: Ktav, 1970), 157–58; Arvid S. Kapelrud, *The Question of Authorship in the Ezra-Narrative: A Lexical Investigation* (Skrifter utgitt av det Norske Videnskaps-Akademi I Oslo 1944; Oslo: Jacob Dybwad, 1944), 9; and David Janzen, "The 'Mission' of Ezra and the Persian-Period Temple Community," *JBL* 119/4 (2000): 619–43, esp. 624–38. Also note that scholars such as Ulrich Kellermann (*Nehemia: Quellen, Überlieferung und Geschichte* [Berlin: Töpelmann, 1967], 62, 68–69) consider only parts of the letter, such as Ezra 7:24–25, to be inauthentic.

fraction," and thus a simple representation of this world is not an adequate reconstruction of the different social strata of Yehud.[38] The texts may have polemical intent or use language about practices such as sacrifice as a stylized language of internal conflict. The interpretive situation is made even more complicated by the geographic scope of this particular project since most of the texts that I am using were probably generated in Jerusalem to talk about how people outside of Jerusalem related to the city in their religious practice. Yet these ideologically skewed and partial narratives do not preclude contemporary historical analysis. Because ancient historical narratives are themselves culturally embedded, and because the residue of its originating culture adheres to them and their semantic field, literary texts are valid sources for history.

In addition, one can also examine archaeological material such as extra-canonical texts, artifacts, and settlement patterns. Such *realia* from the ancient world represent (potentially at least) a larger portion of society and a larger geographical scope than the biblical texts. Yet the use of such material in historical reconstruction has its own challenges, especially for biblical scholars.[39] This particular study, for example, relies on the published reports of the *Kleinefunde* such as figurines and small limestone cuboids found during archaeological excavations, reports that may, on occasion, be incomplete. In addition, there are the obvious risks for text and archaeological scholars when they cross academic boundaries. Yet there are also risks when the two fields are kept separate. A simple example of the necessity of an interdisciplinary approach is the basic issue of the population in the land during the exile. According to the biblical witness, the land was depopulated (2 Kgs 25:21 and Lam 1:3), yet the archaeological evidence shows that most of the population in Benjamin remained in the land.[40] Looking at evidence from both disciplines helps to place limits on possible interpretations for

---

38. See Bruce Lincoln, "Theses on Method," *Method & Theory in the Study of Religion* 8.3 (1996): 225–27, esp. number 8. With regard to this point for Ezra and Nehemiah, see Sara Japhet, "Composition and Chronology in the Book of Ezra-Nehemiah," in *Second Temple Studies 2: Temple Community in the Persian Period* (ed. Tamara C. Eskenazi and Kent H. Richards; JSOTSupp 175; Sheffield: JSOT Press, 1994), 189–216, and idem, "'History' and 'Literature' in the Persian Period: The Restoration of the Temple," in *Ah Assyria . . .: Studies in Assyrian History and Ancient Near Eastern Historiography Presented to Hayim Tadmor* (ed. M. Cogan and I. Eph'al; ScrHier 33; Jerusalem: Magnes, 1991), 174–88.

39. For a helpful discussion of the different nature and protocols of the study of ancient texts and artifacts see William G. Dever, "On Listening to the Text—and the Artifacts," in *The Echoes of Many Texts: Reflections on Jewish and Christian Traditions: Essays in Honor of Lou H. Silberman* (ed. William G. Dever and J. Edward Wright; Brown Judaic Studies 313; Atlanta: Scholars Press, 1997), 1–23.

40. Oded Lipschits, "The History of the Benjaminite Region under Babylonian Rule," *Tel Aviv* 26 (1999): 155–90. See also idem, "Demographic Changes in Judah between the Seventh and the Fifth Centuries B.C.E.," in *Judah and the Judeans in the Neo-Babylonian Period* (ed. Oded Lipschits and Joseph Blenkinsopp; Winona Lake, Ind.: Eisenbrauns, 2003), 323–76.

each body of evidence.[41] Certainly the biblical scholar must avoid the temptation to use excavated artifacts to "second" the text, or consider them simply as items that reflect reality because they also constitute reality. Objects such as figurines and incense altars were not used by ancient people only after reflection upon their central religious tenants, but as items that also helped to construct those beliefs. As Clifford Geertz writes, artifacts are not "reflected, displaced, or even mediated instances of the determinant social reality but are themselves constituents of that social reality."[42]

The problems and risks of integrating the two fields is not particular to biblical studies and the archaeological stratum and sites associated with the biblical world—texts such as *Archaeology and Ancient History: Breaking Down the Boundaries* argue that the research of archaeologists and classicists also suffers from a lack of integration.[43] Although the parameters of the following study clearly have been set by the biblical texts, I have cautiously and respectfully tried to incorporate the archaeological witness (both texts and artifacts) in an attempt to shed additional light on the practice of centrality.

1.3 JERUSALEM'S CENTRALITY PRACTICED IN THE PERSIAN PERIOD

Having laid out the broader historical and theoretical context for the practice of centrality and for how I investigate it, in this section I briefly anticipate my conclusions. The picture of centrality of the Jerusalem temple, as seen in the protocols and practice of sacrifice, use of incense, pilgrimage, and tithing varies considerably throughout the individual sources such that the plural form "centralities" more accurately describes the religious practice of this period. In the midst of a plurality of expression, however, there is a discernible trend in parts of the textual record showing a general reorientation of religious practice toward Jerusalem: notices of some non-central practices decrease in frequency toward the end of the Persian period, while notices of other centralized practices are more frequent.

---

41. Andrew G. Vaughn ("Is Biblical Archaeology Theologically Useful Today? Yes, A Programmatic Proposal," in *Jerusalem in Bible and Archaeology: The First Temple Period* [ed. Andrew G. Vaughn and Ann E. Killebrew; SBL Symposium Series 18; Leiden: Brill, 2003], 407–30, esp. 416–17) makes a similar point in his essay surveying the archaeological evidence for Jerusalem during the First Temple period as part of his larger argument about the need for historical imagination when reading the biblical text.

42. Clifford Geertz, *Interpretation of Cultures* (New York: Basic Books, 1973), 93–94. See also Lee Patterson, *Negotiating the Past: The Historical Understanding of Medieval Literature* (Madison, Wis.: University of Wisconsin Press, 1987), 53. Both of these references were noted by F. W. Dobbs-Allsopp, "Rethinking Historical Criticism," *BibInt* 7 (1999): 235–71, esp. 248–49.

43. Eberhard W. Sauer, ed., *Archaeology and Ancient History: Breaking Down the Boundaries* (New York: Routledge, 2004).

In the biblical texts, Jerusalem is the main place for animal sacrifice, with terminology associated with blood sacrifice such as מזבח ("altar"), זבח ("to sacrifice"), and עולה ("to cause to go up in smoke") mostly related to the Jerusalem cult. The texts show some change in how they speak of Jerusalem as the sacrificial center. Although earlier texts critique the sacrificial cult in Jerusalem for its corruptness (Mal 1:6–14) and speak of sacrifice outside of Jerusalem at vaguely defined places ("there" in Hag 2:14 and "in the valleys" in Isa 57:5), later texts such as Chronicles actively downplay non-Jerusalem sacrifice and uniquely designate Jerusalem as "a house of sacrifice" (בית זבח; 2 Chr 7:12). The letters from the Elephantine colony in Egypt also show a changing attitude toward animal sacrifice outside of Jerusalem by Yahwists such that, while they saw no problem with sacrificing animals prior to 410 B.C.E., by 407 the community explicitly discontinued the practice. Yet additional evidence for Yahwistic cult centers outside Yehud (such as at Mt. Gerizim) indicate that sacrifice and/or worship occurred in other locales.

Religious practices not involving animal sacrifice may also be traced in the biblical texts through reference to the use of incense and images and in the archaeological record through finds of incense altars and figurines. Such evidence shows that, although figurines generally may not have been employed by Yahwistic communities, Yahwists could still use physical objects such as incense and incense burners in their practice of religion. In the textual evidence, acts of devotion such as animal sacrifice seem generally to have been restricted to Jerusalem, yet religious practices still discernible in the extant records such as the use of incense had no geographic boundary.

According to the biblical texts, pilgrimage to Jerusalem (by exiles from Babylon, Jews and Gentiles from outside of Yehud, and residents of Yehud) was encouraged in the Persian period. As with the practice of animal sacrifice, aspects of pilgrimage undergo some amount of change in these texts such that earlier prophetic texts portray pilgrimage to Jerusalem as mostly a future-orientated practice that involves both the Diaspora and Gentiles, and later texts depict pilgrimage as a current practice of the returned (and returning) community. When the textual accounts of pilgrimage are considered in light of the relatively small and undeveloped Jerusalem in the archaeological record of the Persian period, the question arises as to whether they reflect reality or desire, and I suggest that, based on the settlement surrounding other ancient pilgrimage sites, both interpretations are possible.

Finally, alongside pilgrimage and sacrifice, economic concerns express centrality, namely, the payment of offerings or tithes at the Jerusalem temple. Although there is evidence that sometimes such offerings were not made by the community, there is also evidence that the community could be reinvigorated to give to the cult. While it is tempting to postulate that the temple was also a depot for the taxes of the empire, the evidence is not as clear.

In the Persian period, the practices of sacrifice, pilgrimage, and tithing, as well as the use of incense, reveal the geography of YHWH as reflected in the religion of the people, both those who lived in Yehud and those in the further-flung Diaspora. These communal expressions of centrality, as far as they can be discerned in the extant sources, give expression and help to construct adherence to the God who (once again) dwells in Jerusalem.

CHAPTER 2

THE CENTRALITIES OF YAHWISTIC ANIMAL SACRIFICE

Geographical restriction of animal sacrifice is part of the centrality of the Jerusalem temple in religious practice. Limiting a practice to a single place elevates that place ideologically and requires physical journey to it for full participation. In this chapter, I examine the ways in which the biblical texts from this period display a growing concern with sacrifice and a growing limitation of animal sacrifice to the Jerusalem cult. Existing alongside this tradition, albeit less prominently and in a context of negative assessment, are alternate strands in which animals are sacrificed outside Jerusalem. The extra-biblical evidence presents a somewhat different picture. Outside of Yehud, the Yahwistic community at Elephantine explicitly disallows the sacrifice of animals in their cult after 407 B.C.E., yet Yahwistic sacrifice appears to have been practiced at Mt. Gerizim and perhaps also at Lachish and an additional "house of YHW" mentioned in an Aramaic inscription. The following chapter will examine the relevant material, beginning with the biblical text.

2.1 ANIMAL SACRIFICE IN THE BIBLICAL TEXTS

2.1.1 SACRIFICE IN HAGGAI

Chronologically, the first textual witnesses to the second temple in Jerusalem are the prophecies of Haggai and Zechariah 1–8. Alarmed that the city stood without its traditional place of worship, the two men agitated for the temple's rebuilding,[1] a task that was completed in 515 B.C.E. This rebuilding, of course, had implications for the cultic rites associated with the temple. How did sacrifice

---

1. At least this is the implication of Ezra 5:1–2 and 6:14. As Peter Marinkovic points out, however, the prophecies and visions in the book of Zechariah are more concerned with the relationship of YHWH and YHWH's people living in community (Peter Marinkovic, "What does Zechariah 1–8 Tell us about the Second Temple?" in *Second Temple Studies: 2. Temple Community in the Persian Period* [ed. Tamara C. Eskenazi and Kent H. Richards; JSOTSupp 175; Sheffield: JSOT Press, 1994], 88–103).

fit into their messages? The two books maintain different emphases regarding sacrifice and the Jerusalem temple. Zechariah does not include explicit mention of
animal sacrifice, either in Jerusalem or in the proscribed cult in Babylonia. Haggai
also has little to say about sacrifice, yet the text does contain one strong critique
of impure sacrifice practiced in an area identified only as "there." Although the
details surrounding such sacrifice are imprecise, it holds that its ramifications are
dangerous and risks infecting the entire community.

Haggai's relatively small emphasis on sacrifice is seen in the lack of sacrificial
terminology and promises associated with the temple. There is no mention of an
altar or a place of sacrifice in the temple. Further, the promises of future prosperity are most explicitly linked to the actual building not the associated cultic
rites. Although God declares to the people "I am with you" prior to the rebuilding (Hag 1:13), neglect of the temple has caused economic hardship ("You have
sown much, and harvested little. . . ." Hag 1:6; see also 1:9–11; 2:16–17). It is only
upon the completion of the temple that YHWH will take pleasure in it and be
"honored" (Hag 1:8). Once the construction began, YHWH decreed, "I will soon
shake all the nations, so that the treasure of all nations shall come, and I will
fill this house with glory" (Hag 2:6–7), and "in this place, I will give prosperity
(שלום)" (Hag 2:9). Further, the prophet points out that "since the day that the
foundation of YHWH's temple was laid," there has been abundance of seed and
fruit and olives (Hag 2:18–19). Although YHWH promises that the people's economic state will be rectified with the new temple, the linkage between renewed
sacrifice and prosperity is not explicit.[2]

The most explicit mention of sacrifice in Haggai points to the impure practice
of sacrifice that may have occurred outside Jerusalem. After an extended example concerning the contagiousness of holiness and impurity, the prophet quotes
YHWH: "'So it is with this people (העם־הזה), and with this nation (הגוי הזה)
before me,' says YHWH, 'and so with every work of their hands. What they offer
there (ואשר יקריבו שם) is unclean (טמא הוא)'" (Hag 2:14).[3] J. W. Rothstein and
others interpret the condemnation to relate to proto-Samaritans, yet it is more
likely that "this people and this nation" refers to the ancient Jewish community.[4]
Although the term גוי is often used for the non-Israelite nations, it also can refer

---

2. For a fuller discussion of the relation between temple building and fertility in the post exilic
prophets, see Gary A. Anderson, *Sacrifices and Offerings in Ancient Israel: Studies in their Social and
Political Importance* (HSM 41; Atlanta: Scholars Press, 1987), 91–126.

3. LXX adds a phrase at 2:14 that echoes Amos 5:10: ενεκεν των λημματων αυτων των ορθρινων,
οδυνηθησονται απο προσωπου πονων αυτων και εμισειτε εν πυλαις ελεγχοντας ("because of their
quickly won gains, they will suffer for their labors, and you hated those dispensing justice at the city
gate").

4. J. W. Rothstein, *Juden und Samaritaner: Die grundlegende Scheidung von Judentum und
Heidentum. Eine kritische Studie zum Buche Haggai und zur jüdischen Geschichte im ersten nachexilischen
Jahrhundert* (BWAT 3; Leipzig: J. C. Hinrichs, 1908), 5–41. Rothstein argued that "this people . . . this

to the Israelites when they are in disfavor with YHWH.[5] In Jer 7:28, for instance, the people are called גוי in the context of YHWH's charge that their sacrifices are unacceptable because they have rejected YHWH's teaching. The same charge is leveled against the community in Jer 6:19–20, although here they are called "this people" (העם הזה). The two terms, עם and גוי, appear as parallel terms to refer to the disobedient people of God in Isa 1:4 and 10:6.[6] The biblical evidence thus suggests that the interpretation of "this people and this nation" in Hag 2:14 as parallel terms referring to Yahwists is possible.[7]

If this interpretation of the subject in Hag 2:14 is correct, what is the problem with "all the work of their hands" (כל־מעשה ידיהם)? David J. A. Clines argues that this phrase refers to all of the activity of the people: "Haggai seems to go out of his way to insist that everything the Judaeans do is somehow 'unclean' or 'defiled' (2.10–14)."[8] Yet Hag 2:14b indicates that the unclean work is not everything that the people do; according to the text, the cause of the uncleaness is the act of making offerings at some unnamed locale ("what they offer there is unclean"). Similar to Jer 32:30–35, where one of the "work[s] of their hands" (מעשה ידיהם) includes the erection of high places of Baal in order to sacrifice their children to Molech, the "work" in Haggai seems to be a cultic transgression.

A problem remains in identifying the "there" where the sacrifice takes place. Earlier commentators who identified "this nation" as the Samaritans identified the "there" as a Samaritan cult site outside Jerusalem.[9] Others, who saw in "this

---

nation" in Hag 2:14 refers to heterodox Yahwists (i.e., proto-Samaritans) who settled in Israel after 721 B.C.E. (see also Ezra 4:1–5), and that Hag 2:10–14 originated independently of Hag 2:15–19. Rothstein's interpretation is followed by, among others, Wilhelm Rudolph, *Haggai—Sacharja 1–8—Sacharja 9–14—Maleachi* (KAT 13.4; Gütersloh: Gütersloher Verlagshaus Gerd Mohn, 1976) and W. A. M. Beuken, *Haggai—Sacharja 1–8. Studien zur Überlieferungsgeschichte der frühnachexilischen Prophetie* (Assen: Van Gorcum, 1967).

5. See Aelred Cody, "When is the Chosen People called a Gôy?" *VT* 14 (1964): 1–6. Relevant texts include Judg 2:20; Jer 5:9, 29; 9:8; Mal 3:9.

6. Another example of the parallel use of the terms (although not in a context of divine disfavor) is Ps 33:12.

7. Such an interpretation means that the subject of Hag 2:14 would be the same as that of the following verses, Hag 2:15–19. Some have argued that Hag 2:15–19 is a later gloss, or transposed from its original position after Hag 1:14, but Klaus Koch, in his article "Haggais unreines Volk," *ZAW* 79 (1967): 52–66, argues that the whole of Hag 2:10–19 is a single oracle of salvation.

8. David J. A. Clines, "Haggai's Temple, Constructed, Deconstructed and Reconstructed," in *Second Temple Studies* 2, 60–87, esp. 72. As Clines points out, such an expansion of "all the work" entails a "deconstruction" of the message of the book of Haggai: "Must we conclude that the text exhibits a kind of 'bad faith,' according to which the people can never be praised for doing what they are encouraged to, and are required only to do what is impossible for them to do? If they don't build the temple they will be punished for their negligence, and if they do build the temple they will defile it" (p. 76). If, as I argue, "all the work" refers simply to the impure sacrifice indicated in Hag 2:14b, the answer to Clines' question is no.

9. See Beuken, *Haggai—Sacharja 1–8*, 72.

nation" a reference to the Jewish community, identified the "there" as the temple site. Haggai's problem with the "there," according to this judgment, was not its geography but its state of incompletion. Such incompletion of the temple indicates, in this reading, either a laxity that precluded the people's purification or an incorrect assumption that the temple will automatically enact their salvation.[10] Although this is a possible argument, there is no grammatical reason to preclude an extra-Jerusalem location of the "there," even if the worshippers are part of the Yahwistic community. That is, the text may indicate that Yahwists were sacrificing outside of the temple area. Recently, Joseph Blenkinsopp has proposed that the "there" might be Bethel, a place that he thinks might have functioned as an alternative cult site during this period.[11] Unfortunately, the text gives no positive geographical identification. The site of impure sacrifice may be Jerusalem or it may be outside of the city; there is not enough information in this text to insist on a particular site. Because impurity is contagious, however (Hag 2:11–13), those involved in incorrect sacrifice risk infecting the human community and even the temple building itself.

Within the dominant message of Haggai ("Build the temple!"), the text outlines what is at stake for the community. Predominantly, the text emphasizes that the construction will result in the economic prosperity of the people. Although

---

10. On this point, see Janet E. Tollington, "Readings in Haggai: From the Prophet to the Completed Book, a Changing Message in Changing Times," in *The Crisis of Israelite Religion: Transformation of Religious Tradition in Exilic and Post-Exilic Times* (ed. Bob Becking and Marjo C.A. Korpel; Oudtestamentische Studiën 42; Leiden: Brill, 1999), 194–208, esp. 205. According to Herbert G. May ("'This People' and 'This Nation' in Haggai," *VT* 18 [1968]: 190–97), "[f]ailure to rebuild the temple or laxity in the prosecution of the project" did not make the people unclean in the literal sense, but the prophet nevertheless declares that they are "ritually unclean" (ibid., 194). David L. Petersen (*Haggai & Zechariah 1–8: A Commentary* [OTL; London: SCM Press, 1985]) takes a slightly different approach, arguing that the impurity may be a result of the fact that the altar and temple area have not yet been ritually cleansed and rededicated (ibid., 84–85). According to Peter R. Ackroyd (*Exile and Restoration: A Study of Hebrew Thought of the Sixth Century B.C.* [OTL; Philadelphia: Westminster, 1968]), the passage is capable of several interpretations, one of which involves the understanding that "the contagion of uncleanness then implies that so long as the Temple is not adequately put in order the whole condition of the people will be unclean" (ibid., 169). Ackroyd also sets forth an ethical interpretation of the passage, one that is motivated primarily by the gloss attached to Hag 2:14: "Because of their taking of bribes, they shall suffer on account of their evil deeds, 'and you hated those who reprove (or him who reproves) in the gates.'" According to Ackroyd's interpretation, the verse sets forth the idea that "the uncleaness of the people is precisely that kind of moral failure which . . . . [is] potent in making worship unacceptable" (ibid., 170). See also Peter R. Ackroyd, "Studies in the Book of Haggai," *JJS* 3 (1952): 1–13, where he argues that though the temple is "a necessary accessory of new life . . . the Temple is in itself no guarantee of purity of life or immunity from judgment" (ibid., 6).

11. Blenkinsopp's identification is related to his reading of Zech 7:1–3 (for more on which, see below), and he claims that if this reading is correct, the "topographic allusion in Hag 2:14 may very likely be the same [i.e., Bethel]." Joseph Blenkinsopp, "The Judaean Priesthood during the Neo-Babylonian and Achaemenid Periods: A Hypothetical Reconstruction," *CBQ* 60 (1998): 25–43, esp. 33.

sacrifice might be linked to this renewed prosperity since the temple's rebuilding allows for the reinitiation of the sacrificial cult, the text does not make this link explicit. Alongside this emphasis, the text also claims that the building program will stave off the risk of impure sacrifice. It may be that such sacrifice was occurring at the temple site, but the text may also witness to extra-Jerusalem sacrifice. Such impure activity was occurring, and the text is clear that it must be stopped or the whole community is in peril.

2.1.2 SACRIFICE IN ZECHARIAH 1–8

Like Haggai, Zechariah has little to say explicitly about animal sacrifice, yet the text does emphasize that worship in any place other than Jerusalem is inadequate. Bound together with this message is the repeated assertion that YHWH has returned to Jerusalem. The book opens and closes with YHWH declaring that he has returned to the city: "I have returned (שבתי) to Jerusalem with compassion" (Zech 1:16); "I have returned (שבתי) to Zion, and will dwell (ושכנתי) in the midst of Jerusalem" (Zech 8:3; see also Zech 2:14–15). Although these verses might suggest that God is present in the whole city, the temple structure itself is God's particular residence: it is called "the house of YHWH Sebaot" (יהוה צבאות בית; Zech 7:3; 8:9); "my house" (ביתי; Zech 1:16); and "the temple of YHWH" (היכל יהוה; Zech 6:12, 13, 14, 15).[12]

YHWH's presence in the city (even before the temple is rebuilt) and residence in the temple implies that worship in any other place will be inadequate. Such inadequacy is also the message of the strange vision in Zech 5:5–11 in which an angel shows the prophet an *ephah* (a container holding a standard dry volume) with a leaden lid in which a woman sits enthroned (יושבת).[13] The angel names the woman "wickedness" (זאת הרשעה), stuffs her back into the basket, closes it with the lead lid, and then the woman and the basket are borne away by two other women with wings. The angel then declares that the basket is going "To the land of Shinar [i.e., Babylon], to build a house (בית) for it; and when this is prepared, they will set the basket down there on its base (מכנתה)."

The vision criticizes worship sites and practices outside of Jerusalem. The object's house (בית) and base (מכנתה) are cultic terms, so the text indicates that a

---

12. Notice also the terms "this house" (הבית הזה; Zech 4:9) and "the temple" (ההיכל; Zech 8:9). Also note that in Zech 5:4 and 6:10, בית designates simply a house, and in Zech 8:13, 15, and 19, it refers to the house of Judah and/or Israel.

13. Articles on this passage include L. Rost, "Erwägungen zu Sacharjas 7. Nachtgesicht," *ZAW* 17 (1940–1941): 223–28; M. Delcor, "La vision de la femme dans l'epha de Zach., 5, 5–11 à la lumière de la littérature hittite," *RHR* 187 (1975): 137–45; Christoph Uehlinger, "Die Frau im Efa (Sach 5,5–11): Eine Programmvision von der Abschiebung der Göttin," *Bibel und Kirche* 49 (1994): 93–103; and Michael H. Floyd, "The Evil in the Ephah: Reading Zechariah 5:5–11 in its Literary Context," *CBQ* 58 (1996): 51–68.

place of worship will be established for the object in Babylon.[14] Yet the vision disparages such worship; the woman in the ephah basket is called "wickedness," and the lid is forcibly pressed down in her mouth (Zech 5:8). Floyd argues that the vision should be seen in the context of the prior vision of the golden lampstand and two olive trees (Zech 4:1–14), and, when it is, the "wickedness" stuffed into a too-small basket contrasts negatively with the golden temple vessels that are filled by (or flanked by) two olive trees that produce golden oil.[15] The vision also contrasts the limited power of the woman in the ephah to that of YHWH. When the prophet asks his angelic interpreter what the ephah is, the response is "בכל־הארץ עינם" (Zech 5:6). Although the LXX interprets the first term as "their iniquity," the Leningrad codex (supported by the Vulgate) reads "their eyes in all the earth [or land]."[16] This explanation repeats several key terms in the angel's interpreta-

---

14. As noted above, the term for the edifice in which the basket will be placed (בית) is used throughout Zech 1–8 to refer to the temple of YHWH. The object's base (מכנתה) is a term used elsewhere in the Hebrew Bible to designate the place where a cult object is placed for display (1 Kgs 7:27–43 [13x], 2 Kgs 25:13; Jer 27:19; 2 Chr 4:14). Since "wickedness" (הרשעה) can indicate cultic sins such as idolatry (Deut 8:18–20; 9:4), some scholars would also include this with the other cultic terms. See Ackroyd, *Exile and Restoration*, 204–5. Scholars who prefer a non-cultic sense of this term include Theophane Chary, *Aggee-Zacharie, Malachie* (Paris: Librairie Lecoffre, 1969), 102–3 ("méchanceté," or "perversité"), and Margaret Barker, "The Evil in Zechariah," *HeyJ* 19 (1978), 12–27 (on p. 23 Barker links this vision to the prophet's concern with "the economic situation which accompanied the rebuilding"). Finally, S. Marenof ("Note Concerning the Meaning of the Word 'Ephah,' Zechariah 5:5–11," *AJSLL* 48 [1931–32]: 264–67), suggests that the *"ephah"* might refer to a cella atop a ziggurat (the Sumerian term for the shrine of Nin-Girsu at Lagash is *E-pa*), and, although most scholars have not adopted this, commentators such as Carol L. Meyers and Eric M. Meyers suggest that that "at best, the word may be a *double entendre*, partly meaning an idolatrous cult room but also inescapably evoking the image of a grain container" (*Haggai, Zechariah 1–8: A New Translation with Introduction and Commentary* [AB 25B; Garden City, N.Y.: Doubleday, 1987], 296).

15. Floyd, "The Evil in the Ephah," 52–53. According to Floyd, this vision is also related to that of the scroll. The oversized flying scroll, "going out over the face of the whole land" (Zech 5:3), represents the word of God and the covenantal norms of communal identity and is capable of destroying any household (בית) that does not follow its precepts. Floyd argues that this vision negatively contrasts with the more passive *ephah* (itself a standardized measure based on communal norms), undersized for its contents, dependent for its transportation on the women with wings, and leaving the land to have a temple (בית) built for it. In this vision, the prophet criticizes the program of basing one's identity on anything other than the torah. In relation to the vision of the lampstand and the scroll, the vision of the *ephah* "appears to caricature a popular alternative to the form of Jewish communal life represented by these two symbols [i.e., the lampstand and the scroll]. The lampstand represents the restored royal temple in Jerusalem, viewed as the only legitimate place for offering sacrificial worship, in its solely legitimate aniconic form, to Yahweh, the only legitimate God. The torah scroll represents scriptural instruction, viewed as the primary form of communal activity and the primary means of maintaining in every locality, whether back home in Judah or elsewhere, a worldwide community based on covenantal norms" (Floyd, "The Evil in the Ephah," 53–54, 57–58, 66–67). Given the scope of my particular work, Floyd's discussion of the scroll will not be addressed here.

16. The Latin reads *oculus eorum* (noted by Floyd, "The Evil in the Ephah," 55). For more on the versions, see Lars Gösta Rignell, *Die Nachtgeschichte des Sacharja* (Lund: Gleerups, 1950), 189–90.

tion of the prior lampstand vision in which the seven lamps are described as "the eyes of YHWH that range through all the earth [or land]" (עינם . . . בכל־הארץ; Zech 4:10b). Although English versions such as the NRSV obscure the parallel by choosing the LXX reading for Zech 5:6 and translating בכל־הארץ first as "through the whole earth" (Zech 4:10b), then as "in all the land" (Zech 5:6), the parallel in the Hebrew text clearly makes a point about the power and place of God over against other divinities. God's presence, embodied in seven eyes, radiates from the Jerusalem temple and is active in all the land (בכל־הארץ). In contrast, the power of the eyes of the others is radically contained—first stuffed into a basket, then removed from the land in order to be "housed" in Babylon.

Although some have argued that the message of the *ephah* vision concerns prohibitions against goddess worship such as Ištar or the "queen of heaven," I suggest that its main message has to do with geography.[17] Namely, any kind of worship involving iconographic representations of the deity in Babylonia is unsanctioned and ultimately powerless. Although some circles asserted that YHWH was once present in Babylonia (Ezek 1), after YHWH "returned to Jerusalem" in Zech 1:16, the prophet's visions proclaim that there will be no subsequent migration of the deity outside Jerusalem. The book of Zechariah claims that YHWH's cult is centered in the one city alone. God can be present in other places, and, like the informants of the Persian emperor, his "eyes" go in all the land (בכל־הארץ; Zech 4:10b).[18] Yet Jerusalem is the only legitimate cult center.

Some have proposed that the book of Zechariah also may witness to Bethel's function as a cult site in the early-post-exilic period (that is, in the time before the Jerusalem temple was built). According to Blenkinsopp's reading of Zech 7:1–3, during the fourth year of King Darius, "Sareser, Regemmelech and his men had sent to Bethel [Leningrad Codex: וישלח בית־אל שר־אצר ורגם מלך] to entreat the favor of Yahweh and to ask the priests who belonged to the house of Yahweh Sebaot and the prophets, 'Should I mourn [weep] in the fifth month and practice abstinence as I have been doing for these many years?'"[19] Although

---

17. For those who understand the woman in the *ephah* as a representation of a goddess (and thus relating the vision to idolatry), see Hinckley G. Mitchell, John Merlin Powis Smith, and Julius A. Bewer, *A Critical and Exegetical Commentary on Haggai, Zechariah, Malachi and Jonah* (ICC 22; New York: Scribners' Sons, 1912), 173–74; Delcor, "Vision de la femme," 144; Ackroyd, *Exile and Restoration*, 205; and Uehlinger, "Die Frau im Efa," 93–103. For a creative discussion of the text as an accusation that YHWH murdered Asherah his wife see Diana Edelman, "Proving Yahweh Killed his Wife (Zechariah 5:5–11)," *BibInt* 11 (2003): 3–44.

18. See A. L. Oppenheim, "The Eyes of the Lord," *JAOS* 88 (1968): 173–80. The relation of the rhetoric of Persian emperors to this passage is made by Floyd, "The Evil in the Ephah," 58.

19. Blenkinsopp, "Judaean Priesthood," 25–43, specifically 32–33. For a similar translation, see Francis Sparling North, "Aaron's Rise in Prestige," *ZAW* 66 (1954): 191–99. For the additional textual evidence outside the book of Zechariah that Blenkinsopp cites, see the section on sacrificial sites within Yehud at the end of this chapter.

Blenkinsopp's reading has the support of the Greek and Targum,[20] equally valid readings of the text include the one preserved by the Leningrad Codex ("[the people of] Bethel had sent Sharezer...") or, alternatively, one proposed by Julius Wellhausen ("Bethelsareṣer sent...").[21] Because the text is not a sure witness to a cult place at Bethel, and because no archaeological remains of this cult area have been found within the city (see below), it is difficult to make definitive claims.[22] It seems clearest to read with the Leningrad Codex and interpret the passage to indicate that a delegation was sent from Bethel to ask the prophets and priests in Jerusalem an oracular question about a rite of lamentation ("Should I weep in the fifth month...?").

Zechariah's emphasis on the temple and on YHWH's presence in Jerusalem effectively precludes any mention of other cult centers (although 7:1–3 may point to an earlier cult at Bethel). In this regard, it is significant that even the particular critique against worship in Babylonia (Zech 5:5–11) does not mention animal sacrifice.

2.1.3 Sacrifice in Malachi

Malachi emphasizes several times that YHWH's influence transcends geographic and national bounds. YHWH announces "my name is great among the nations" (Mal 1:11 [2×]), and "my name is reverenced among the nations" (Mal 1:14) and predicts that the people themselves will say "Great is YHWH beyond the borders of Israel!" (Mal 1:5). Yet this affirmation of a religious life that stretches beyond Jerusalem is coupled with an emphasis on the centralization of sacrifice—although the cult needs to be purified, the text maintains that the Jerusalem temple is still the only place for sacrifice. In addition, Malachi asserts that such sacrifice provides food for YHWH and agricultural abundance for the people.

As part of its concern with sacrifice, the text includes a sharp critique of the priests and lay persons who offer second-grade animals. YHWH accuses the priests of scorning the divine name by offering lame or blind animals (Mal 1:6–8) and curses the "cheat" who sacrifices a blemished animal when there is an unblemished animal in the herd (Mal 1:14). Yet this critique is not a call for

---

20. Both the Targum and the LXX of Zech 7:2 render the place name with an accusative of direction.

21. Meyers and Meyers, *Haggai, Zechariah 1–8*, translate "Bethel sent Sar-ezer . . ." (p. 379), and the NRSV is similar: "Now the people of Bethel had sent Sharezer . . . ." For Wellhausen's translation, see his *Die kleinen Propheten: übersetzt und erklärt* (Berlin: de Gruyter, 1963), 186. This translation is adopted by, among others, Petersen, *Haggai & Zechariah 1–8*, 281.

22. See also Klaus Koenen, *Bethel: Geschichte, Kult und Theologie* (Orbis Biblicus et Orientalis 192; Freiburg: Universitätsverlag, 2003), 62–64, and Francisco Oscar Garcia-Treto, "Bethel: The History and Traditions of an Israelite Sanctuary," (Th.D. diss., Princeton Theological Seminary, 1967).

the cessation of sacrifice in Jerusalem. Even YHWH's cry "Oh that someone of you would shut the doors so that you would not kindle fire on my altar in vain!" (Mal 1:10) speaks only of the current futility of sacrifice and not of the permanent destruction of the altar. Instead of calling for a permanent end of the Jerusalem cult, Malachi looks forward to the day when YHWH will send a messenger and when YHWH "will suddenly come to this temple" (Mal 3:1) and purify the Levites so that they may again present the "offering (מנחת) of Judah and Jerusalem" (Mal 3:3–4).

The problem with second-grade sacrifices is not only that they dishonor YHWH (Mal 1:8, 14), but that they also risk polluting God since they function as divine food.[23] Such a function is seen in the terminology for the sacrificial area and YHWH's possessive relation to it: "YHWH's table" (שלחן יהוה; Mal 1:7), "the Lord's table" (שלחן אדני; Mal 1:12), "my altar" (מזבחי; Mal 1:7, 10) and "YHWH's altar" (מזבח יהוה; Mal 2:13). When YHWH accuses the priests of offering "polluted bread" (לחם מגאל) upon his altar, they reply by asking, "How have we polluted you (גאלנוך)?" (Mal 1:7).[24] YHWH subsequently accuses the people of profaning "the table of the Lord" (שלחן אדני) when they say that "his food" (אכלו) can be despised (Mal 1:12). This relation of sacrifice to food, seen here in its divine aspect, also has a human aspect: according to Mal 3:10–11, when the people bring the full tithe into the temple ("so that there may be food [טרף] in [YHWH's] house"), they will also receive "an overflowing blessing" from heaven (Mal 3:10) in the form of YHWH's rebuke of the locust and the fertility of the vines.

Thus, although these texts do not expressly forbid animal sacrifice outside Jerusalem, they should be read as assuming at least that the city's cult area ("this temple") is the preeminent place, and possibly the only sanctioned place, for sacrifice. Like Haggai, Malachi also links the temple to agricultural abundance for the people, although Malachi includes within this equation the explicit function of sacrifice as food for YHWH.

2.1.4 SACRIFICE IN TRITO-ISAIAH

Although the contradictory perspectives embedded within this book make a descriptive statement about sacrifice in Trito-Isaiah difficult, the text nevertheless witnesses to and soundly criticizes animal sacrifice that occurs outside the Jerusalem temple. Sacrifice within the city is also criticized, but, like Malachi, the author foresees its purification rather than its cessation.

---

23. For a discussion about the sacrifice's function as food for the gods in the Hebrew Bible and the ancient Near East, see Anderson, *Sacrifices and Offerings*, 14–19.

24. Its seems that the LXX wants to avoid this reading and translates instead "polluted it" (followed by NRSV): ηλισγησαμεν αυτους.

In particular, two passages specifically criticize the practice of animal and non-animal sacrifice outside the city, Isa 57:1–13 and 65:1–12. The latter contains a polemic against those who "sacrifice (זבחים) in gardens and offer grain (or food) offerings on platforms (מקטרים על־הלבנים), who sit inside tombs . . ." (65:3–4).[25] The reference to "gardens" and "tombs" in this passage motivates the translation of על פני in 65:3a not as the technical term for the central sanctuary, but rather as "openly" (so Whybray), that is, outside of the Jerusalem temple.[26] Such extra-temple sites for sacrifice are also criticized in Isa 57, although here they are mentioned along with impure sacrifice in the city itself. According to this text, the sons of the sorceress (עננה) have slaughtered (שחטי) their children in the valleys and under the clefts of the rocks, poured out a drink offering (נסך) and brought a grain offering (מנחה) to the smooth stones of the valley (Isa 57:3–6). In addition, they went to a high mountain "to offer sacrifice (לזבח זבח)" (Isa 57:7). Although Paul Hanson interprets the entire passage as a critique of sacrifice within the Jerusalem cult, it seems that sacrifice both within and outside the temple is in view. Impure worship and sacrifice outside Jerusalem is indicated by the phrases "among the oaks," "under every green tree," and "in the valleys, under the clefts of the rocks" (vv. 5–6). Impure worship and sacrifice within Jerusalem is primarily indicated by placing the worship "upon a mountain high and lofty" (v. 7), a description reminiscent of other descriptions of Zion (Mic 4:1; Isa 2:2; Ezek 40:2). In addition, vv. 7 and 8 refer to a "bed" (משכב) around or on which sacrifice is made, and the singular form may be in deliberate distinction from the plural במות that the prophets often rail about. Finally, the reference to the cult's "door and doorpost," may be more applicable to the Jerusalem temple structure than other open-air sanctuaries.[27] Both Isa 57:3–6 and 65:1–12, then, reveal that animal and other offerings are made outside Jerusalem, although the texts do not give sufficient detail to identify a particular cult center. In 57:7–8, sacrifice within the city itself is also condemned.

---

25. Although some translations render מקטרים על־הלבנים as "burn incense on tiles [or bricks]" (so JPS and NRSV), קטר in the *piel* seems most properly to refer to the offering of other agricultural products. For discussion, see Julius Wellhausen, *Prolegomena to the History of Israel* (New York: Meridan Books, 1957), 64–65, n. 2; Menahem Haran, *Temples and Temple Service in Ancient Israel: An Inquiry into Biblical Cult Phenomena and the Historical Setting of the Priestly School* (Winona Lake, Ind.: Eisenbrauns, 1985), 233–34; idem, "The Uses of Incense in the Ancient Israelite Ritual," *VT* 10 (1960): 113–29, esp. 116–17; Diana Edelman, "The Meaning of *qiṭṭēr*," *VT* 35 (1985): 395–404; and Wolfgang Zwickel, *Räucherkult und Räuchegeräte* (OBO 97; Freiburg: Universitätsverlag, 1990), 336–39.

26. R. N. Whybray, *Isaiah 40–66* (New Century Bible; London: Oliphants, 1975), 269; contra Paul D. Hanson, *The Dawn of Apocalyptic: The Historical and Sociological Roots of Jewish Eschatology* (Philadelphia: Fortress, 1975), 147.

27. According to Hanson (*Dawn of Apocalyptic*, 198–202), the passage compares the temple cult to "a gigantic bed of prostitution, a brothel upon Mt. Zion."

Yet even given such condemnations, Trito-Isaiah ultimately does not renounce the sacrificial cult in Jerusalem. A larger oracle about the importance of maintaining justice and keeping the Sabbath (Isa 56:1–8) contains a verse about the divine acceptability of the sacrifices of foreigners in the city: YHWH promises to bring those foreigners (בני הנכר) who keep the Sabbath and the covenant "to my holy mountain . . . their burnt offerings and their sacrifices (עולתיהם וזבחיהם) will be accepted on my alter (על־מזבחי); for my house shall be called a house of prayer for all peoples" (Isa 56:7). Significantly, this text prioritizes the geography of sacrifice (along with ethics) over ethnicity. Acceptable sacrifices are those performed by covenant-keeping foreigners "on my holy mountain" and "on my altar."

Although the perspective on sacrifice in Trito-Isaiah is more complex than that found in the shorter texts of Haggai, Zechariah, and Malachi, there are discernable links. The condemnation of sacrifice in Jerusalem does not entail its ultimate cessation (similar to Malachi)—the text's vision of future restoration includes the offerings of animals in the city even by righteous foreigners (Isa 56:7). In addition (and in a manner similar to Hag 2:14), extra-Jerusalem locales for sacrifice, too vague to locate precisely ("in the valleys," "under the clefts of the rocks"), are noted and sharply criticized.

2.1.5 SACRIFICE IN EZRA

In contrast to other Persian-period biblical texts, Ezra never refers to sacrifice outside Jerusalem. Instead, all such activity takes place within the city, and the book includes many examples of the community and even rival groups sacrificing in Jerusalem.

Notices of animal sacrifice begin at the very point that the first group of returnees arrive in Jerusalem. After gathering together in the city, Joshua, Zerubbabel, and his relatives "set out to build the altar (מזבח) of the God of Israel in order to offer burnt offerings on it (להעלות עליו עלות)" (Ezra 3:2). When they set the altar upon its foundation, they proceeded to "offer (ויעל) burnt sacrifices (עלות) upon it to YHWH, morning and evening" (Ezra 3:3). The community also kept the festival of booths, and the text lists the many other sacrifices which succeeded those of the festival: the daily "burnt offerings (עלת) . . . and after that the regular burnt offerings (עלת), and those at the new moon and at all the sacred festivals of YHWH, and those of everyone who made a freewill offering to YHWH. From the first day of the seventh month they began to offer burnt offerings (עלות להעלות) to YHWH" (Ezra 3:4–6).

The text also relates that sacrifice in Jerusalem predated not only the rebuilt temple, but perhaps even the first returnees as part of exilic worship in the land. While the community was rebuilding the temple, "the adversaries of Judah and Benjamin" approached the builders with a request to join in the project. As justification for their request, they report, "for we worship your God as you do, and

we have been sacrificing (אנחנו זבחים) to him[28] ever since the days of King Esar-
haddon of Assyria who brought us here" (Ezra 4:2). Although the precise place of
sacrifice is not given, a Jerusalem site for this sacrifice is certainly implied. Despite
the rebuff of the returnees ("You shall have no part with us in building a house to
our God . . ."; Ezra 4:3), the report implies that sacrifice took place in Jerusalem
before the exiles came back from Babylon.

By disclaiming the validity of such sacrifices, Ezra 4 indicates that social
boundaries are built on criteria other than worship practices and the geography of
such practices. Although the requesting group claims relationship via cultic practice ("we worship your God as you do, and we have been sacrificing to him . . ."),
the building group denies that they worship the same God ("your God" vs. "our
God"). As such, "the adversaries" are prevented from joining in building a place
of worship "to our God." The two groups might have worshiped in the same
way (i.e., with sacrifice in Jerusalem), and the requesting group saw an affinity
with the building group, yet the building group denied such affinity seemingly on
grounds other than the practice of Jerusalem sacrifice. Although the containment
of sacrifice to Jerusalem emphasizes the city's centrality in practice, this account
implies that group distinctions were based on issues not entirely related to the
geography of worship.

Yet such a position is not entirely maintained throughout the book. Following the incident in Ezra 4, and following also various delays in building, the
rebuilt temple is dedicated with a great number of sacrifices (one hundred bulls,
two hundred rams, four hundred lambs, and twelve male goats; Ezra 6:16–18).
After this celebration the priests were set in their divisions and the Levites in their
courses (Ezra 6:18). Then followed the offerings of the Passover festival in the first
month, when "they killed (וישחטו)[29] the Passover lamb for all the returned exiles,
for their fellow priests, and for themselves" (Ezra 6:20). In contrast to Ezra 4, here
the Passover sacrifice was open to outsiders, at least those who "separated themselves from the pollutions of the nations of the land to worship YHWH" (Ezra
6:21).

This more inclusive account of the practice is followed by the story of the
return of Ezra and his party to Jerusalem, an account that likewise emphasizes
sacrifice in the city. Although some have pointed to the cultic designation of
"the place" (המקום) as Casiphia in Babylon from which Ezra recruited priests to
accompany his party to Jerusalem (Ezra 8:17), the linguistic evidence is too vague
to identify the site as an area for animal sacrifice.[30] More clear is the notice that

---

28. Although the Leningrad Codex has ולא, I read ולו with the LXX, 1 Esdras, Syriac, and the Vulgate.

29. The subject of this verb is unclear. It probably refers to the Levites, although the priests may
also be implied.

30. Although המקום can designate sacred space, and is sometimes associated with altars and sacrifice
(Gen 13:3; Deut 12:13, 14; Jer 7:14), its connection with animal sacrifice is not always clear (Gen 28:11,

when the group reached Jerusalem "they offered burnt offerings (הקריבו עלות) to the God of Israel, twelve bulls for all Israel, ninety-six rams, seventy-seven lambs, and as sin offerings twelve male goats; all this was a burnt offering (עולה) to YHWH" (Ezra 8:35).

This large sacrifice, seen in conjunction with the other sacrifices made in Jerusalem throughout the book of Ezra, manifests the book's emphasis on the practice. Unlike the books of Haggai and Zechariah, the practice of sacrifice is central in Ezra. And unlike Trito-Isaiah and Haggai, Ezra never explicitly mentions sacrifices that occur outside Jerusalem. Yet even given its centrality in the book, the geographical containment of animal sacrifice is not the only defining aspect of community in Ezra. Although the group that had sacrificed in Jerusalem prior to the return were excluded from the worshipping community (Ezra 4), others were later allowed to join the returnees in the Passover sacrifice held within the city (Ezra 6).

2.1.6 SACRIFICE IN NEHEMIAH

The book of Nehemiah mentions the practice of sacrifice only twice. It is first mentioned by Sanballat, who, with his army of Samaria, mocked the community engaged in building the walls of Jerusalem: "What are these feeble Jews doing? Will they restore things? Will they sacrifice (היזבחו)?" (Neh 3:34). Sanballat's question implies that the community was not sacrificing up until that point and that sacrifice was somehow dependent upon the building of the city walls. The relation of walls to sacrifice is strengthened with the realization that the only recorded act of sacrifice in Nehemiah is at the dedication of these walls. During the celebration of dedication, the community "offered . . . great offerings (ויזבחו . . . זבחים גדולים)" (Neh 12:43). It could be argued that this single mention of the act of sacrifice is meant to reveal more about the importance of the walls in the book of Nehemiah than about the lack of sacrifice in the people's religious practice. That is, it might be that the author deliberately recounts only one act of sacrifice in order to highlight the significance of the walls rather than recording the actual lived practice of the people. The temple dedication is immediately followed ("on that day") with the establishment of temple responsibilities to maintain the treasuries for the gifts, first-fruits, and tithes for the temple cult and its personnel (Neh 12:44–47). Thus, once the wall was dedicated, the structures were in place to maintain the sacrificial cult.

Unlike Ezra, the book of Nehemiah assigns responsibility for the support of the sacrificial cult in Jerusalem to the people. Ezra emphasizes repeatedly that

---

16, 19). See Laurence E. Browne, "A Jewish Sanctuary in Babylonia," *JTS* 17 (1916): 400–401; Ho Chong Joong, "Were There Yahwistic Sanctuaries in Babylonia?" *Asia Journal of Theology* 10 (1996): 198–217; Ackroyd, *Exile and Restoration*, 156 fn. 11.

the sacrificial cult in Jerusalem was supported and subsidized by the Persian emperors: Darius promised that "whatever is needed [for the temple]—young bulls, rams, or sheep for burnt offerings (לעלון) to the God of heaven, wheat, salt, wine, or oil, as the priests in Jerusalem require—let that be given to them [from the royal treasury] day by day without fail, so that they may offer pleasing sacrifices (די־להון מהקרבין ניחוחין) to the God of heaven . . ." (Ezra 6:9–10). Artaxerxes' letter to Ezra similarly offered money from the royal treasury (as well as from others living in Babylon) for Ezra to "buy bulls, rams, and lambs, and their grain offerings and their drink offerings, and you shall offer (ותקרב) them on the altar (על־מדבחה) of the house of your God in Jerusalem" (Ezra 7:17). This is in contrast to the situation in Nehemiah: although the Persian emperors are forthcoming with support for the city walls and gates (Neh 2:8), they do not directly fund the cult. And, although "the governor" makes a contribution of gold, basins, and priestly robes to the treasury, the account specifies only that the gifts were intended for "the work" and not specifically the temple (Neh 7:69). According to Neh 10, the people agree to supply the money and supplies for the sacrificial cult. The covenant agreement is signed by officials, priests, and Levites and joined with "the rest of the people, the priests, the Levites, the gatekeepers, the singers, the temple servants, and all who have separated themselves from the peoples of the lands to adhere to the law of God, their wives, their sons, their daughters, all who have knowledge and understanding" (Neh 10:1–29). The provisions to which the people agree are quite detailed. They lay on themselves the obligation to provide the temple cult with one-third of a shekel annually to fund the rows of bread, the regular grain (מנחת) and burnt offerings (עולת), the offerings for the Sabbaths, new moon, appointed festivals, sacred donations, and the sin offerings (Neh 10:33–34). In addition, the community arranges to transport to the temple their offerings of wood, the first fruits of the field, flock, family, and dough, as well as contributions of fruit, wine, and oil (Neh 10:35–38).

In sum, although sacrifice occurs only once in the book of Nehemiah, its prominence is marked by the occasion on which it is performed and the subsequent detailed arrangement for its support by the temple functionaries and the people. As such, this one story of sacrifice sets up a future of regular sacrifice, supported by the people, at the one place where God is worshipped.

2.1.7 SACRIFICE IN CHRONICLES

As Isaac Kalimi has noted, "little happens in Chronicles without some connection to Jerusalem," and this especially applies to the practice of animal sacrifice.[31] The author's emphasis on centralized sacrifice comes through in sev-

---

31. Isaac Kalimi, "Jerusalem – The Divine City: The Representation of Jerusalem in Chronicles Compared with Earlier and Later Jewish Compositions," in *The Chronicler as Theologian: Essays*

eral different ways, most obviously in the explicit designation of the temple as "a house of sacrifice" (בית זבח), unique biblical nomenclature put into the mouth of YHWH as a direct quote: "I have chosen this place for myself as a house of sacrifice" (2 Chr 7:12). Significantly, this designation comes as a response to Solomon's dedicatory prayer in which the king never referred to sacrifice, offerings, or even the "ritual function" of the temple.[32] Yet, in contrast to Solomon's reticence about sacrifice, YHWH makes clear just what the temple should be—a house of blood sacrifice.

The author's emphasis on sacrifice in Jerusalem is also evident when the text is compared to parallel accounts in Kings. In the retelling of history, Chronicles includes slightly more references to sacrifices at the temple (including an expanded account of a major sacrifice), and fewer references to sacrifices that occurred outside the holy precincts. Although some of the differentiation between the accounts may be attributed to a different *Vorlage* or even stylistic preferences, the amount and consistency of differences in the accounts pertaining to sacrifice are striking.[33]

The expansion of the number and occasions of sacrifice at the Jerusalem temple includes the account of David's erecting an "altar to YHWH" (מזבח ליהוה) under the command of an angel of YHWH (1 Chr 21:18 = 2 Sam 24:18)[34] and presenting "burnt offerings and offerings of well-being" (ויעל עלות ושלמים; 1 Chr 21:26 = 2 Sam 24:25). After David calls upon YHWH, the two parallel accounts diverge somewhat, with 1 Chr 21 including more emphasis on sacrifice. In answer to David's call, 2 Sam 24:25 claims that YHWH "answered his supplication for the land." In Chronicles, however, God answered with fire from heaven "on the altar of burnt offering" (על מזבח העלה; 1 Chr 21:26). This is followed by a passage that

in Honor of Ralph W. Klein (ed. M. Patrick Graham, Steven L. McKenzie, and Gary N. Knoppers; JSOTSupp 371; London; T&T Clark International [Continuum], 2003), 189–205. Related articles include Panc Beentjes, "Jerusalem in the Book of Chronicles," in *The Centrality of Jerusalem: Historical Perspectives* (ed. Marcel Poorthuis and Chanda Safrai; Kampen, The Netherlands: Kok Pharos, 1996), 15–28; H. G. M. Williamson, "The Temple in the Books of Chronicles," in *Studies in Persian Period History and Historiography* (FAT 38; Tübingen: Mohr Siebeck, 2004), 150–61.

32. Sara Japhet, *The Ideology of the Book of Chronicles and Its Place in Biblical Thought* (trans. Anna Barber; BEATAJ 9; Frankfurt am Main: Peter Lang, 1989), 79.

33. For examples of how some differences between the Chronicles text and that of Samuel and Kings might be more adequately explained by either stylistic preferences or a different *Vorlage*, see Werner E. Lemke, "The Synoptic Problem in the Chronicler's History," *HTR* 58 (1965): 349–63. See also Andrew G. Vaughn, *Theology, History, and Archaeology in the Chronicler's Account of Hezekiah* (Archaeology and Biblical Studies 4; Atlanta: Scholars Press, 1999) and Jonathan Rosenbaum, "Hezekiah's Reform and the Deuteronomistic Tradition," *HTR* 72 (1979): 23–43 for arguments that some of the material in Chronicles that is absent in Samuel–Kings may include factual material omitted in Samuel–Kings because the Dtr historian deemed it unnecessary or in conflict with his work's ideology.

34. Note, however, that in 2 Sam 24:18 the order of the terms is reversed: David is instructed to build ליהוה מזבח.

has no parallel in Samuel: "When David saw that YHWH had answered him at the threshing floor of Ornan the Jebusite, he made his sacrifices (ויזבח) there. For the tabernacle of YHWH, which Moses made in the wilderness, and the altar of burnt offering (ומזבח העולה) were at that time in the high place at Gibeon; but David could not go before it to inquire of God, for he was afraid of the sword of the angel of YHWH" (1 Chr 21:28–30). The story concludes with David declaring, "Here shall be the house of the God YHWH and here the altar of burnt offering (מזבח לעלה) for Israel" (1 Chr 22:1), a part of the story that again has no parallel in the Samuel text. David's life concludes in Chronicles with more sacrifice, a detail absent in the Kings account (1 Chr 29:21; 1 Kgs 2). According to Chronicles, on the day after David's deathbed speech "they sacrificed to YHWH sacrifices (ויזבחו ליהוה זבחים), and offered burnt offerings to YHWH (עלות ליהוה ויעלו), a thousand bulls, a thousand rams, and a thousand lambs, with their libations, and sacrifices in abundance for all Israel" (1 Chr 29:21).

Additional notices of sacrifice occur in the Chronicler's account of Solomon's reign. When Solomon moved the ark and dedicated the temple, the author repeats the account of the great number of sacrifices included in Kings (2 Chr 5:6; 7:4–5, 7 = 1 Kgs 8:5, 62–64) and also includes several more notices that highlight the practice. According to Kings, YHWH's glory "fills the temple" when the priests came out of the holy place before Solomon's prayer of dedication (1 Kgs 8:10). In the Chronicler's version, however, this event happens after Solomon's prayer and is preceded by a dramatic display of the divine acceptance of the sacrifice in the temple: "fire came down from heaven and consumed the burnt offering and the sacrifices; and the glory of YHWH filled the temple" (2 Chr 7:1).

The significance of sacrifice in Jerusalem is also emphasized in the accounts of the Passover celebrations of Hezekiah and Josiah (2 Chr 30; 35:1–19), accounts found either in a summary form or not at all in the Kings material (2 Kgs 18; 23:22–23).[35] In the Chronicler's accounts, there is a noticeable emphasis on the

---

35. Like the author of Ezra, the Chronicler adopts the centralization program of Deuteronomy and moves the location of the Passover celebration from the home to Jerusalem (Deut 16:1–8; contra Exod 12:1–20 and Num 9). Linked with the emphasis on the central place for Passover is the emphasis on the role of the priests and the Levites in the celebration since they are related to the temple cult. In the Torah's instructions for Passover, the actual sacrifice and the sprinkling of blood are the responsibilities of the laity. In Exodus, "the whole assembled congregation of Israel shall slaughter it at twilight" and "they shall take some of the blood and put it on the two doorposts…" (Exod 12:6, 7). For all the emphasis on the central location of the Passover in Deuteronomy, the text nevertheless assumes that the sacrificers include the laity as well: "you shall offer the Passover sacrifice" (Deut 16:2). The Chronicler, however, highlights the role of the clergy in both the sacrificing and the sprinkling of blood in the Jerusalem temple. At Hezekiah's Passover, the people began to slaughter the Passover offering, but this sight so upset the priests and Levites that they were "ashamed and they sanctified themselves and brought burnt offerings into the house of YHWH" (2 Chr 30:15). It was also the explicit role of the priests to "dash the blood" of the offerings (2 Chr 30:16; see also Lev 3:2). The role of the priests and Levites is highlighted

number of participants, their geographical breadth, and the large number of sacrifices. The celebrants at Hezekiah's Passover consisted of "many people" (2 Chr 30:13), and the crowd came from both the south and the north. There were Judahites, "a few" from Asher, Manasseh, and Zebulun (2 Chr 30:11–12), celebrants from Ephraim and Issachar (2 Chr 30:18), as well as resident aliens from Israel and Judah (2 Chr 30:25). Josiah's passover in Jerusalem likewise included celebrants from both Israel and Judah (2 Chr 35:18). The large numbers at both celebrations is emphasized in the amount of sacrifices. At Hezekiah's Passover, the king and the officials presented 2,000 bulls and 17,000 sheep; so many that the priests had to sanctify themselves "in great numbers" (2 Chr 30:24). At Josiah's celebration, the text records that Josiah provided 30,000 lambs and kids with 3,000 bulls, and Josiah's officials supplied additional offerings for the people as well as 7,600 lambs and kids and 800 bulls for the priests and Levites (2 Chr 35:7–9). In the account of both festivals, the celebration concludes with the regularization of sacrifice at the temple. After Hezekiah's celebration, the king appointed the divisions of priests and Levites "for burnt offerings and peace offerings, to minister in the gates of the camp of YHWH and to give thanks and praise," and established the system of tithes and offerings for the temple sacrifices and the welfare of the priests and Levites (2 Chr 31:2–19). The account of Josiah's festival concludes with the note that "after all this, when Josiah had set the temple in order . . ." (2 Chr 35:20), and it seems probable that such "putting in order" would include the means of sacrifice as well. With the emphasis on the great number of sacrifices and a system by which sacrifices could regularly be maintained in the reigns of Josiah and Hezekiah, the Chronicler highlights sacrificial worship by the nation at the Jerusalem temple.

This emphasis on centralized sacrifice is evident not only in the enlargement of the notices in Kings, but it is also found in the suppression of notices of sacrifice outside Jerusalem. For instance, the Chronicler delays the erection of a high place in Judah from the time of Rehoboam (1 Kgs 14:22–24) to the time of Jehoram (2 Chr 21:11). In addition, reference to non-Jerusalem sacrifice is generally avoided in the royal summaries. The summaries in Kings include four notices that sacrifice outside Jerusalem was practiced by the people during the reigns of Joash/Jehoash, Amaziah, Azariah/Uzziah, and Jotham ("the high places were not taken away, the people continued to sacrifice and make offer-

---

in the account of Josiah's Passover: the instruction to "slaughter (וְשַׁחֲטוּ) the Passover lamb" was issued to the Levites (2 Chr 35:3, 6), and, in the description of the celebration, the immediate referent of "they slaughtered the Passover lamb" is the priests and the Levites (2 Chr 35:10–11). In addition, the account specifies that "the priests . . . were occupied in offering the burnt offerings and the fat parts until night" (2 Chr 35:14). The priests also "dashed the blood" of the offerings (2 Chr 35:11). Thus, although there is some sacrifice performed by laity in Hezekiah's Passover, the emphasis in both accounts is on the role of the clergy and Jerusalem as the place of the festival.

ings on the high places [מזבחים ומקטרים בבמות]"; 2 Kgs 12:4; 14:4; 15:4; 15:35).[36] In Chronicles' summaries of the reigns of Joash/Jehoash, Amaziah, and Azariah/ Uzziah, the notice is simply absent. In the case of Jotham, the people's worship is cast in a negative light, yet there is no explicit mention of sacrifice: "The people still followed corrupt practices" (2 Chr 27:2).[37] Even when Chronicles includes a negative assessment of Jehoram not found in Kings, there is still no explicit reference to sacrifice outside of Jerusalem: "He made high places in the hill country of Judah, and led the inhabitants of Jerusalem into unfaithfulness, and made Judah go astray" (2 Chr 21:11). The Chronicler's reticence to use the phrase from Kings is found also in the contradictory account of the reign of Jehoshaphat. According to Kings, during his reign "the people still sacrificed and made offerings on the high places (מזבחים ומקטרים בבמות)" (1 Kgs 22:44). The account in Chronicles is complicated since in one reference the king destroyed the high places and *asherim* (2 Chr 17:6; see also 2 Chr 19:3), yet the account in 2 Chr 20:33 claims that the high places were *not* removed during his reign. According to Japhet, this inconsistency may be the result of the author's reverence for Solomon and his successors mixed with his dependence on the sources in Kings.[38] Yet even in its contradictory versions in Chronicles, accounted for by whatever means, it is significant that the story does not include the explicit description of sacrifice at the high places.[39]

Even when the Chronicler speaks of sacrifice outside Jerusalem, the accounts downplays its significance and frequency vis-á-vis sacrifice in the temple. When Solomon goes to Gibeon to sacrifice, for instance, the account in Kings reminds

---

36. The Chronicler praises Joash/Jehoash's restoration of the temple (2 Chr 24:4–14) yet also relates the king's subsequent falling away and the nation's serving of "the asherim and the idols" (2 Chr 24:18). In the Chronicler's account of Amaziah, no sacrifice at the high places is recorded (although his defeat in battle against Jehoash of Israel is attributed to God as punishment for worshiping the gods of Seir "and making offerings to them [ולהם יקטר]" [2 Chr 25:14, 20]). Similarly, although there is no notice of the people's sacrifice during the reign of Azariah/Uzziah, the Chronicler includes the note that when the king "grew proud" and "false to YHWH," he attempted "to make offering on the altar of incense" but was ordered out of the temple by the priests and afflicted with a skin disease by YHWH (2 Chr 26:16–21).

37. This is similar to the Chronicler's treatment of Rehoboam. Although the summary in Kings does not explicitly mention sacrifice, the account comes very close: "Judah did what was evil in the sight of YHWH . . . they built for themselves high places, pillars, and asherim on every high hill and under every green tree . . . they committed all the abominations of the nations . . ." (1 Kgs 14:22–24). The Chronicler modifies this statement by eliminating explicit mention of worship outside Jerusalem: "[Rehoboam] did evil, for he did not set his heart to seek YHWH" (2 Chr 12:14).

38. Japhet, *Ideology*, 220–21.

39. Although the Chronicler avoids mentioning non-Jerusalem sacrifice five times (when compared to the narratives in Kings), the author retains the two notices of sacrifice in the reigns of Manesseh and Amon (although there are some differences between the accounts). The Chronicler includes a story absent in Kings when Manesseh had a change of heart and restored YHWH's altar in Jerusalem "and

the reader that, since the temple was not yet built, the site "was the principal high place" (1 Kgs 3:4). The Chronicler does not include this reminder, but accounts for Solomon's worship at Gibeon by claiming that the site was the location of God's own "tent of meeting" and the bronze altar made by Bezalel (2 Chr 1:3–5). Thus, Gibeon was not a kind of "stand-in" while the nation was waiting for the construction of the temple but was the place of YHWH's tabernacle, God's portable shrine, and a legitimate site for the worship of God in the land. In addition, the Chronicler reduces the number of verbs used to describe Solomon's sacrifice at Gibeon. According to the account in Kings, Solomon went to Gibeon "to sacrifice (לזבח) there . . . Solomon offered (יעלה) a thousand burnt offerings on that altar" (1 Kgs 3:4). The account in Chronicles includes only one verb of sacrifice: "he offered (ויעל) a thousand burnt offerings . . ." (2 Chr 1:6).[40]

Extra-Jerusalem sacrifice is also included in the account of Ahaz, although here again the report differs from that found in Kings. Second Chronicles 28:4 repeats the notice in 2 Kgs 16:4 that Ahaz "sacrificed and made offerings on the high places (ויזבח ויקטר בבמות), on the hills, and under every green tree." The Chronicler adds a notice that Ahaz encouraged offerings outside Jerusalem: "In every city of Judah he made high places to make offerings (לקטר) to other gods" (2 Chr 28:25). Yet, according to Kings, Ahaz built an altar according to the design of the altar at Damascus and placed this before the temple, and offered "his burnt offering and his grain offering and poured his drink offering, and dashed the blood of his offerings of well-being against the altar" (2 Kgs 16:10–14). The Chronicler does not include these stories but merely records that Ahaz "sacrificed to the gods of Damascus" (2 Chr 28:23). By keeping the detail of the foreign altar out of the story, the desecrating object is kept out of the temple area and the sacred space is maintained.

The contradictory account of Asa in Chronicles also includes a centralizing slant. According to Kings, Asa was a good king, "but the high places were not taken away" (1 Kgs 15:14). This summary is repeated in Chronicles ("But the high places were not taken out of Israel;" 2 Chr 15:17), although preceded with a story of Asa's centralizing religious reform: The king "took away the foreign altars and the high places . . . he also removed from all the cities of Judah the high places

---

offered on it offerings of well-being and of thanksgiving" (2 Chr 33:16). In spite of this, the people practiced noncentralized sacrifice, although the Chronicler adds a telling detail: "The people, however, still sacrificed at the high places, but only to YHWH their God" (2 Chr 33:17). Whereas the account of Amon in Kings stipulates that "he served the idols that his father served, and worshiped them" (2 Kgs 21:21), the Chronicler's account specifies that Ammon "sacrificed to all the images that his father Manasseh had made" (2 Chr 33:22).

40. Japhet notes that the Targum plays down the sacrificial nature of the Gibeon high place. Instead of translating "במה" as במטיא or במתיא (which is the usual translation) in passages about Gibeon, the term is translated to designate a house of assembly or synagogue: במקדשא דבגבעון (1 Chr 21:29), רמתא דבגבעון (2 Chr 1:3, 13), and בית כנשתא דבגבעון (1 Chr 16:19; Japhet, Ideology, 219, n. 77).

and the incense altars" (2 Chr 14:3–4). He also put away the idols in Judah, Benjamin, and Ephraim, repaired the altar of YHWH (2 Chr 15:8), and gathered Judah and Benjamin (as well as those from Ephraim, Manasseh, and Simeon who were residing as aliens) to Jerusalem where "they sacrificed . . . 700 oxen and 7,000 sheep . . . [and] entered into a covenant to seek YHWH" (2 Chr 15:11–12). Similar to the treatment of Ahaz, Asa's retention of the high places is joined with a unique story about the king's emphasis on centralized sacrifice.

When compared to the texts of Kings, the book of Chronicles emphasizes centralized sacrifice through expansion and suppression—accounts of sacrifice in Jerusalem are added and expanded, while accounts of non-Jerusalem sacrifice are omitted or suppressed. Because it is not clear what version of Kings the author was using as a source, it is difficult to tell which of these differences were deliberate modifications, but the general emphasis of the Chronicler is clearly on the centralization of animal sacrifice at the Jerusalem temple.

According to the biblical texts, then, animal sacrifice is largely limited to Jerusalem and becomes increasingly emphasized in the later Persian period. In the earlier texts of Haggai and Zechariah, the practice and its cultic accoutrements do not receive much attention, although both texts contain critiques of worship outside Jerusalem (sacrifice "there" in Hag 2:14 and nonsacrificial worship in Babylon in Zech 5:5–11). Whereas Malachi is more supportive of nonsacrificial worship outside Jerusalem than is Zechariah, the prophet still maintains the restriction of sacrifice to Jerusalem and directs that the cult be purified. Trito-Isaiah likewise rebukes impure sacrifice in Jerusalem (Isa 57:7–8) but includes with this rebukes against extra-Jerusalem sacrifice (Isa 57:3–6; and see also 65:1–12). In all of the accounts of sacrifice outside Jerusalem included in these texts, the authors provide no specific location or name of a rival site. Within the texts of Ezra, Nehemiah, and Chronicles there is a marked decline in the mention of non-Jerusalem sacrifice: only Chronicles refers to the practice, but the author may deliberately have altered the literary sources to suppress some of the accounts. Alongside this deemphasis of sacrifice outside Jerusalem is the emphasis on sacrifice in the city. Occasions of sacrifice in Jerusalem are referred to throughout Chronicles and Ezra, and, even though it is celebrated only once in Nehemiah, it is coupled with the book's highest moment, the celebration of the walls. Nehemiah also includes protocols for the community to continue to supply the sacrificial cult (Neh 12:44–47; 10:33–38). Taken together, the biblical texts reveal an evolving landscape in which Jerusalem emerges more dominantly as a sacrificial center and rival sites disappear.

Having examined the biblical texts, I now turn to archaeological evidence, specifically the textual and archaeological evidence for areas used by Yahwists in Yehud and the Diaspora for the purposes of animal sacrifice. In this body of evidence, the portrait of Jerusalem differs from that found in the biblical texts. For context, I begin by briefly surveying the evidence for non-Yahwistic cult areas in Persian-period Palestine.

2.2 ANIMAL SACRIFICE IN ARCHAEOLOGICAL EXCAVATION

Many cultic installations in the ancient Near East are marked by specialized architecture such as benches, raised platforms, and plastered drains, and/or by cultic accoutrements or votive gifts such as statuettes. Examples from the Persian period include Sarepta,[41] Tel Michal,[42] Makmish,[43] Dan,[44] and Mizpe Yammim.[45]

---

41. At Sarepta a small structure (6.5 m x 2.5 m), oriented east–west, was found. Along the longer walls were benches made of plastered fieldstone, 20 cm high and 30–40 cm wide, probably used for votive objects. The opening was at one of the narrow ends, and at the other end was a raised platform, probably where cult objects were placed. The sanctuary also contained nineteen inscriptions, one of them reading "the statue which Shillem son of Mapa'al son of 'Izai made for Tanit 'Aštart." Also, the base of a stone altar records an inscription to Eshmoun. See James B. Pritchard, *Recovering Sarepta, A Phoenician City* (Princeton: Princeton University Press, 1978); Josette Elayi, "The Phoenician Cities in the Persian Period," *JANES* 12 (1980): 13–28; Olivier Masson, "Pèlerins Chypriotes en Phénicie (Sarepta et Sidon)," *Sem* 32 (1982): 45–49, pl. 7.1–2; Maria Giulia Amadasi Guzzo, "Two Phoenician Inscriptions Carved in Ivory: Again the Ur Box and the Sarepta Plaque," *Or* 59 (1990): 58–66; Stern, *Archaeology*, 480–81, 486.

42. A small building with benches was found on the east side of Tel Michal. A nearby favissa contained a bronze seal and other objects. See *Excavations at Tel Michal, Israel* (ed. Ze'ev Herzog, George Rapp, Jr. and Ora Negbi; Publications of the Institute of Archaeology 8; Minneapolis: The University of Minnesota Press and Tel Aviv: The Sonia and Marco Nadler Institute of Archaeology, 1989); Ze'ev Herzog, "Michal, Tel," *NEAHL* 3:1036–41, esp. 1039; Stern, *Archaeology*, 483.

43. Makmish, a small area 400 m northeast of the mound of Tel Michal, is believed to be a cultic area for the city. In the Persian-period layers is a large building made of undressed stone with ashlar square posts for the door, oriented north–south, and constructed on top of Iron Age remains. The building has one large room, 15 m long and 6.5 m wide, with a small chamber on the north side that was added later. Outside to the east of the building is a courtyard in which was found two large sunken plastered basins (1.1 m and 1.5 m in diameter) that were probably added in the second phase of construction. There is also an open plastered drain that runs east-west, of which a length of 5.2 m is still preserved. The drain was probably used in connection with the basins. A basalt round base was found out of context near the drain. Finds associated with this area include beads of semi-precious stones, faience objects, glass pendants shaped as human heads, a set of twelve bronze bracelets, and many male and female figurines. See Nahman Avigad, "Makmish," *IEJ* 8 (1958): 276; idem, "(סקירה ראשונה) החפירות במכמיש," *BIES* 23 (1959): 48–52; idem, "Excavations at Makmish, 1958: Preliminary Report," *IEJ* 10 (1960): 90–96, pls. 9–12; idem, "Excavations at Makmish, 1960: Preliminary Report," *IEJ* 11 (1961): 97–100, pl. 25; idem, "Makmish," *NEAEHL* 3:932–34; Ephraim Stern, *Material Culture of the Land of the Bible in the Persian Period, 538–332 B.C.* (Warminster, Wiltshire: Aris & Phillips, 1982), 61.

44. See Avraham Biran, *Biblical Dan* (Jerusalem: Israel Exploration Society; Hebrew Union College-Jewish Institute of Religion, 1994), 214–16; fig. 175; pl. 39; Stern, *Archaeology*, 484–85.

45. At Mizpe-Yammin a broad-house edifice was found. The main room, with an entrance on the north side, measured 6 m x 13.7 m, and a secondary room measured 4.8 m x 10.4 m. Two raised platforms were found in the main room, and benches ran along the east, south, and north walls (some hewn from bedrock). There were also many animal bones found outside the building (95% sheep/goat) and several skulls inside the temple next to the westernmost platform. The site was active in the Persian period, as seen by the associated pottery within and around the temple such as juglets, bottles, and storage jars. The shrine was in use for several periods: to the west of the temple were found some

Additional cultic areas outside Yehud are known through inscriptional evidence. Along with a favissa of statuettes at Acco was found an inscription instructing that a metal basin be given to "the overseer of the shrine" (אש על אשרת).[46] An inscribed cow scapula found at Dor indicates that there was a temple in the city,[47] and a dedicatory inscription, "to the 'Ashtorim of the Sharon" (*l'strm zy dšrn'*), on a bronze bowl was found at Eliachin.[48] Further down the coast, an inscription was found at Jaffa telling of the erection of a temple to Ba'al-Ashmun in the city.[49] In addition, a receipt was found at Nebī Yūnis that may record a donation (*dšn'*) of sheqels to the god Ba'l Ṣūr, and may indicate that there was a sanctuary in the area.[50]

2.2.1 YAHWISTIC SACRIFICE OUTSIDE YEHUD

The archaeological evidence for non-Yahwistic cult areas, along with the allusions to sacrifice outside of Jerusalem in Persian period biblical texts, sets the context for the archaeological findings of Yahwistic sacrifice at Elephantine, the "house of YHW," Lachish, and Mt. Gerizim. The clearest evidence for animal sacrifice by Yahwists (prior to 410 B.C.E.) comes from the papyri found on the island of Elephantine in Egypt, a military colony just north of the first cataract of the

---

pottery sherds from Iron II and two Tyrian coins from the fourth and second centuries. According to the excavator, major activity at this site decreased in the second century B.C.E.; subsequent finds include a Roman pit, a Byzantine coin, and weak Mameluke walls. See Rafael Frankel, "Miẓpe Yammim, Mount," *NEAEHL* 3:1061–63; idem, "המקדש מן התקופה הפרסית בהר מצפה-ימים," *Qadmoniot* 30.1 (1997): 46–53; Rafael Frankel and Raphael Ventura, "The Mispe Yamim Bronzes," *BASOR* 311 (1998): 39–55; Stern, *Archaeology*, 483–84, 497, 500–501.

46. M. Dothan, "A Phoenician Inscription from 'Akko," *IEJ* 35 (1985): 81–94. Also at the site was a large pottery vessel stamped with the sign of Tanit. See idem, "A Sign of Tanit from Tel 'Akko," *IEJ* 24 (1974): 44–49; idem, "Tel Acco," *NEAEHL* 1:17–24, esp. 22; Stern, *Archaeology*, 485–86.

47. Ephraim Stern, "A Phoenician-Cypriote Votive Scapula from Tel Dor: A Maritime Scene," *IEJ* 44 (1994): 1–12; idem, *Dor, Ruler of the Seas: Nineteen Years of Excavations at the Israelite-Phoenician Harbor Town on the Carmel Coast* (trans. Joseph Shadur; Jerusalem: Israel Exploration Society, 2000); idem, "Dor," *NEAEHL* 1:357–68; idem, *Archaeology*, 486.

48. R. Deutsch and M. Heltzer, "New Phoenician and Aramaic Inscriptions from the Sharon Plain," in *Forty New Ancient West Semitic Inscriptions* (Tel Aviv: Archaeological Center Publication, 1994), 69–88, esp. 80–83.

49. Stern, *Archaeology*, 486.

50. According to Frank Moore Cross Jr. ("An Ostracon from Nebi Yūnis," *IEJ* 14 [1964]: 185–86, pl. 41.h), the text reads:

     b'lṣd (or b'lṣr) tq[ln X]   Ba'līṣīd (or Ba'l Ṣūr) sheq[els X]
     dšn'   Donation

The first term is either a personal name or, reading the final letter as a *resh*, the name of the deity Ba'l Ṣūr, the god of Tyre. The final term is a Persian loan word in Imperial Aramaic, used in Egyptian and later Aramaic texts to signify "gift" or "present." Cross dates the ostracon on paleographical grounds to the second half of the fourth century B.C.E. See also Stern, *Archaeology*, 486–87.

Nile inhabited by Babylonians, Persians, Egyptians, and Yahwists. Information about the religious practices of Yahwists at this site is detailed in a lengthy letter that survives in two drafts written to Bagavahya, governor of Yehud, in 407 B.C.E. (TAD A4.7 and A4.8). In this letter the community relates that they worshipped in a temple dedicated to YHW, and that this temple was in existence from at least 525 B.C.E. until its destruction in 410 B.C.E. by the Egyptian priests of Khnum with the local Persian authorities.[51] Since the destruction, they have not been able to sacrifice offerings of grain, incense (or frankincense), and animals (ועלוה מנחה לבונה). The letter also relates that the colony had written other letters prior to this one. They had sent an earlier letter to the governor, which may be TAD A4.5, written in 410 B.C.E. to "our Lord" describing an act of destruction that year. In addition, they wrote to the Jerusalem establishment—to Yehohanan the High Priest and the priests in Jerusalem and to Ostanes the brother of Anani and the nobles of the Jews/nobles of Yehud (TAD A4.7.18–19 and A4.8.17–18).[52] Apparently, neither of these letters received a response; after the list specifying to whom Elephantine wrote (the governor, high priest, and nobles) comes the curt line "they did not send us a single letter" (TAD A4.7.19 and A4.8.18). This same letter mentions that the community also sent a copy of "all these words" to Delaiah and Shelemiah, sons of Sanballat, governor of Samaria (TAD A4.7.29; A4.8.28).

The letter to Bagavahya details the sacrifices that the Yahwists of Elephantine made in their temple. Before the destruction they would offer up (עבדו) meal-offerings (מנחה), incense (or frankincense) offerings (לבונה), and burnt-animal offerings (עלוה) in the temple (באגורא; TAD A4.7.21–22 and A4.8.21). They promise that they will again offer these sacrifices (this time in the name of the governor) upon rebuilding, specifically, "the meal-offering and the incense and the burnt-offering on the altar (על מדבחא)" (TAD A4.7.25–26 and A4.8.25–26).

Finally, years after the initial destruction, the colony received a reply; not a letter per se, but a copy of a memorandum from the governors Bagavahya and Delaiah (TAD A4.9). In this memorandum, the two Persian authorities allow for the rebuilding of a house of offering at Elephantine as it was "formerly," complete with the reinstitution of the meal-offering (מנחתא) and the incense-offering (לבונתא; lines 9–10). Significantly absent from the directive is permission to engage in meat sacrifice. This omission is crucial; although on the surface the authorities allow for the "restoration" of Elephantine worship to earlier practice

---

51. TAD A4.7.13–14 and A4.8.12–13 relate that the temple was built prior to Cambyses' conquering of Egypt in 525 B.C.E. For an account of the original establishment of the temple at Elephantine, see Bezalel Porten, "Settlement of Jews at Elephantine and the Arameans at Syene," in *Judah and the Judeans*, 451–70.

52. TAD A4.7.19 reads "nobles of the Jews" (והרי יהודיא), but this is replaced in TAD A4.8.18 with "nobles of Yehud" (והרי יהוד).

(indeed, they insist twice that they are returning to "former practice," לקדמין and לקדמן), the directive in fact sets up radical changes.

What is implicit in the directive from Bagavahya and Delaiah is explicit in an offer of payment for the reconstruction of the Temple, written sometime after 407 B.C.E. by five men, including Jedaniah son of Gem[ariah] (TAD A4.10). Referring to themselves as "Syenians who are heredi[tary-property-hold]ers in Elephantine the fortress," they write to their lord that if "our temple (אגורא) of YHW the God be rebuilt in Elephantine the fortress as it was former[ly bu]ilt—and sheep, ox, and goat are [n]ot made there as burnt-offering but [they offer there] (only) incense (and) meal-offering—and should our lord mak[e] a statement [about this, then] we shall give to the house of our lord si[lver . . . and] a thousa[nd] ardabs of barley." Although Jerusalem may have been silent on the matter of rebuilding the Elephantine temple, both the Persian authority and property holders in Elephantine voiced their opinion: burnt offerings were not to be continued in the new worship area.

The Elephantine material is significant in several ways to the discussion of Jerusalem's centrality in animal sacrifice. First, as part of their initial attempts to deal with the destruction, the Yahwists in Elephantine immediately wrote to the political and cultic establishment in Jerusalem: "at the time that this evil was done to us, a letter we sent (to) our lord, and to Jehohanan the High Priest and his colleagues the priests who are in Jerusalem, and to Ostanes the brother of Anani and the nobles of the Jews/nobles of Yehud" (TAD A4.7.17–19 and A4.8.16–18). They waited for a response for three years, but their letter went unanswered. When they wrote another letter to Bagavhaya in 407 B.C.E., they emphasized Jerusalem's nonresponse with the phrase "A single letter they did not send us" (TAD A4.7.19; A4.8.18). The alacrity with which they initially wrote ("at the time that this evil was done to us, a letter we sent . . ."), the three years they allowed to pass before sending out another round of letters, and their sense of surprise when Jerusalem did not reply all manifest the bonds that Elephantine felt toward Jerusalem. They also manifest Elephantine's expectation that Jerusalem felt these same bonds. Such bonds may also be seen in the architectural orientation of the YHW temple towards Jerusalem.[53]

Most significant for this chapter, the letters reveal that the Yahwists were sacrificing animals in Elephantine until their temple was destroyed in 410 B.C.E., and

---

53. Bezalel Porten, "The Structure and Orientation of the Jewish Temple at Elephantine: A Revised Plan of the Jewish District," *JAOS* 81 (1961): 38–42; idem, "Settlement of Jews at Elephantine," 451–70; Cornelius von Pilgrim, "Textzeugnis und archäologischer Befund: Zur Topographie Elephantines in der 27. Dynastie," in *Stationen: Beiträge zur Kultgeschichte Ägyptens: Rainer Stadelmann Gewidmet* (ed. H. Guksch and D. Polz; Mainz: von Zabern, 1998), 485–97; idem, "Der Tempel des Jahwe," in "Stadt und Tempel von Elephantine: 25./26./27. Grabungsbericht," *Mitteilungen des Deutschen Archäologischen Instituts Abteilung Kairo* 55 (1999): 142–45.

that they apparently did not feel any need to hide this from the authorities in Jerusalem and Samaria. They are explicit in their desire again to sacrifice animals in their letter to Bagavahya (and presumably to the Samarian governors as well)—they relate their history of offering incense, meal, and animals in the temple and promise that, if Bagavahya allows the temple to be rebuilt, they will offer "the meal-offering and the incense and the burnt-offering . . . on the altar of YHW the God" in Bagavahya's name (TAD A4.7.25–26; A4.8.24–26).

The documents thus maintain that, although animal sacrifice occurred prior to 410 B.C.E. (indeed, the community seems not to have recognized that Jerusalem would have a problem with this), and although the immediate cause of its cessation was not originally welcomed by the Yahwists at Elephantine, the community actively supported the limitation of their cult to the offering of grain and incense three years later. The letters give no explicit reason for the limitation, and no one has yet to offer an explanation that is fully convincing.[54] Yet, it might be possible to link the cessation with the thread in the biblical books that limits animal sacrifice to Jerusalem.

Another piece of inscriptional evidence (albeit much briefer and more oblique) tells of a "house of YHW" in the area south and west of Yehud. The Aramaic ostracon reads, "The hill/ruin which is below the House of 'Z' // and the strip/rope (of land) of the House of YHW (בית יהו) . . .," and goes on to list other properties whose fields had, apparently, not been cultivated. The text can be dated to the fourth century and indicates that a temple of YHWH was located in this area.[55]

The most straightforward interpretation of this text is that it refers to a sacrificial cult site outside Jerusalem. Other ostraca from the same geographical area contain personal names with Yahwistic theophorics, supporting the interpretation that Yahwists lived in this vicinity,[56] and they may have worshipped at this

---

54. Veneration of the ram god by the Khnum priests would not preclude all animal sacrifice, and Persian aversion to blood sacrifice did not preclude sacrifice prior to 410 B.C.E. For more, see I. Kottsieper, "Die Religionspolitik der Achämeniden und die Juden von Elephantine," in *Religion und Religionskontakte im Zeitalter der Achämeniden* (ed. Reinhard G. Kratz; Gütersloh: Kaiser, Gütersloher Verlagshaus, 2002), 150–78, esp. 169–75; and Reinhard G. Kratz, "The Second Temple of Jeb and of Jerusalem," in *Judah and the Judeans in the Persian Period* (ed. Oded Lipschits and Manfred Oeming; Winona Lake, Ind.: Eisenbrauns, 2006), 247–64, esp. 262.

55. André Lemaire, *Nouvelles inscriptions araméennes d'Idumée au Musée d'Israël* (Paris: Gabalda, 2002), 149–56; idem, "New Aramaic Ostraca from Idumea and their Historical Interpretation," in Lipschits and Oeming, *Judah and the Judeans in the Persian Period*, 413–56, esp. 416–17.

56. Examples include יהונתן in ostraca from Arad (dated paleographically to the mid-fourth century B.C.E.); and יהוכל. See Joseph Naveh, "The Aramaic Ostraca from Tel Arad," in *Arad Inscriptions* (Yohanan Aharoni, in cooperation with Joseph Naveh; Judean Desert Studies; Jerusalem: Israel Exploration Society, 1981), 153–76; and Lemaire, "New Aramaic Ostraca," 423–24.

site. Yet it is not absolutely clear that this "house of YHW" was used for the purposes of animal sacrifice—at the end of the fifth century, Yahwists at Elephantine continued to refer to their temple as "our temple of YHW our God" (יהו אלהא אגורא זי) even after animal sacrifice was explicitly disallowed from the area.[57] Regardless, and with the lack of other evidence, it seems most likely to assume that the "house of YHW" inscription points to a sacrificial site outside Jerusalem.

Another possible site for Yahwistic sacrifice outside Jerusalem is Lachish. During the excavations at the site in the 1930s, J. L. Starkey concluded that a large building (27 m × 17 m) with a courtyard, two sets of stairs, floor drains, and several limestone altars was a shrine in use during the Persian period.[58] Starkey's date was partially determined by the features of the building he considered to be associated with solar worship, such as its E–W orientation and an altar decorated with a life-size hand and a figure with upstretched hands. Such features indicated, for Starkey, the "intrusive" influence of Persian worship, and so the building was dated to the Persian period and interpreted to be a "solar shrine."[59] The date was also indicated by the finds of a bronze lamp, limestone altars, and a fragment of a horse-and-rider figurine within the building complex.[60] Nearby was a large building, "the Residency."

Scholars after Starkey have debated the shrine's date, although there is consensus that a cultic building existed in Lachish in the mid- and late-Persian period. In the excavation report published after Starkey's death, Olga Tufnell was less willing to date the structure to the Persian period because of the second century coins and pottery found with the building. According to Tufnell, the cultic objects that date to the Persian period (the bronze lamp and altars) were reused in the later building.[61]

When Aharoni reinvestigated the site in 1966 and 1968, he also preferred a date later than Starkey's and argued that the structure was Hellenistic based on his finds of Persian and Hellenistic pottery found in the building's foundation trenches and in the fill under the paved floors. Most notably, he found a Persian-period cooking pot (which he dated to the fifth to third centuries) under the eastern wall of the court of the building and a few Hellenistic pottery fragments.[62]

---

57. TAD A4.10.8. For references to אגורא זי יהו אלהא in texts that predate the community's decision to ban animal sacrifice from the temple, see TAD A4.7.24 and A4.8.24.

58. J. L. Starkey, "Lachish as Illustrating Bible History," *PEQ* 69 (1937): 171–79, esp. 171–72.

59. Starkey, "Lachish as Illustrating," 172.

60. Olga Tufnell (with contributions by Margaret A. Murray and David Diringer), *Lachish III (Tell Ed-Duweir): The Iron Age* (Oxford: Oxford University Press, 1953), 141–45; pls. 42:8, 9; 64:7.

61. Tufnell, *Lachish III*, 61, 142. For the floor plan and photos of the structure, see pls. 24:1–4 and 121.

62. For a brief summary of these finds, see Yonahan Aharoni et al., *Investigations at Lachish: The Sanctuary and the Residency (Lachish V)* (Publications of the Institute of Archaeology 4; Tel Aviv: Gateway Publishers, 1975), 4–5. See also Aharoni, "Trial Excavation," 157–69 and pl. 9.a.

In addition, his report argued that it is not necessary to connect the building with the "intrusive" solar cult associated with Persian worship; the motifs on the altar (the hand and the figure with the upraised arms) can also be associated with non-solar worship,[63] and comparison with the earlier temple at Arad (excavated after Starkey's work at Lachish) shows similarities both in floor plan and in E–W orientation.[64] Like Tufnell, Aharoni surmised that cultic objects from the Persian period found in the "solar shrine" were brought from another earlier building. Aharoni's investigation does not, however, preclude a Persian-period cult at Lachish: in his report he suggested that the public cult may have been practiced in building 10 (or, alternatively R/Q/S.15/16), an earlier forerunner to the "solar shrine."[65] This structure has dimensions similar to the "solar shine" (25 m × 16 m), was also built on an E–W axis with a large courtyard, and in it was found a small limestone altar.[66] Distinct from the "solar shrine," however, building 10 has a long cella with pillars along the N–S wall and a rounded stone structure that may have served as a *bamah* or some kind of small, elevated platform. Based on associated pottery, the original excavation report dates the building's probable construction to some time after 588 B.C.E., with use continuing into the third century.[67]

More recently, Ephraim Stern has redated the "solar shrine" to the Persian period, arguing that the buried Persian-period cooking pot excavated by Aharoni is an early style and should be dated to the sixth or early fifth centuries. Thus, according to Stern, the founding of the structure can be dated to the mid-fifth century, with use continuing into the Hellenistic period.[68]

The most recent and thorough excavation report on the site presents both datings of the "solar shrine." In his report of the excavations at the site (carried out from 1973–1994), David Ussishkin dates the building to the Persian period, and relates it to the building campaign initiated by the Persian government in the early-fourth century, a campaign that included also fortifications and the large palatial building ("the Residency").[69] He defends this date of the "solar shrine"

63. Yigael Yadin, "Symbols of Deities at Zinjirli, Carthage and Hazor," *Near Eastern Archaeology in the Twentieth Century* (ed. James A. Sanders; Garden City, N.Y.: Doubleday, 1970), 199–231; Nahum M. Sarna, "The Chirotonic Motif on the Lachish Altar," in Aharoni, *Lachish V*, 44–46.

64. For the Arad parallel, see Aharoni, *Lachish V*, 1.

65. Aharoni, *Lachish V*, 9–11; pl. 1.1.

66. Aharoni, *Lachish V*, 9–11, pl. 1:1; Tufnell, *Lachish III*, 146–49, 384 (where the find spot seems to be erroneously designated as the "Solar Shrine"); pls. 42:6, 64:11.

67. Tufnell, *Lachish III*, 146–49, pls. 24:5–6. 42.6; 64.11, 123. As Aharoni notes (*Lachish V*, 11), although the altar is listed with the contents of building 10 and not included with the contents of the "solar shrine," the original excavation report erroneously also lists it as an item found in the "solar shrine" in the section on altars (Tufnell, *Lachish III*, 384).

68. Stern, *Material Culture*, 61–63; idem, *Archaeology*, 479–80.

69. David Ussishkin, *The Renewed Archaeological Excavations at Lachish (1973–1994)* (vols. 1–5; Publications of the Institute of Archaeology 22; Tel Aviv: Emery and Claire Yass Publications in Archaeology, 2004), 1:95–97. For more details on the Residency, see 2:840–47.

on the basis of Stern's study, the architectural similarities of the shrine with the firmly-dated Residency (particularly the barrel corbelling) and the relatively meager and stratigraphic unclarity of some of Aharoni's ceramic evidence. Yet, in their report on the pottery from the Hellenistic and Persian periods at the site included in the Ussishkin volumes, Fantalkin and Tal argue for a later date (late Persian or early Hellenistic). They claim that Stern's argument based on the earlier date of the cooking pot is "misleading" because the form is late Iron Age, and the Persian and Hellenistic dates of other sherds found in pits below the shrine's floors make the later date more likely.[70]

Regardless of whether one wants to locate the public worship area for Persian-period Lachish in the "solar shrine" (with Starkey, Stern, and Ussishkin) or building 10 (with Aharoni), both options affirm the existence of a public worship area in the city during the mid- to late-Persian period. However, the two buildings give different evidence for the nature of this worship, specifically with regards to animal sacrifice. In the "solar shrine," two floor drains were found in the innermost room, one at the entrance to the inner sanctuary and the other in a plastered niche in the south wall of the inner sanctuary.[71] These drains may indicate that animals were sacrificed in this area. Since building 10 has no floor drains, the practice of animal sacrifice is not as obvious.

These findings are significant because it is likely that a Yahwistic community lived in Lachish during the Persian period along with other communities. According to Neh 11:30, returnees from Babylon settled in the town. In addition, the similarity of the "solar shrine" with the Arad temple may indicate a cultural connection with Yahwistic worship that was expressed in cultic architecture either in the Persian period or later in the Hellenistic period.[72] Finally, a small incense altar from the Persian period found at Lachish may be inscribed with the Yahwistic name "Maḥalyah" (מחליה).[73] The whole text reads,

לבנתא י[א]
ש בנ מח
ליה מל[א ר ב̇] [כ ר ש]

---

70. Alexander Fantalkin and Oren Tal, "The Persian and Hellenistic Pottery of Level I," in Ussishkin, *Renewed Archaeological Excavations at Lachish*, 4:2174–96, esp. 2191; idem, "Redating Lachish Level I: Identifying Achaemenid Imperial Policy at the Southern Frontier of the Fifth Satrapy," in Lipschits and Oeming, *Judah and the Judeans in the Persian Period*, 167–97, esp. 171–77.

71. See Tufnell, *Lachish III*, 141, and pl. 121.

72. Dating the "solar shrine" to the Hellenistic period does not necessarily mean that there were no Yahwists in the city until then, but only that some of their cultic heritage was not expressed architecturally until the Hellenistic period.

73. Yohanan Aharoni, "מזבח הלבונה מלכיש," *Lěšonénu* 35 (1971): 3–6; and Aharoni, *Lachish V*, 5–7. See the name Maḥli (מחלי), perhaps a hypocoristicon of Maḥalyahu, in Exod 6:19; 1 Chr 23:23; 24:30;

Although scholars agree on the identity of the radicals at the end of line 2 and beginning of line 3, they link them in different combinations with the preceding and following letters (A. Dupont-Sommer reads ". . . *mḥ*[*r*] *lyh* . . ." [". . . Meḥ[ir] à Yah . . ."]; Frank Moore Cross reads ". . . *m*[*ḥ*]*ly hml*'[*k*]" [". . . Maḥalī the courier"]; Edward Lipiński reads ". . . *nm ḥyh mn* '[*š*]" [". . . fall asleep . . . agreeable because of fire"]).[74] Aharoni proposes that the relevant letters be linked as the personal name מחליה and the text translated as "Incense (altar). Ya'ush son of Maḥalyah from Lachish."[75] Because a word division between the *h* and the *m* in the last line is not precluded in the published photographs, I see no problem with Aharoni's reading. Yet, even if one preferred to read with Cross, Dupont-Sommer, or Lipiński, the existence of adherents of YHWH in the town may still be indicated by Neh 11:30 and perhaps by the architecture of the "solar shrine."

In summary, what can be said about Yahwistic worship during the Persian period at Lachish? Assuming that there was a Yahwistic community in the city, they may have practiced their public cult in a large building (either the "solar shrine" or building 10). Although the community probably offered up incense (see chapter 3), sacrifice of animals is not as much in evidence. The remains of the "solar shrine" indicate that animals were probably sacrificed, but this cultic activity is harder to see in building 10. And the evidence does not clearly indicate whether such worship was related to YHWH. All that can be said for sure is that the local Yahwistic community at Lachish may have engaged in animal sacrifice outside of Jerusalem.

The final area to be considered in the context of Yahwistic sacrifice outside Yehud is Mt. Gerizim. According to the excavator, Yitzhak Magen, parts of the sacred precinct and temple date to the Persian period, and the establishment of the site dates to the first half of the fifth century B.C.E.[76] Although there was a break between the two communities in later periods, religious and cultural features of the populace of Samaria show continuities with Yahwists in Yehud, continuities that include a similar system of scripts, a significant overlap of per-

---

and Ezra 8:18. The inscription was originally published in Tufnell, *Lachish III*, 226; pls. 49:3; 68:1; with an article by A. Dupont-Sommer in the same volume, "Aramaic Inscription on an Altar," 358–59.

74. Dupont-Sommer, "Aramaic Inscription," 358–59; Frank Moore Cross, "Two Notes on Palestinian Inscriptions of the Persian Age," *BASOR* 193 (1969): 19–24, esp. 23. Edward Lipiński, *Studies in Aramaic Inscriptions and Onomastics* (Orientalia Lovaniensia Analecta 1; Leuven: Leuven University Press, 1975), 1.142–45.

75. Aharoni, "מזבח הלבונה," 3–6; idem, *Lachish V*, 7.

76. This date is partially established by pottery remains and coins, one of which dates to 480 B.C.E. See Yitzhak Magen, *Mount Gerizim Excavations* (vol. 1; JSP 2; Jerusalem: Israel Antiquities Authority, 2004), 1:1–12; idem, "הר גריזים – עיר מקדש," *Qadmoniot* 33 (2000): 74–118, esp. 113–14, 117; Ephraim Stern and Yitzhak Magen, "השלב הראשון של המקדש השומרוני בהר גריזים: עדויות ארכיאולוגיות חדשות," *Qadmoniot* 33 (2000): 119–24; idem, "Archaeological Evidence for the First Stage of the Samaritan Temple on Mount Gerazim," *IEJ* 52 (2002): 49–57.

sonal names, and Yahwistic theophorics in these names.[77] At Gerizim, these continuities are likewise reflected: the faunal remains from the Persian period consist of sheep and goat (with some pigeons and cattle) but no swine, inscriptions include personal names with Yahwistic theophorics such as Yehoḥanan and Yehonatan, and a silver ring (most likely from the Late Roman/Byzantine period) probably inscribed yhwh 'ḥd ("YHWH is one").[78] Most significant for the purposes of this investigation, animal sacrifice at Mt. Gerizim is indicated by an inscription referring to "the house of sacrifice" (בבית דבחא), and perhaps also by the large amount of animal bones (often burned) and ash.[79]

Having briefly examined the evidence for possible sacrificial sites outside of Yehud used by Yahwists, this study now moves to possible sites within the province, specifically Bethel, Tell en-Naṣbeh, and Jerusalem.

2.2.2 Yahwistic Sacrifice within Yehud

As noted above, Joseph Blenkinsopp has recently argued that there might have been a cult area at Bethel in the early post-exilic period, taking over the administrative functions from the site of Mizpeh, an earlier administrative center under the Babylonians.[80] As discussed earlier in the section on Zechariah in this chapter, Blenkinsopp's translation of Zech 7:1–2 forms part of his argument

---

77. For a brief summary of the evidence, see Gary N. Knoppers, "Revisiting the Samarian Question in the Persian Period," in Lipschits and Oeming, *Judah and the Judeans in the Persian Period*, 265–89, esp. 273–79.

78. Magen, *Mount Gerizim Excavations*, 1:1–12, 30–41 and inscriptions 7, 20, 170, 33 and 47 (with examples for both names written in both lapidary Aramaic and Proto-Jewish [i.e., Proto-Hasmonean] script), inscription 391.

79. Magen, *Mount Gerizim Excavations*, 1:9, and inscription 199. Magen also proposes that it is reasonable to suppose that the expression זי הקרב ("that which offered") on many of the inscriptions "stems from their proximity to the actual sacrifices offered at the temple" (ibid., 17).

80. Joseph Blenkinsopp, "Judaean Priesthood," 25–43. See also his article, "Bethel in the Neo-Babylonian Period," in Lipschits and Blenkinsopp, *Judah and the Judeans in the Neo-Babylonian Period*, 93–107. According to Blenkinsopp's reconstruction, after Ishmael's attempted coup against Gedaliah, Bethel may have taken over the administrative as well as the cultic functions from Mizpeh. Although I find Blenkinsopp's evidence for a sacrificial center at Bethel suggestive, the evidence for an earlier cult center at Mizpeh is less strong, at least if the cult center is understood as a place to sacrifice animals. This is primarily because the biblical texts present Mizpeh as a place for meeting and prayer and not for sacrifice. In Judg 20:1–10, an assembly of Israelites gathered at Mizpeh to give "advice and counsel" in the wake of the outrage at Gibeah, and subsequently swear an oath (Judg 21:1; see also 21:5). In addition, 1 Sam 10:17–25 makes no explicit mention of sacrifice, but only the gathering of the nation, inquiring of YHWH, and the acclamation of Saul as king. Furthermore, even if the pilgrims in Jer 41:4–5 were journeying to Mizpeh instead of being interrupted on their way to Jerusalem (plausible, considering that the Jerusalem temple was destroyed and the altar was contaminated by corpses according to Lam 2:6–7, 20), the geographical designation of the group nevertheless is absent in the text, as is mention of

("Sareser, Regemmelech and his men had sent to Bethel [Leningrad Codex: מלך
וישלח בית־אל שר־אצר ורגם] to entreat the favor of Yahweh and to ask the priests .
. .").[81] In addition, Blenkinsopp cites several texts in Judges 20–21 that may have
been retrojected onto the site to boost its cultic significance[82]—the tribes of Israel
gathered at Bethel "before YHWH" (Judg 20:18, 26–27; and 21:2–4), built an
altar (מזבח, Judg 21:4), and sacrificed (יעלו עלות ושלמים, Judg 20:26; 21:4).[83] Blenkinsopp dates these texts to the Neo-Babylonian or early-Persian period based
linguistic evidence in Judg 20–21 (namely the use of עדה and קהל),[84] conduct
such as fasting and weeping and the threat of death for those who did not appear
at the gathering (Judg 21:5),[85] and concerns with marriage and "delinquent
conduct."[86] Although this evidence is intriguing, it is difficult to use stereotypi-
cal worship practices such as fasting, lamentation, and weeping as indicators of
date. Also, comparing the violent deaths of the concubine, the Benjamites and
the Gibeonites with the exile of foreign wives in Ezra-Nehemiah for purposes of
dating these texts seems strained.[87] In addition, as I pointed out in the section on
Zechariah, there is no compelling reason to prefer Blenkinsopp's reconstruction

---

animal sacrifice. According to the text, the group's intended offering was only grain and incense, and
no mention of animals is made. If they did intend to offer animals, perhaps the pilgrims intended to
buy them at the place of sacrifice (see Deut 14:24–26 which permits this for pilgrims who must travel
some distance to the cult center). The text, however, does not indicate that the pilgrims were carrying
money for such an expenditure—indeed, when ten of the men barter with Ishmael to save their life,
they offer him neither silver nor animals, but rather the stocks of wheat, barley, oil, and honey that they
had hidden in a field (Jer 41:8). As the text stands, it seems that the group was not planning to offer
animals. Later textual evidence also supports a lack of sacrificial associations with this site. According
to 1 Maccabees, Israel gathered at Mizpeh before battle "to be ready for battle and to pray and ask for
mercy and compassion . . . because Israel formerly had a place of prayer (τόπος προσευχῆς) at Mizpeh
(1 Macc 3:44, 46, my emphasis). Indeed, the only explicit sacrifice at Mizpeh is in 1 Sam 7:9–10 where
the nation gathered for prayer and Samuel sacrificed a lamb. From the textual evidence, Mizpeh seems
to have been predominantly a place for prayer and coming "before YHWH" and not a place for animal
sacrifice.

81. Blenkinsopp, "Judean Priesthood," 32–33.

82. See also Patrick M. Arnold, S.J., *Gibeah: The Search for a Biblical City* (JSOTSupp 79; Sheffield:
Sheffield Academic Press, 1990), 63–69, where he examines the redactions of Judg 19–21 by Dtr and P.

83. Blenkinsopp, "Judean Priesthood," 30.

84. Blenkinsopp points out that the term עדה ("gathering") is used in Judg 20:1; 21:10, 13, 16, and
is frequent within P. The term קהל ("assembly") is used in Judg 20: 2; 21:5, 8, and throughout Ezra and
Nehemiah (Ezra 2:64; 10:1, 8, 12, 14; Neh 5:13; 7:66; 8:2, 17; 13:1).

85. This situation parallels Ezra 10:8 since those who did not appear were banished from the
community, a situation that Blenkinsopp construes as a "social death."

86. Blenkinsopp, "Judean Priesthood," 31.

87. In addition, while the term קהל is indeed mostly found in exilic and post-exilic texts (including
P, Chr, Ezek, etc.), it also appears in texts that are difficult to date, such as Ps 89:6 and Gen 49:6. Thus
the term cannot function as a sure peg for dating.

of Zech 7:1–2 over that of the Leningrad Codex, where it is the people of Bethel who sent Sharezer.[88]

When Blenkinsopp's proposal is evaluated in light of the extant archaeological evidence, it can be neither confirmed nor denied. There is no evidence of a cult area in the town during the early-Persian period prior to the destruction layer in the mid- to late-sixth century, although the excavation is difficult to interpret.[89] Of course, as Blenkinsopp points out, the cult area could have been outside the city itself (perhaps even shared with Mizpeh).[90] Yet at this point there is not enough evidence, textual or archaeological, to make sure claims about Bethel as a place of animal sacrifice for Yahwists in the early-Persian period.

Another site of interest is Tell en-Naṣbeh (biblical Mizpeh), since Jeffrey R. Zorn has recently redated to the Persian period an area thought to be cultic.[91]

---

88. As discussed above, most translators do not read בית־אל as a destination (accusative of direction) but rather as a term to designate the city's inhabitants: "[the people of] Bethel had sent Sharezer . . ." (so NRSV and Meyers and Meyers, *Haggai, Zechariah 1–8*, 379), or as the beginning of the personal name Bethelsareṣer (Wellhausen, *Die kleinen Propheten*, 186).

89. See the published reports in James L. Kelso, with chapters by William F. Albright, Lawrence A. Sinclair, Paul W. Lapp, and James L. Swauger, *The Excavation of Bethel (1934–1960)* (AASOR 39; Cambridge, Mass.: American Schools of Oriental Research, 1968), 37–38, 52; and James Leon Kelso, "Bethel," *NEAEHL* 1:192–94. See also Nadav Na'aman, "Beth-acen, Bethel, and Early Israelite Sanctuaries," *ZDPV* 103 (1987): 13–21; Stern, *Material Culture*, 31, and idem, *Archaeology*, 432.

90. Perhaps indicated by the close proximity of the cities and the tradition of building cultic areas outside of city centers (Blenkinsopp, "Judean Priesthood," 33–34).

91. Jeffrey Ralph Zorn, "Tell en-Naṣbeh: A Re-Evaluation of the Architecture and Stratigraphy of the Early Bronze Age, Iron Age and Later Periods" (4 vols.; Ph.D. diss., University of California at Berkeley, 1993); idem, "Naṣbeh, Tell en-," *NEAEHL* 3:1098–1102; idem, "Estimating the Population Size of Ancient Settlements: Methods, Problems, Solutions, and a Case Study," *BASOR* 295 (1994): 31–48; idem, "An Inner and Outer Gate Complex at Tell en-Nasbeh," *BASOR* 307 (1997): 53–66; and idem, "Mizpeh: Newly Discovered Stratum Reveals Judah's Other Capital," *BAR* 23.5 (September/October 1997): 28–38, 66.

In his reevaluation, Zorn detected an archaeological layer (stratum II, 586–ca. 400 B.C.E.) on top of the IA material noted in the original publication reports (see Chester Charlton McCown, with contributions by James Muilenburg, Joseph Carson Wampler, Dietrich von Bothmer, and Margaret Harrison, *Tell en-Naṣbeh I: Archaeological and Historical Results* [Berkeley: The Palestine Institute of Pacific School of Religion and the American Schools of Oriental Research, 1947] and Joseph Carson Wampler, with a chapter by Chester Charlton McCown, *Tell en-Naṣbeh II: The Pottery* [Berkeley: The Palestine Institute of Pacific School of Religion and the American Schools of Oriental Research, 1947]). This layer contains the remains of what could be interpreted as a provincial capital during this period. Finds within this stratum include a large building with a stone paving, storehouses, larger and finer houses (some built over part of the earlier gate complex), and thirty M(W)ṢH seal impressions. Although much of the new building activity seems to date to the beginning of the Babylonian period, occupation in the Persian period is marked by fragments of late-sixth to fifth century B.C.E. Greek pottery, late local forms including mortaria, and twenty-four YHW(D) stamp impressions (Zorn, "Naṣbeh, Tell en-," 1102; idem, "Mizpeh," 37). Stratum II seems to end with destruction, marked by crushed store-jars in a four-room house (Building B; Zorn, "Mizpeh," 36).

According to the original excavator, William Frederic Badè, part of the site was an Iron Age cultic installation, where the bedrock was carved with circular "cup marks" and channels used to hold offerings and to drain the blood of sacrifices. The excavation report, published after Badè's death, was less enthusiastic about this designation and concludes that, because no other cultic material (such as altars and favissae) was found associated with the cup holes, and because the holes and channels were found elsewhere at the site, the area was probably of a secular nature.[92] As part of his full reevaluation of the stratigraphy in the reports, Zorn redated this area to the Babylonian–Persian period. Yet Zorn also maintained its secular nature, arguing that the distinctive marks in the stone were associated with the processing of agricultural products.[93] Although a small incense altar was found at the site (see chapter 3), there is no recognizable Persian-period cult area or cultic structure in this city.[94] Thus, although Mizpeh may have remained an administrative center until the time of Nehemiah (according to Neh 3:7),[95] the extant evidence is insufficient to conclude that the site also housed a cult center.

Ironically perhaps, the archaeological record preserves nothing specifically cultic within the city of Jerusalem during this period. Although there is archaeological evidence for Persian-period settlement and activity in the city, its cult area is evident only in textual sources. According to the archaeological remains, the population and settled area of the city during this period was much smaller than it was at the end of the Iron Age (although the inhabitants may have made use of older walls that enclosed more area than the population currently occupied).[96] At the beginning of the Persian period the population was scant, and the settled area (not including the Temple Mount) comprised about 50 to 60 dunams and

92. For an account of the cup holes and channels, see McCown, *Tell en-Naṣbeh I*, 206–8.

93. Zorn, "Tell en-Naṣbeh," 900–901.

94. Zorn, "Tell en-Naṣbeh," 360. One three-roomed structure that may have had a cultic use is Building 142.04, but this dates to Stratum 3. (The cultic nature of the building may be indicated by an assemblage of an ostracon with one inscribed character, the base of a hand-burnished stand, a cosmetic mortar, two pinched-face figurine fragments, and a human skull with additional charred bone fragments near a hearth in Room 616; and fragments of a human and an animal figurine in Room 622). See ibid., 360–61, 654–55. For analysis of other cult objects found throughout the various strata at the site, see McCown, *Tell en-Naṣbeh I*, 233–48, 273, pls. 84–90; Wampler, *Tell en-Naṣbeh II*, 52–53, 184–85, pls. 78–79.

95. Neh 3:7 speaks of the men of Gibeon and Mizpeh "לכסא פחת עבר הנהר" (translated by the NRSV as "who were under the jurisdiction of the governor of the province Beyond the River"). This verse is somewhat difficult to translate, but scholars who interpret this verse to indicate that the governor maintained a seat at Mizpeh (perhaps used on state visits to Transeuphrates) include Blenkinsopp ("Judaean Priesthood," 29, n. 11; see also n. 48 on page 42; idem, *Ezra-Nehemiah* [(OTL: Philadelphia: Westminster Press, 1988], 235) and H. G. M. Williamson (*Ezra, Nehemiah* [WBC 16, Waco, Tex.: Word Books, 1985], 205). See also Neh 3:15, 19.

96. David Ussishkin, "The Borders and *De Facto* Size of Jerusalem in the Persian Period," in Lipschits and Oeming, *Judah and the Judeans in the Persian Period*, 147–66.

was limited to the ridge of the City of David. This situation looks similar to that described in Neh 7:4 where the city dwellers are "few." At its height in the Persian period, the settled area in and around the city increased to about 110 dunams.[97] Given this small settled area and the absence of cultic remains, Jerusalem's significance to its adherents (particularly vis-à-vis the practice of animal sacrifice) is obvious only in the biblical texts.

2.3 THE GEOGRAPHIC PROTOCOLS OF ANIMAL SACRIFICE FOR YAHWISTS

Before the recent publication of the excavations at Mt. Gerizim, it was possible to claim that the archaeological evidence fit with the biblical picture of a growing concern for the centralization of animal sacrifice in Jerusalem in the Persian period. Although Yahwists at Elephantine engaged in the practice prior to 410 B.C.E., their archives indicate that they explicitly disavowed it after 407 B.C.E. Perhaps the community in Egypt came to support the program emerging in the biblical texts (especially seen in Ezra, Nehemiah, and Chronicles) for the geographic restriction of animal sacrifice to Jerusalem alone. Although some of the earlier biblical texts make vague references to sacrifice outside the city ("there" in Hag 2:14; "gardens" in Isa 65:3), the great majority of references to the sacrificial cult involve Jerusalem. Even Malachi, a book that affirms the worship of YHWH outside the traditional boundaries of Israel and strongly criticizes the temple cult (Mal 1:10), maintains that animal sacrifice must be contained within Jerusalem. Although the few references to extra-Jerusalem sacrifice in Chronicles might indicate its continued practice, the text puts great emphasis on animal sacrifice in the temple, even referring to it as בית זבח (2 Chr 7:12).

The evidence from Mt. Gerizim (considered along with evidence from Lachish and perhaps also the reference to the "house of YHW" in an Aramaic ostracon), indicates that not all Yahwists outside Yehud enacted similar decisions about religious practice as those pursued at Elephantine. The emerging impulse in the biblical texts to confine sacrifice to Jerusalem is not matched uniformly in

---

97. Oded Lipschits, "Demographic Changes in Judah Between the Seventh and the Fifth Centuries B.C.E.," in Lipschits and Blenkinsopp, *Judah and the Judeans in the Neo-Babylonian Period*, 323–76, esp. 329–33. Evidence for settlement includes Persian-period pottery, seal impressions, some walls, and a great quantity of limestone chips that may indicate quarrying activity. For the ceramic analysis, see Alon De Groot and Donald T. Ariel, "Ceramic Report," in *Excavations at the City of David* (ed. Donald T. Ariel; Qedem 40; Jerusalem: The Hebrew University of Jerusalem, 2000), 91–154, esp. 98 and figures 28–29. For a discussion of the limestone chips, see in the same volume Donald T. Ariel, Hannah Hirschfeld, and Neta Savir, "Area D1: Stratigraphic Report," 33–72, esp. 59–62. See also Yigal Shiloh, *Excavations at the City of David* (Qedem 19; Jerusalem: The Hebrew University of Jerusalem, 1984), 7–9, 14, 20, 29. For the seal impressions, see Nahman Avigad, *Bullae and Seals from a Post-Exilic Judean Archive* (trans. R. Grafman; Qedem 4; Jerusalem: Institute of Archaeology, The Hebrew University of Jerusalem, 1976). See also Stern, *Archaeology*, 434–36.

the archaeological evidence from outside Yehud, which shows that this central-izing tendency was only partially realized. Indeed, it may be that this variation between the texts and the archaeological remains accounts for the rising promi-nence of Jerusalem in texts such as Chronicles: the author's portrayal of the city is a "promotion" of Jerusalem in a context of rival shrines. In such a context, the author had to argue for "the authority and privilege of the Jerusalem temple," and part of this argument was the relegation of animal sacrifice to the city.[98]

---

98. Gary N. Knoppers, "'The City Yhwh Has Chosen': The Chronicler's Promotion of Jerusalem in Light of Recent Archaeology," in Vaughn and Killebrew, *Jerusalem in Bible and Archaeology*, 307–26, esp. 321.

CHAPTER 3

CENTRALITY AND THE RELIGIOUS USE OF INCENSE AND FIGURINES: THE GEOGRAPHIC PROTOCOLS OF NON-SACRIFICIAL WORSHIP

B esides animal sacrifice, how did those who lived outside Jerusalem enact their religious belief in ways still detectable in the textual and archaeological records? Is it possible to see additional religious activities and protocols pursued outside of Jerusalem that attest to the city's centrality? In the previous chapter, I presented evidence for the various enactments of the curtailment of animal sacrifice by Yahwists outside Jerusalem. In this chapter, I examine two additional religious practices with different geographical enactments, namely, the use of incense and figurines.[1] After briefly examining the evidence for the religious use of aromatics in the larger ancient Near East, I present the findings for the practice by Yahwistic communities both within Yehud and the wider Diaspora. In the final section of this chapter, I present the evidence for the religious use of figurines by Yahwists within and outside Yehud.

Whereas most of the extant textual evidence (Hebrew Bible and Elephantine) privileges Jerusalem as the setting for animal sacrifice, there is a greater diversity regarding incense: texts such as Chronicles is against its use outside of Jerusalem, yet Malachi and Elephantine indicate that this was accepted by at least some parts of the community. Like animal sacrifice, there is limited archaeological evidence

---

1. Although it would be possible to include an examination of the use of other potentially religious artifacts such as chalices, model furniture, and rattles, the use of such evidence is not as clear nor the items as prolific in the relevant archaeological evidence. For discussions of such artifacts, see John S. Holladay, Jr., "Religion in Israel and Judah under the Monarchy: An Explicitly Archaeological Approach," in *Ancient Israelite Religion: Essays in Honor of Frank Moore Cross* (ed. Patrick D. Miller Jr., Paul D. Hanson, and S. Dean McBride; Philadelphia: Fortress, 1987), 249–99; and P. M. Michèle Daviau, "Family Religion: Evidence for the Paraphernalia of the Domestic Cult," in *The World of the Aramaeans II: Studies in History and Archaeology in Honour of Paul-Eugène Dion* (ed. P. M. Michèle Daviau, John W. Wevers, and Michael Weigl; JSOTSupp 325; Sheffield: Sheffield Academic Press, 2001), 199–229.

for the religious use of incense outside Jerusalem. The use of figurines has a different textual and archaeological profile than both the sacrifice of animals and incense because they are condemned throughout the entire textual corpus and not attested in archaeological excavation (at least within the provinces of Yehud and Samaria). Examining all three practices together reveals distinct and nuanced religious geographies at play in the enactment of Yahwism during the Persian period.

3.1 THE RELIGIOUS USE OF INCENSE IN THE ANCIENT NEAR EAST

Textual evidence outside the Hebrew Scriptures indicates that aromatics such as incense and frankincense were used in worship contexts throughout various periods in the ancient Near East. Although they could be used to perfume the air or one's body and to heal wounds, they were also used for worship and ritual purification in the public and domestic cult.[2] For example, incense was used to purify the temple of Bel and Beltiya on the fifth day of the Babylonian New Year festival, and, in the temple that Shalmaneser I built, aromatics were mixed into the mortar used for the first bricks.[3] In the domestic sphere, a Babylonian wisdom text instructs the head of the family to worship his god daily at the house shrine with "the proper accompaniment of incense."[4]

Scholars often link this textual evidence for the religious use of aromatics with stone and clay platforms or burners found in archaeological excavations. In Iron Age strata, these burners are fairly large, often with a "horn" fashioned at each corner.[5] In the Persian period, the platforms are usually smaller (most are about 10–20 cm square), with a shallow basin and fashioned either as a cuboid or as a taller rectangular object, sometimes inscribed with geometric decoration and/or figures.[6] The small platforms have been found throughout the ancient

---

2. Kjeld Nielsen, *Incense in Ancient Israel* (VTSupp 38; Leiden: Brill, 1986), 89–94.

3. Nielsen, *Incense in Ancient Israel*, 32–33.

4. Quoted in Karel van der Toorn, *From Her Cradle to Her Grave: The Role of Religion in the Life of the Israelite and the Babylonian Woman* (trans. Sara J. Denning-Bolle; The Biblical Seminar 23; Sheffield: JSOT Press, 1994), 45.

5. For the archaeological and biblical record of incense stands in the pre-exilic and exilic periods, see Wolfgang Zwickel, *Räucherkult und Räuchergeräte: Exegetische und archäologische Studien zum Räucheropfer im Alten Testament* (OBO 97; Freiburg: Universitätsverlag, 1990); Seymour Gitin, "Incense Altars from Ekron, Israel and Judah: Context and Typology," *EI* 20 (1989): *52–*67; idem, "New Incense Altars from Ekron: Context, Typology and Function," *EI* 23 (1992): 43–49; Nielsen, *Incense in Ancient Israel*, 38–51.

6. For studies of the altars see Kurt Galling, *Der Altar in den Kulturen des alten Orients. Eine archäologische Studie* (Berlin: Karl Curtius Verlag, 1925); Franz Josef Stendebach, "Altarformen im kanaanäisch-israelitischen Raum," *BZ NS* 20 (1976): 180–96; Michael O'Dwyer Shea, "The Small Cuboid Incense-Burner of the Ancient Near East," *Levant* 15 (1983): 76–109 (note A. R. Millard's

Near East in domestic as well as public-cult contexts. They have been excavated in Mesopotamia at Babylon, Assur, Uruk, Ur, and Nippur,[7] at Arabian sites such as Hureidha in Hadhramaut and at Baraqish in Yemen,[8] and in Egypt at Tell er-Retabeh.[9] Within extra-Yehudian Palestine, the small cuboid platforms have been found in the south (thirteen from Tell Jemmeh,[10] two from Tell el-Far'ah [S],[11] ten from Tell Abu Salima/Sheikh Zuweid,[12] one from Tel Sera' [Tell Esh-Shari'a],[13]

---

corrective of Shea's dating of some of the examples from Ur in "The Small Cuboid Incense-Burners: A Note on Their Age," *Levant* 16 [1984]:172–73); and Stern, *Material Culture*, 182–95. For diagrams of some incense *thymiateria* (including Egyptian, Old-Babylonian, Assyrian, Neo-Babylonian and Palestinian censers), see Nielsen, *Incense in Ancient Israel*, 4 and 28.

7. Stern, *Material Culture*, 183; Liselotte Ziegler, "Tonkästchen aus Uruk, Babylon und Assur," *ZA* 47 (1942): 224–40.

8. Richard LeBaron Bowen Jr., "Dating the Hureidha Irrigation Ruins," in *Archaeological Discoveries in South Arabia* (Richard LeBaron Bowen and Frank P. Albright et al.; Publications of the American Foundation for the Study of Man 2; Baltimore: The John Hopkins Press, 1958), 149–53; Gertrude Canton Thompson, *The Tombs and Moon Temple of Hureidha (Hadhramaut)* (Reports of the Research Committee of the Society of Antiquaries of London 13; Oxford: Oxford University Press, 1944), 36, 49–50, 58, 152–53, pls. 12, 16–17; Gus W. Van Beek, "Monuments of Axum in the Light of South Arabian Archaeology," *JAOS* 87.2 (1967): 113–22, esp. 114, 119; Sabina Antonini, "Nuovi incensieri iscritti Yemeniti," *OrAnt* 27 (1988): 133–41, pls. 4–6. Some of these platforms are later than the Persian period.

9. Unfortunately it was found in an unstratified context: W. M. Flinders Petrie, *Hyksos and Israelite Cities* (London: Office of School of Archaeology, University College and Bernard Quaritch, 1906), 34, pl. 36c:13; Stern, *Material Culture*, 185.

10. These are dated typologically to the Persian period. See Flinders Petrie, *Gerar* (London: British School of Archaeology in Egypt, 1928), 18–19; pls. 40–41, 42:5–6; James B. Pritchard, "An Incense Burner from Tell es-Sa'idiyeh, Jordan Valley," in *Studies on the Ancient Palestinian World* (ed. J. W. Wevers and D. B. Redford; Toronto: University of Toronto Press, 1972), 3–17, esp. 10–11; Gus W. Van Beek, "The Reexcavation of Sites: Tell Jemmeh," *Biblical Archaeology Today, 1990: Proceedings of the Second International Congress on Biblical Archaeology, Jerusalem, June–July 1990* (ed. Avraham Biran and Joseph Aviram; Jerusalem: Israel Exploration Society, 1993), 575–80; Shea, "The Small Cuboid Incense-Burner," 85–86; fig. 1; Stern, *Material Culture*, 184 fig. 303, 185; idem, *Archaeology*, 513.

11. Although the altars are not discussed in the excavation report, they are depicted in J. L. Starkey and Lankester Harding, "Beth-Pelet Cemetery," in *Beth-Pelet II* (Publications of the Egyptian Research Account and British School of Archaeology in Egypt 52; London: British School of Archaeology in Egypt, 1932), 22–32, esp. pls. 88:14 and 93:662. One was from an unstratified context, and one was in a tomb that Stern redates to the beginning of the fifth century B.C.E. See Stern, *Material Culture*, 75–76, 185; and see also Shea, "The Small Cuboid Incense-Burner," 85–86.

12. Although W. M. Flinders Petrie dates the group of objects from 470–15 B.C.E. (*Anthedon: Sinai* [London: British School of Egyptian Archaeology, 1937], 10, pl. 26:24–33), the stratigraphy of this site is problematic. According to typological analysis, the group can be dated to the late fifth century B.C.E., with a floruit in the fourth through third centuries B.C.E., and use continuing into later periods (Shea, "The Small Cuboid Incense-Burner," 85–86). See also Stern, *Material Culture*, 185.

13. Eliezer D. Oren, "Ziglag: A Biblical City on the Edge of the Negev," *BA* 45 (1982): 155–66, esp. 158; Stern, *Material Culture*, 184, fig. 304, 185; idem, *Archaeology*, 512–13.

and additional examples from Tel Beer-Sheba[14]), one in the Transjordan at Tell es-Saʿidiyeh,[15] and, along the coast, one from Tell es-Samak/Shiqmona,[16] four from Makmish,[17] and eight from Tel Michal.[18] Significantly, there are also some examples from the province of Samaria, with several found in the capital city[19] and two

---

14. Ephraim Stern ("Limestone Incense Altars," in *Beer-Sheba 1: Excavations at Tel Beer-Sheba, 1969–1971 Seasons* [ed. Yohanan Aharoni; Publications of the Institute of Archaeology 2; Tel Aviv: The Tel Aviv University Institute of Archaeology, 1973], 53–54, pls. 29, 52, esp. 52–53; pls. 29:1–2 and 52:6), identifies one example from the Persian-period stratum. Shea ("The Small Cuboid Incense-Burner," 86, 102), includes five additional burners that compare typologically to late-fifth through early-fourth century examples (see Stern, "Limestone Incense Altars," pls. 29:3–6; 52:1–3, 5; and Yohanan Aharoni, "Excavations at Tel Beer-Sheba: Preliminary Report of the Fourth Season, 1972," *TA* 1 [1974]: 34–42, pl. 8, esp. pl. 8.6).

15. This was found in a large public building, inscribed with a private name ("*lzkwr*") in lapidary Aramaic script that dates paleographically, according to Frank Moore Cross, between the late-sixth and fourth centuries B.C.E. See James B. Pritchard, *Tell Es-Saʿidiyeh: Excavations on the Tell, 1964–1966* (University Museum Monograph 60; Philadelphia: The University Museum, The University of Pennsylvania, 1985), 62–63, 66–68; figs. 18.22; 174:1–6; idem, "An Incense Burner from Tell es-Saʿidiyeh, Jordan Valley," in *Studies on the Ancient Palestinian World* (ed. J. W. Wevers and D. B. Redford; Toronto: University of Toronto Press, 1972), 3–17; Stern, *Material Culture*, 185, 190 fig. 309.1; idem, *Archaeology*, 513; Shea, "The Small Cuboid Incense-Burner," 86–88. For information on subsequent excavations in the "acropolis" area where the object was found, see Jonathan N. Tubb and Peter G. Dorrell, "Tell Es-Saʿidiyeh 1993: Interim Report on the Seventh Season of Excavations," *PEQ* 126 (1994): 52–67.

16. A cuboid-shaped example was found in stratum II (fourth century). In addition, an object that also may have been used for incense, shaped as a round bowl with dentil decoration, was found in stratum I (late-sixth to early-fifth centuries). It was found in a room with at least fifty Cypriot-influenced pottery vessels, which, according to the excavator, was a storeroom for locally produced spices. See Joseph Elgavish, שקמונה (Tel Aviv: Hakibbutz Hameuchad, 1994), 85, 88; Stern, *Material Culture*, 184; idem, *Archaeology*, 513; and Shea, "The Small Cuboid Incense-Burner," 84.

17. Two altars were found in a stratified context that dates to the Persian period, and two were discovered prior to the archaeological excavation. See Nahman Avigad, "(סקירה ראשונה) במכמיש החפירות," *BIES* 23 (1959): 48–52; idem, "Makmish," *IEJ* 8 (1958): 276; idem, "Makmish," *NEAEHL* 3:932–34; Stern, *Material Culture*, 185; Shea, "The Small Cuboid Incense-Burner," 85.

18. The objects were found in Persian-era strata IX–VI (525–300 B.C.E.). Two are made of basalt. See Lily Singer-Avitz, "Stone and Clay Objects," in *Excavations at Tel Michal, Israel* (ed. Zeʾev Herzog, George Rapp, Jr., and Ora Negbi; Publications of the Institute of Archaeology 8; Minneapolis: The University of Minnesota Press and Tel Aviv: The Sonia and Marco Nadler Institute of Archaeology, 1989), 350–60, esp. 356–57; figs. 31.6:1, 2, 4–9; pl. 77.5. It is not clear to me whether the two fragments of stone incense altars discussed by Steven Derfler ("Area C: The Eastern Hillock," 136–40 in Zeʾev Herzog, ed., "Excavations at Tel Michal 1978–1979," *TA* 7 [1980]: 111–52, pls. 29–35) are included in Singer-Avitz's discussion. See also Zeʾev Herzog, Ora Negbi, and Shmuel Moshkovitz, "Excavations at Tel Michal, 1977," *TA* 5 (1978): 99–130, pls. 33–39, esp. 115; 127 fig. 15.7.

19. See George Andrew Reisner, Clarence Stanley Fisher, and David Gordon Lyon, *Harvard Excavations at Samaria: 1908–1910* (2 vols.; Cambridge: Harvard University Press, 1924) 1.333; 2. pl. 80:a–c (a limestone cuboid was found along with other objects that also may have served as incense altars or "incense cups"). The authors claim that, although the stratification of the cuboids is difficult to ascertain, the assemblage is "without doubt Preherodian" (ibid., 1.333). For another limestone cuboid

bronze *thymiateria* found in and around Persian-period tombs at Shechem.[20] The use of these objects continued into the Hellenistic era, with examples found at sites such as Ashdod, Acco, Caesarea, Ashkelon, and Dor.[21]

Despite the ubiquity of these objects in Persian-period strata, neither term of the description "incense altar" is without debate. Scholars such as William F. Albright have argued that they were used to burn incense but in a secular context to perfume the body (see also Ps 45:9; Esth 2:12; Song of Songs 3:6).[22] Mervyn Fowler also argues that many examples were used for secular functions, including room fresheners, insect repellents, and braziers (see Jer 36:22–23; Ezek 23:41), or as a portable hearth for cooking and heating liquids.[23] On the other hand, Menahem Haran argues that they were cultic objects but used for the ritual burning of grain instead of incense.[24] Because the items have been excavated in the contexts of the public cult at sites such as Makmish and Lachish,[25] as well as in domestic

---

(found under a floor with Hellenistic pottery), see J. W. Crowfoot, G. M. Crowfoot, and Kathleen M. Kenyon, *The Objects from Samaria* (Samaria-Sebaste; Reports of the Work of the Joint Expedition in 1931–1933 and of the British Expedition in 1935 3; London: Palestine Exploration Fund, 1957), 466, 468, fig. 119.2; Stern, *Material Culture*, 184; idem, *Archaeology*, 513; Shea, "The Small Cuboid Incense-Burner," 84–85.

20. See Ephraim Stern, "Achaemenian Tombs from Shechem," *Levant* 12 (1980): 90–111, pls. 13–15; idem, *Archaeology*, 510–11. One of the bronze thymiaterion was found in a tomb (in a coffin); the other artifact was collected from the area around this tomb, and, according to Stern, probably came from another tomb contemporaneous with the first (Stern, "Achaemenian Tombs," 102). Stern dates the items to the second quarter of the fifth century B.C.E. on the basis of three Attic *lekythoi* sherds found within the coffin.

21. These are discussed by L. Y. Rahmani, "Hellenistic Brazier Fragments from Israel," *IEJ* 34 (1984): 224–31; and J. Gunneweg and I. Perlman, "Hellenistic Braziers from Israel: Results of Pottery Analysis," *IEJ* 34 (1984): 232–38. See also Moshe Dothan and David N. Freedman, *Ashdod I: The First Season of Excavations, 1962* ('Atiqot 7 [English Series]; Jerusalem: Department of Antiquities and Museums, 1967): 26–27; fig. 9:8; pl. 9:14; Moshe Dothan, *Ashdod II–III: The Second and Third Seasons of Excavations, 1963, 1965* ('Atiqot 9–10 [English Series]; Jerusalem: Department of Antiquities and Museums, 1971): 44, 70; fig. 27.7, 8; pl. 22:7, 8; Stern, *Material Culture*, 185.

22. William F. Albright, "The Lachish Cosmetic Burner and Esther 2:12," in *A Light unto My Path: Old Testament Studies in Honor of Jacob M. Myers* (ed. Howard N. Bream, Ralph D. Heim and Carey A. Moore; Gettysburg Theological Studies 4; Philadelphia: Temple University Press, 1974), 25–32.

23. Mervyn D. Fowler, "Excavated Incense Burners: A Case for Identifying a Site as Sacred?" *PEQ* 117 (1985): 25–29; idem, "Excavated Incense Burners," *BA* 47 (1984): 183–86.

24. Menahem Haran, "'Incense Altars' – Are They?" *Biblical Archaeology Today, 1990: Proceedings of the Second International Congress on Biblical Archaeology, Jerusalem, June–July 1990* (ed. Avraham Biran and Joseph Aviram; Jerusalem: Israel Exploration Society, 1993), 237–47; and idem, "Altar-ed States: Incense Theory Goes Up in Smoke," *BR* 11 (1995): 30–37, 48.

25. At the Makmish cultic area, northeast of Tell Michal and referred to earlier in this chapter and in chapter 2, four incense altars were found: two in a stratified context that dates to the Persian period, and two discovered prior to the archaeological excavation. See Avigad, "החפירות במכמיש," 48–52; idem, "Makmish," *IEJ* 8 (1958): 276; idem, "Makmish," *NEAEHL* 3:932–34; Stern, *Material Culture*, 185; Shea, "The Small Cuboid Incense-Burner," 85.

contexts, the archaeological find sites alone are not sufficient to settle the issue regarding these objects' purpose.

Although the items were probably not relegated to a single use, the preponderance of evidence indicates that they were used for an incense ritual. Their use as platforms upon which incense was burned is indicated by the inscription of terms such as "frankincense" or "balsam" on some of the cubes.[26] In addition, some of the objects have a fragrant resinous residue in their basin.[27] Not all cubes have this residue, however, and many lack all traces of burn marks—of the eight found at Tell Kheleifeh, for example, only two have burn marks in their basins,[28] as do only a few from the more than two hundred examples found at

---

At Lachish, several were found in the "solar shrine" complex (Tufnell, *Lachish III*, 141–44; pl. 64:7. In addition, a larger version inscribed with a large hand and a figure with outstretched arms was found on the stairs of the "solar shrine." See J. L. Starkey, "Lachish as Illustrating Bible History," *PEQ* 69 (1937): 171–79, esp. 172; Tufnell, *Lachish III*, 141–44, 383–84, pls. 42:8, 9; and Nahum M. Sarna, "The Chirotonic Motif on the Lachish Altar," in Yonhanan Aharoni et al., *Investigations at Lachish: The Sanctuary and the Residency* (Lachish V) (Publications of the Institute of Archaeology 4; Tel Aviv: Gateway Publishers, 1975), 44–46. Although the date of this temple is disputed (see the chapter on sacrifice), scholars agree that these objects date to the Persian period. An additional stand carved with door panels flanked by pillars was found in R/Q/S 15/16, a building which Aharoni argues is a Persian-period shrine. See Tufnell, *Lachish III*, 146–49 (where it is listed with the contents of the building) and 384 (where the find spot seems to be designated erroneously as the "Solar Shrine"), pls. 42:6, 64:11; Aharoni, *Lachish V*, 9–11.

26. One altar from Lachish has a three-line inscription, the first term of which is "*lbnt*" ("the incense," or, "the frankincense"). Although not all scholars have translated the text identically, there is general consensus on these radicals. See A. Dupont-Sommer, "Aramaic Inscription on an Altar," in Tufnell, *Lachish III*, 358–59 (also 226, 383–84; 49:3; 68:1); William F. Albright, "Some Recent Publications," *BASOR* 132 (1953): 46–47; Frank Moore Cross, "Two Notes on Palestinian Inscriptions of the Persian Age," *BASOR* 193 (1969): 19–24; Yohanan Aharoni, "מזבח הלבונה מלכיש" *Lĕšonénu* 35 (1971): 3–6; idem, *Lachish V*, 5–7; Edward Lipiński, *Studies in Aramaic Inscriptions and Onomastics* (Orientalia Lovaniensia Analecta 1; Leuven: Leuven University Press, 1975), 1.142–45. In a later article, Albright changed his translation of the first term from "incense" to "belonging to the daughters of. . . ." (Albright, "The Lachish Cosmetic Burner," 25–32).

For the inscription "*ḏrw*" ("balsam") on an example from South-Arabia, see A. Jamme, "Deux autels à encens de l'Université de Harvard," *Bibliotheca Orientalis* 10 (1953): 94–95, pl. 14. For a bibliography of altars with incense terminology found in south Arabia, see Bowen and Albright, *Archaeological Discoveries in South Arabia*, 151, pl. 96. For additional altars inscribed with related terms from Baraqish, see Antonini, "Nuovi incensieri," 133–41, pls. 4–6.

27. On a cache of these objects found at Hueidha was a dark greasy residue that emitted a fragrant odor when heated. See Caton Thompson, *Tombs and Moon Temple*, 50. In a more recent analysis, when charcoal and frankincense were heated on ceramic vessels, the vessels became sooty with an oily residue that could not be removed with various instruments (Daviau, "Family Religion" 207).

28. Nelson Glueck, "Incense Altars," in *Translating and Understanding the Old Testament* (ed. Harry Thomas Frank and William L. Reed; Nashville and New York: Abingdon, 1970), 325–29, pls. 1–5, figs. 1–4, esp. 326, 329, pls. 3.1, 3; fig. 2.2, 3; idem, "מזבחות־קטורת," *EI* 10 (1971): 120–25, figs. 1–4. On the

Lachish.[29] Based on an example from Nineveh, some have suggested that a bowl could have been placed on the altar in which the incense or offering was burned, but this theory works best only for the larger "horned" altars of the Iron Age or perhaps some of the fenestrated stands.[30]

Any theory regarding the use of these objects must take into account both the presence and absence of burn marks, and I suggest that their use in religious rituals involving a costly item such as incense can make the most sense of this evidence. Not only are the cuboids too small for cooking, it is difficult to understand how those without burn marks were used to perfume rooms or bodies. A more plausible explanation might be that chips of aromatic resin were placed in the bowl of the platform, and these chips may or may not have been lit with fire. Since the resins were generally imported from southern Arabia or Africa,[31] they were an expensive commodity for a family unit, and one can imagine that some households would choose not to burn away the precious substance in their worship. The practice of "offering up" a commodity that is not burned with fire has conceptual parallels to activities done within the context of the ancestor cult—for example, the ne-IZI-gar festival practiced in Nippur and Larsa,[32] the daily Mesopotamian *kispum* ritual,[33] and some Asian practices[34]—where food was set out for

---

other hand, most of the ten examples found at Tell Abu Salima/Sheikh Zuweid have signs of burning (see Petrie, *Anthedon*, 10, pl. 26:24–33).

29. According to the original excavation report, "The majority [of tapered stands"] . . . seldom showed traces of burning or discoloration" (Tufnell, *Lachish III*, 383). Yet one example, carved with door panels flanked by pillars, had a "cracked and charred top surface," which the authors attribute to the burning of incense (idem, 384; cf. pls. 42:6; 64:11).

30. William F. Albright, *The Excavations of Tell Beit Mirsim, III. The Iron Age* (AASOR 21–22; New Haven, Conn.: American Schools of Oriental Research, 1943), 30; Gitin, "New Incense Altars," 47*.

31. Nielsen, *Incense in Ancient Israel*, 19–24, 27. Helga Weippert (*Palästina in vorhellenistischer Zeit* [Handbuch der Archäologie, Vorderasien 2.1; München: C. H. Beck, 1988], 717) suggests that the greater availability during the Persian period would have lead to a reduction in the price of these aromatics, leading to their broader use. Despite this possible price reduction, aromatics still would have been a luxury item. Based on figures from the second century c.e., Gus W. Van Beek ("Frankincense and Myrrh," *BA* 23 [1960]: 70–95) estimates that one pound of frankincense would cost approximately 2.5–5% of a minimal annual salary (pp. 86–88).

32. During this festival the spirits of the ancestors would return to their former homes, and, guided by torches, participate in a ceremonial meal served by the living family. See Mark E. Cohen, *The Cultic Calendars of the Ancient Near East* (Bethesda, Md.: CDL Press, 1993), 456–57.

33. Old Babylonian texts mention *kispum* as a daily ritual in which water and a bowl of fine flour would be offered to the ancestors. See Karel van der Toorn, *Family Religion in Babylonia, Syria and Israel: Continuity and Change in the Forms of Religious Life* (Studies in the History and Culture of the Ancient Near East 7; Leiden: Brill, 1996), 49.

34. Some Japanese Buddhists daily offer portions of food at the ancestral altar before the family eats (Robert J. Smith, *Ancestor Worship in Contemporary Japan* [Stanford: Stanford University Press, 1974], 90–91).

the ancestors, and, once they had fed on it, taken away. The fact that such food is not visibly altered does not mean that it does not perform its function of edifying the ancestors or the gods and marking the worshipper as devout. Likewise in the case of the incense—even if it was not burned, this does not mean that it did not perform its purpose. Of course, the worshippers could choose to light the chips, and this choice is also reflected in the extant altars with burn marks. The variety of find sites (public cult and private home) coalesces with this evidence since one can imagine that a religious ritual involving incense occurred in both venues.[35]

Having reviewed a portion of the evidence for the religious use of incense in the ancient Near East, I now turn to Persian-period Yehud and the Yahwistic communities both within and outside its borders. To preview the conclusion briefly, although Chronicles condemns the religious use of aromatics outside Jerusalem, this condemnation, evaluated along with the other biblical texts and archaeological finds (such as Mal 1:11, the texts from Elephantine, and perhaps some incense burners as well) indicates that such a practice was engaged in by Yahwists outside the city.

3.2 The Religious Use of Incense by Yahwists in the Biblical Texts

The Hebrew Bible mentions incense (קטרת) and frankincense (לבונה) most frequently in religious contexts,[36] the burning of which is usually indicated by the root קטר in the *hiphil*.[37] The aromatics were offered either with the cereal offering (Lev 2:1, 2, 15, 16; 6:8) or as a separate offering burned in censers or on altars (מקטרת, מחתה and חמנים;[38] Lev 10:1; Num 16:6; Lev 26:30; Isa 17:8; 27:9; Ezek

---

35. According to Shea ("The Small Cuboid Incense-Burner," 95), the small incense burners found in domestic settings were "a portable version" of the larger incense altars found in temples.

36. For the nonreligious use of incense (such as medicinal or cosmetic) referred to in the Hebrew Bible, see Nielsen, *Incense in Ancient Israel*, 89–94.

37. Infrequently, הקטיר can also refer to grain offerings (Jer 33:18) or animal sacrifices (Lev 17:6; Num 18:17; 1 Sam 2:15, 16). Although some English translations render the *piel* form of קטר as "burn incense," this form seems most properly to refer to the offering of other agricultural products. For discussion, see Julius Wellhausen, *Prolegomena to the History of Israel* (New York: Meridan Books, 1957), 64–65, n. 2; Menahem Haran, *Temples and Temple Service in Ancient Israel: An Inquiry into Biblical Cult Phenomena and the Historical Setting of the Priestly School* (Winona Lake, Ind.: Eisenbrauns, 1985), 233–34; idem, "The Uses of Incense in the Ancient Israelite Ritual," *VT* 10 (1960): 113–29, esp. 116–17; Diana Edelman, "The Meaning of *qiṭṭēr*," *VT* 35 (1985): 395–404; and Zwickel, *Räucherkult*, 336–39.

38. For an argument that חמנים / חמן are shrines rather than incense altars, see Volkmar Fritz, "Die Bedeutung des Wortes *ḥammān/ḥmn*," in *Wort und Wirklichkeit: Studien zur Afrikanistik und Orientalistik* (ed. Brigitta Benzing, Otto Böcher, and Günter Mayer; Meisenheim am Glan: Anton Hain, 1976), 41–50; and idem, "The Meaning of the Word *Ḥammān/ḥmn*," *Folio Orientalia* 21 (1980): 103–15.

6:4, 6; 8:11; 2 Chr 26:19; 30:14; 34:4, 7).[39] Scholars have argued about the date when incense was incorporated into the ceremony of the official cult, but all agree that it was part of the ritual of the Second Temple.[40]

Many biblical texts emphasize that the burning of aromatics for religious purposes is performed most properly in the central cult. Further, although there is some discrepancy as to the particular rank (probably related to the specific type of incense offering), many texts also emphasize that this burning is to be performed by the clerical classes. According to Exod 30:1–10, the high priest is to burn aromatic incense (והקטיר ... קטרת סמים) on the incense altar (מקטר קטרת מזבח) twice a day in the sanctuary, and Lev 16:12–13 includes an additional mention of an incense rite in the holy place on the Day of Atonement. According to the Korah incident in Numbers 16, only Aaronites can offer incense, yet Levites are appointed to offer incense to YHWH in Deut 33:8–10, and local priests are to "burn incense" (להקטיר קטרת) at the Shiloh sanctuary in 1 Sam 2:28. The book of Jeremiah twice mentions laity bringing frankincense (לבונה) to the Jerusalem temple: once as a vision of the future (Jer 17:26), and another time when men from Shechem, Shiloh, and Samaria brought meal-offerings and frankincense to present at the House of YHWH (Jer 41:5). Although the frankincense was in the hands of laity in this account, it is clearly in transit to the temple, presumably to be burned by priests.

Exceptions to these rules of geography and ordained personnel are strongly critiqued in texts that predate the Persian period. As part of the "vile abominations" that the prophet sees in Ezek 8:9–11, seventy elders of Israel, along with Jaazaniah son of Shaphan, each hold a censer (מקטרתו) and create "a thick cloud of incense smoke" (הקטרת) that ascends in front of walls depicting "creeping things and beasts and all the fetishes of the House of Israel." The area of this wall is somewhere near the temple courtyard and not, presumably, in the temple itself (Ezek 8:7–9). Although the ritual context of this vision is not clear,[41] the vision

---

39. Haran (*Temples and Temple Service*, 231–45, and "The Uses of Incense," 114–29) makes a careful distinction between the two types of aromatic offerings sacrificed on their own (distinct from the aromatics mixed with the grain offering): that burned in a censer usually within the temple precincts ("censer-incense," referred to simply as *qeṭōret* in the biblical text, e.g., Lev 10:1), and that burned on the altar of gold inside the tabernacle ("altar-incense," referred to as *qeṭōret sammîm*; e.g., Exod 30:7).

40. According to Wellhausen (*Prolegomena*, 63.2), incense offerings in the cult are referred to only in later texts. Based on texts such as Deut 33:20 and 1 Sam 2:28, however, Haran (*Temples and Temple Service*, 235, and "The Uses of Incense," 118) argues for an earlier date, as does Nielsen (*Incense in Ancient Israel*). More recently, Paul Heger (*The Development of Incense Cult in Israel* [BZAW 245; Berlin, New York: Walter de Gruyter, 1997]) has claimed that, although incense was used in earlier auxiliary cultic rites, it developed into a more regular rite in the official worship of the larger community only in the late Second Temple period.

41. Susan Ackerman ("A Marzēaḥ in Ezekiel 8:7–13?" *HTR* 82 [1989]: 267–81) argues that it depicts a ritual *marzēaḥ* feast celebrated by Israelite aristocracy.

criticizes the use of incense by laity outside the temple in the worship of engraved images. As Walther Zimmerli points out, the inappropriateness of this lay use of incense is emphasized with the term מקטרת ("censer"), a rare word used only here and in 2 Chr 26:19 where a similar critique is levied against the laity.[42] Further, when Aaron brought out the incense from the tent of meeting into the midst of the congregation, the text makes clear that this is an exceptional circumstance, motivated to "make atonement" for the people so that the consuming wrath of YHWH might be stopped (Num 17:11–13).

3.2.1 INCENSE IN CHRONICLES

Persian-period texts such as Chronicles retain these geographical and professional protocols and include condemnatory notices when such protocols are transgressed. In concert with the regulations of the Pentateuch, the Chronicler emphasizes that "making offerings . . . on the altar of incense" (על־מזבח הקטרת ... מקטירים) in the tabernacle is part of the duties of the Aaronic priesthood (1 Chr 6:34). Some of the Levites were appointed to be in charge of various cultic accoutrements for the house of God, including the flour, wine, and "the frankincense and the spices" (הלבונה והבשמים), and other priests prepared the mixing of these spices (1 Chr 9:29, 30). In the plan of the temple that David gave to Solomon, the sacred area was to include an "altar of incense" (מזבח הקטרת) made of refined gold (1 Chr 28:18), and Solomon subsequently told Huram of Tyre that he wanted to dedicate the temple "for the offering before him [YHWH] of fragrant incense" (להקטיר לפניו קטרת־סמים) as well as burnt offerings (2 Chr 2:3). In his speech claiming legitimacy and power over the North (not included in the Kings account), Abijah proclaimed in Ephraim that the South retained Aaronites and Levites to serve YHWH and daily burn offerings and "fragrant incense" (סמים־קטרת; 2 Chr 13:11). In a similar vein, part of Hezekiah's reforms included the reinstitution of incense offerings (לא־הקטירו) in the holy place (2 Chr 29:7), and the king instructed the Levites to "make offerings" to YHWH (ומקטרים; 2 Chr 29:11). Via such notices, the Chronicler emphasizes that the care for and burning of incense is the proper task of the Aaronites and Levites and that such tasks are a necessary part of worship in the central sanctuary.[43]

Alongside these texts emphasizing centralized geography and priestly personnel are stories that condemn the religious use of incense outside the official Jerusalem Temple cult by non-priests. In 2 Chr 26:16–21, a story not found in

---

42. Walther Zimmerli, *Ezekiel 1: A Commentary on the Book of the Prophet Ezekiel, Chapters 1–24* (trans. Ronald E. Clements; Hermeneia; Philadelphia: Fortress, 1979), 241.

43. These emphases can also be seen as part of the author's attempt to link both the first and second temples. See Peter R. Ackroyd, "The Temple Vessels – A Continuity Theme," in *Studies in the Religion of Ancient Israel* (Leiden: Brill, 1972), 166–81.

Kings, Uzziah tries to offer incense on the incense altar in the temple. He is smitten by leprosy as punishment for not respecting the Aaronic exclusivity of the incense offering. It may be that this story, relating the near-offering of incense by a lay person, was intended not only to condemn Uzziah alone but also to threaten other laypersons who wanted to offer incense with severe punishment.

Chronicles also denounces the use of incense outside the central cult, associated with worship at high places or shrines (במות), and approves when such practice is eradicated. Ahaz is criticized for a variety of cultic sins, including making offerings (הקטיר) in the valley of Ben-Hinnom as well as sacrificing and making offerings (ויקטיר) "on the high-places, and on the hills and under every green tree" (2 Chr 28:3, 4). The removal of such incense altars is part of the cultic reforms of Asa, Hezekiah, and Josiah. According to 2 Chr 14:4, Asa removed "from every town of Judah the high places and the incense altars" (החמנים). During Hezekiah's reforms, the people threw "all the incense altars" (המקטרות־כל) that were in Jerusalem into the Wadi Kidron (2 Chr 30:14). In Judah and Jerusalem, Josiah destroyed the high places and "the incense altars" (החמנים) that stood above the altars to Baal and hewed down "all the incense altars" (החמנים־כל) throughout Israel (2 Chr 34:4, 7).

In relating the destruction of these altars, the author indicates that incense was a part of worship throughout Judah and Israel. Although the Chronicler espouses restrictions for the religious use of incense (only in the central sanctuary and only by the proper priests) and emphasizes that these cultic precepts were maintained during the reign of Hezekiah, the book also indicates that incense was offered outside the central cult. The fact that the reforming kings (Hezekiah and Josiah, as well as Asa) destroyed incense altars demonstrates both their pervasiveness in worship throughout the land and the author's assessment of the sinfulness of the practice. It may be that, by including narratives not found in Kings about bodily harm associated with laity offering incense (2 Chr 26:16–21) and the ongoing offering of incense by Aaronites and Levites in the Jerusalem temple cult (2 Chr 13:11), the author reveals his/her particular anxieties in a context in which incense was being offered by the laity or it was offered outside Jerusalem.

3.2.2 INCENSE IN NEHEMIAH

Additional textual evidence that aromatics were associated with the worship of the second temple in Jerusalem comes from the book of Nehemiah. According to Neh 13:5, frankincense (הלבונה) was kept in a temple storeroom, along with the cereal offering, vessels, and tithes of grain, new wine, and fine oil for the Levites. When Nehemiah left Jerusalem for a period of time, Eliashib, the priest who was in charge of these storerooms, cleared out these items to make room for Tobiah. Upon his return to the city, Nehemiah found this situation unacceptable, and, after cleaning and purifying the rooms, threw Tobiah out and restored the vessels, cereal offering, and frankincense (Neh 13:7–9). In this story of a power struggle between early leaders of the second temple community, frankincense appears as a necessary part of the cultic accoutrement of the temple, just as vital as the temple vessels and the materials for grain offerings.

3.2.3 INCENSE IN TRITO-ISAIAH

The priestly use of aromatics in worship may also be inferred from the critique in Isa 66:3: "the one who makes a memorial offering of frankincense (לבנה מזכיר), blesses an idol." This verse occurs in the context of a larger condemnation of sacrificial practices in Isa 66:1–4 ("the one who slaughters [שוחט] an ox, kills a human being . . . the one who presents a grain offering [מעלה מנחה], [offers] swine's blood . . ."), referred to earlier in chapter 2. The passage is specifically directed to the clerical classes who regularly engage in the ritual slaughter of animals and offering of grain. YHWH's subsequent announcement that he will "take" part of the nation returning from distant lands "for priests and for Levites" (Isa 66:21) indicates that these classes are so corrupt as to need a complete replacement. Although the author seems to indicate that the current practitioners of the frankincense offering are corrupt, the text nevertheless maintains that such a duty is properly the task of the priests and Levites. Just as the ritual slaughter of oxen, the sacrifice of lambs, and the ritual offering of grain are all reserved for the clerical classes, so too is the offering of frankincense. In this context of harsh critique, Isa 66 indicates that the religious use of aromatics properly belongs to the sphere of priests and Levites.

3.2.4 INCENSE IN MALACHI

Although most Persian-period texts in the Hebrew Bible emphasize that the religious use of aromatics is most properly the task of priests and Levites operating in the Jerusalem cult, there is one notable exception. In Mal 1:11, YHWH proclaims that "From the rising of the sun to where it sets, great is my name among the nations, and in every place (where) incense is offered (מקטר מגש)[44] to my name, even a pure offering (ומנחה טהורה). For great is my name among the nations." In this description of worship "among the nations," outside the bounds of the temple ("From the rising of the sun to where it sets . . . and in every place . . ."), the author speaks only of the non-animal offering of incense (מקטר). In its immediate literary context, this worship contrasts with the impure animal and non-animal sacrifices made in the Jerusalem temple, namely, the "defiled food" (לחם מגאל) offered to YHWH at the altar such as blind or lame or sick animals (Mal 1:7–8, 12–13), and the offering (מנחה) that YHWH rejects (Mal 1:10; see

---

44. I translate the first *hophal* participle as a substantive and the second as an intransitive passive, as with the LXX (θυμίαμα προσάγεται). For a brief discussion of other interpretations, see Beth Glazier-McDonald, *Malachi: The Divine Messenger* (SBLDS 98; Atlanta: Scholars Press, 1987), 55–57.

also 2:13). Thus, both the geography and the content of sacrifice are in play—the impure animal sacrifice presently practiced in Jerusalem is condemned and the pure incense sacrifice practiced everywhere else is praised. Yet even in the context of a severe critique of the Jerusalem cult, the prophet maintains that pure sacrifice outside the city does not include the offering of animals. Although this text may be open enough to apply to both Jews in the Diaspora and/or the Gentiles,[45] the vision of worship is circumscribed such that religious sacrifice outside Jerusalem includes only incense.

According to these biblical texts, the religious use of aromatics was part of Yahwistic worship during the Persian period both within and outside Jerusalem. The book of Chronicles, most notably, strictly prescribes that it be offered only by the clergy at the central shrine, but, in its denouncement of lay presenters and use at alternate cult sites, the text also seems to provide negative evidence for such practice. Other texts, such as Mal 1:11, reveal that during this period the religious use of incense outside of Jerusalem was considered, in some circles at least, an acceptable form of YHWH worship.

3.3 THE RELIGIOUS USE OF INCENSE BY YAHWISTS IN THE ARCHAEOLOGICAL RECORD

The archaeological evidence generally supports the biblical texts of this period that describe the use of incense in Yahwistic religion. Extra-biblical texts and artifacts indicate that the religious use of aromatics outside Jerusalem, condemned in Chronicles but not in Malachi, occurred in what are most likely Yahwistic communities. The following pages first briefly discuss the finds of Persian-period altars within Yehud at Gezer and Tell en-Naṣbeh and then turn to the evidence for the use of aromatics by Yahwistic communities living outside Yehud in Lachish and Elephantine.

3.3.1 INCENSE USED BY YAHWISTS WITHIN YEHUD

Twelve small cuboid altars dating to the Persian period were found at Gezer in tombs.[46] An additional cuboid burner was found at Tell en-Naṣbeh, and,

---

45. According to James Swetnam ("Malachi 1, 11: An Interpretation," *CBQ* 31 [1969]: 200–209), the text refers to the contemporary worship of the Jewish Diaspora. Others see in this text a reference to the present or future worship of the Gentiles. See Carl Friedrich Keil, *The Twelve Minor Prophets* (trans. James Martin; Biblical Commentary on the Old Testament; Grand Rapids: Eerdmans, 1949), 437–39; Robert C. Dentan, "The Book of Malachi," *IB* 6:1117–44, esp. 1128; Rex Mason, *The Books of Haggai, Zechariah, and Malachi* (Cambridge Bible Commentary; Cambridge: Cambridge University Press, 1977), 144.

46. R. A. Stewart Macalister, *The Excavation of Gezer* (3 vols.; London: J. Murray, 1912), 2.442–45, figs. 524–26; 3.225:9; 1:357–58, fig. 185 (tomb 147); 1.358; 3.107.2 (tomb 153); 1.363 (tomb 156);

although the date is somewhat difficult to ascertain, it probably dates to the Persian period as well. The difficulty of dating relates to the problematic stratigraphy of the site and lack of clarity regarding the exact find site. According to the written excavation report, the item was found "in the wall" between Rooms 405 and 406, but, according to the plan of the site, there are two walls to which this might refer: either the west wall of Room 405 or the east wall of Room 406.[47] In addition, there is a small area that divides the two walls, and, because fifteen other objects are assigned the same find spot, the altar and these items may have come from this area between the two walls. In the original excavation report, the two rooms are dated ca. 600–450 B.C.E., although the two walls are dated ca. the ninth through sixth century B.C.E.[48] In his reexamination of the site's stratigraphy, Jeffrey Zorn assigns these walls and rooms to Stratum 3A (800–586 B.C.E.), noting that Room 406 is later than Room 405 and perhaps even part of Stratum 2 (post-586 B.C.E.).[49] Thus, if the altar was used as material for one of the walls, or by one

---

1.371; and 3.114.1a–d (tomb 176). Macalister assigned most of these to the "Persian and Hellenistic" period (which he dated to 550–100 B.C.E.), and later scholars have dated these examples typologically to the Persian period (Stern, *Material Culture*, 184; Shea, "The Small Cuboid Incense-Burner," 85). One exception is the example from tomb 153, assigned by Macalister to the "Fourth Semitic" period (dated 1000–550 B.C.E.), but redated by Stern to late sixth through early fifth centuries B.C.E. on the basis of the ceramics found in the tomb and the typology of the altar (Stern, *Material Culture*, 73–75, 80–84). In addition, the date of a cuboid found in tomb 147 is contested by L. Y. Rahmani who argues that its handle stump places the object in the seventh through early eighth centuries C.E. (see Macalister, *Gezer*, 1:357–58, fig. 185; Stern, *Material Culture*, 183; L. Y. Rahmani, "Palestinian Incense Burners of the Sixth to Eighth Centuries C.E.," *IEJ* 30 [1980]: 116–22, pls. 12, 13). Finally, there is note of a "Sandstone Cube, No. 142" found in Field II in a mixed locus with Iron II, Persian, and Hellenistic items during the subsequent excavations of the site. See William G. Dever, H. Darrell Lance, and G. Ernest Wright, *Gezer I: Preliminary Report of the 1964–66 Seasons* (Annual of the Hebrew Union College Biblical and Archaeological School in Jerusalem; Jerusalem: Keter Publishing, 1970), 104.

47. Chester Charlton McCown, with contributions by James Muilenburg, Joseph Carson Wampler, Dietrich von Bothmer and Margaret Harrison, *Tell en-Naṣbeh Excavated under the Direction of the Late William Frederic Badè: Archaeological and Historical Results* (Berkeley and New Haven: The Palestine Institute of Pacific School of Religion and The American Schools of Oriental Research, 1947), 236–37; fig. 61a; pl. 84.14. See also the site plan included with the volume.

48. Note that the material under the floor of Room 406 is dated to 900–500 B.C.E., although the material is considered "mixed and uncertain" (Joseph Carson Wampler with Chester Charlton McCown, *Tell en-Naṣbeh Excavated under the Direction of the Late William Frederic Badè: The Pottery* [Berkeley and New Haven: The Palestine Institute of Pacific School of Religion and the American Schools of Oriental Research, 1947], 122).

49. Jeffrey Ralph Zorn, "Tell en-Naṣbeh: A Reevaluation of the Architecture and Stratigraphy of the Early Bronze Age, Iron Age and Later Periods" (4 vols.; Ph.D. diss., University of California at Berkeley, 1993); idem, "Mizpeh: Newly Discovered Stratum Reveals Judah's Other Capital," *BAR* 23.5 (September/October 1997): 28–38, 66; idem, "Tell En-Naṣbeh and the Problem of the Material Culture of the Sixth Century," in Lipschits and Blenkinsopp, *Judah and the Judeans in the Neo-Babylonian Period*, 413–47. I am most grateful for Prof. Zorn's helpful emails to me in March and April, 2004.

of the room's occupants, it would date stratigraphically to the ninth through early sixth century B.C.E. (although the stratigraphic date would be later if Room 406 is assigned to Stratum 2). If, however, the altar was part of the fill between the two walls that leveled the area in preparation for the construction of Stratum 2 in the sixth century, then its stratigraphic date would be closer to the mid-500s B.C.E. Given the number of ceramics that were also assigned the same find spot ("in the wall" between Rooms 405 and 406), it is most likely that the item was part of the leveling fill from the mid-sixth century. This later date is also supported with typological analysis.[50] Thus, although the date of the object cannot be assigned with certainty, a Persian-period date is possible.

3.3.2 INCENSE USED BY YAHWISTS OUTSIDE YEHUD

Outside Yehud, is it possible that incense was used by Yahwists in their worship at Lachish. As discussed in the chapter on sacrifice, a population of Yahwists in the city may be indicated by the notice in Neh 11:30 that exiles returned to the city and by what I read as the Yahwistic name "Maḥalyah" (מחליה) inscribed on an incense cuboid.[51] More than two hundred other small Persian-period altars, some in explicitly cultic contexts, were found at Lachish. Ten were found in the rooms associated with the "solar shrine," and a larger example was found on the inner stairs of the building.[52] (Even if, as Tufnell, Aharoni, and Fantalkin and Tal [see p. 46 n. 70] argue, this building is later than the Persian period, these altars may be considered, along with the bronze lamp, some of the objects from the Persian period reused in the later building.) Another stand, decorated with a carving of door panels flanked by pillars, was found in the Persian-period structure R/Q/S 15/16 ("Building 10"), a building that Aharoni argues functioned as the public worship area for the city during this period.[53] Part of approximately 170 altars, mostly tapered stands and mostly fragmentary, were found in Cave 534 along with Persian-period pottery.[54] In addition, thirty were found in Cave 515 and

---

50. This is the conclusion of G. E. Wright (McCowan, *Tell En-Naṣbeh I*, 237) but note that Shea ("The Small Cuboid Incense-Burner," 85) thinks that the object may date as late as the Hellenistic period.

51. This is following Aharoni's reading, "Incense (altar). Ya'ush son of Maḥalyah (מחליה) from Lachish." See Aharoni, "מזבח הלבונה מלכיש," 3–6; and idem, et al., *Investigations at Lachish: The Sanctuary and the Residency (Lachish V)* (Publications of the Institute of Archaeology 4; Tel Aviv: Gateway Publishers, 1975), 5–7. As discussed in chapter 2, scholars read the radicals מחליה identically, although they translate the text differently.

52. Tufnell, *Lachish III*, 141–44, 384, pls. 42:8, 9; 64:7.

53. Aharoni, *Lachish V*, 9–11, pl. 1:1; Tufnell, *Lachish III*, 146–49 (where the stand is listed with the contents of the building) and 384 (where the find spot seems to be erroneously designated as the "Solar Shrine"); pls. 42:6, 64:11.

54. Tufnell, *Lachish III*, 226, 358–59, 383–84; pls. 42:4–5; 49:3; 68; 69; 70; 71:17, 20–27; Ephraim Stern, "Note on a Decorated Limestone Altar from Lachish," *'Atiqot* 11, English Series (1976): 107–9.

thirteen more in Deposit 506.[55] The report of the most recent excavations at the site lists the find of another possible censer (a small shallow limestone bowl-like object with traces of burning) that may also date to the Persian period.[56]

Although these finds of altars in both shrines and favissae indicate that incense was used in the worship at Lachish, the evidence that such worship was Yahwistic is suggested mainly by the proposed reading of the theophoric name on one altar. (It could be that the other altars were used by devotees of Qos or other gods in the city.) The textual evidence from Elephantine that incense was used in the public cult of YHWH is much more clear. As already discussed in chapter 2, in their letter to Bagavahya the Yahwists in the colony write that since the destruction of their temple in 410 B.C.E. the community has not been able to offer up frankincense offerings (לבונה) along with meal-offerings (מנחה) and burnt offerings (עלוה) in their temple (TAD A4.7.21–22 and A4.8.21). They promise to offer these offerings in the name of the governor in the rebuilt temple (TAD A4.7.25–26 and A4.8.24–25). In the memorandum from Bagavahya and Delaiah, the two Persian authorities permit the rebuilding of a house of offering at Elephantine along with the reinstitution of the meal-offering (מנחתא) and the frankincense-offering (לבונתא; TAD A4.9.9–10). In their offer to pay for the Temple's reconstruction, written sometime after 407 B.C.E., five property holders in Elephantine insist that no animals be offered in the new building, only frankincense and meal-offerings (לבונה מנחה; TAD A4.10.10–11). Although animal sacrifice is not allowed, none of the records indicates that offering aromatics in a religious context outside Jerusalem was problematic. Even when their religious practices were significantly altered after 407 B.C.E., the use of frankincense (along with grain offerings) was still permitted by the political authorities of Yehud and Samaria. The community itself, represented in the letter from the five property holders, was amenable to such a change.

The combined evidence for aromatics, both from the Hebrew Bible and archaeological excavation, suggests that they were used by Yahwists in their religious worship during the Persian period. The evidence also suggests that there was some dispute about this. While indicating that incense was used throughout Judah and Israel and "under every green tree," Chronicles strongly condemns the use of incense outside the centralized cult. This condemnation is not reflected in Malachi, where the use of incense outside Jerusalem is endorsed. The texts from Elephantine also testify to this geographical openness, such that the political lead-

---

55. For Cave 515, see Tufnell, *Lachish III*, 221, 383, pl. 71:19; for Deposit 506, see ibid., 220, 383.

56. The object is ascribed to levels II–I (from area R, locus 6170, an area with habitation remains in level II). See Benjamin Sass "Section A: Vessels, Tools, Personal Objects, Figurative Art and Varia," in David Ussishkin, *The Renewed Archaeological Excavations at Lachish (1973–1994)* (vols. 1–5; Publications of the Institute of Archaeology 22; Tel Aviv: Emery and Claire Yass Publications in Archaeology, 2004), 4:1983–2057, esp. 1990–2001, fig. 28.3:9 and Table 28.10:8.

ers of Yehud and Samaria as well as the local Yahwistic community in the colony see no problem with offering up frankincense in their temple in Egypt. These biblical and extra-biblical texts, when combined with the incense cuboids from Gezer, Tell en-Naṣbeh, and Lachish, indicate that Yahwists within and outside the boundaries of Yehud used incense in their religious practice outside Jerusalem.

3.4 THE RELIGIOUS USE OF FIGURINES BY YAHWISTS IN THE ARCHAEOLOGICAL RECORD

The textual and archaeological evidence for the use of figurines by worshipping Yahwists is not nearly as extensive as that for incense. Like incense altars, figurines are found throughout the ancient Near East, and Persian-period figurines usually depict either women or bearded men on horseback.[57] Some of the many sites within Palestine and the northern Sinai where favissae and/or stratified finds of such figurines have been found include Dan and Mount Miẓpe Yammim in the north;[58] Tel Megadim, Dor, Makmish, and Ashkelon along the coast;[59] Tel Ẓafit, Tel Ẓippor, Tel 'Erani, Maresha, Tel el-Ḥesi, Tel Haror, Tel Sera' (Tell Esh-Shari'a), and Tel Halif further inland;[60] and a cultic area near Raphia in the Sinai.[61]

---

57. For a discussion about the statuettes and figurines found in Persian-era strata, including the delineation of the eastern group from the western group based on stylistic features, see Stern, *Material Culture*, 158–82; idem, *Archaeology*, 490–507.

58. For the figurines found at Dan, see Avraham Biran, *Biblical Dan*, 214–16; fig. 175; pl. 39; Stern, *Archaeology*, 489. For the figurines found at Mount Miẓpe Yammim, see Rafael Frankel, "Miẓpe Yammim, Mount," *NEAEHL* 3:1061–63; Rafael Frankel and Raphael Ventura, "The Mispe Yamim Bronzes," *BASOR* 311 (1998): 39–55; Stern, *Archaeology*, 497, 500–501.

59. For Megadim, see Magen Broshi, "Megadim, Tel," *NEAEHL* 3:1001–3; Stern, *Archaeology*, 392. Two Persian-period favissae with figurines were found at Dor. See Ephraim Stern, "A Favissa of a Phoenician Sanctuary from Tel Dor," *JJS* 33 (1982): 35–54; idem, *Dor, Ruler of the Seas: Nineteen Years of Excavations at the Israelite-Phoenician Harbor Town on the Carmel Coast* (trans. Joseph Shadur; Jerusalem: Israel Exploration Society, 2000); idem, "Dor," *NEAEHL* 1:357–68, esp. 360–62; idem, *Archaeology*, 500–503, 506. For the many male and female figurines found at Makmish (a cultic area for the nearby city of Tel Michal), see Avigad, "החפירות במכמיש," 48–52; idem, "Makmish," *IEJ* 8 (1958): 276; idem, "Excavations at Makmish, 1958: Preliminary Report," *IEJ* 10 (1960): 90–96, pls. 9–12; idem, "Excavations at Makmish, 1960: Preliminary Report," *IEJ* 11 (1961): 97–100; idem, "Makmish," *NEAEHL* 3:932–34; Stern, *Archaeology*, 497, 500. For the finds at Ashkelon, see W. J. Phythian-Adams, "Report on the Stratification of Askalon," *PEFQS* (1923): 60–84; J. H. Iliffe, "A Hoard of Bronzes from Askalon c. Fourth Century B.C.," *Quarterly of the Department of Antiquities in Palestine* 5 (1935): 61–68, pls. 29–34; Lawrence E. Stager, "Ashkelon," *NEAEHL* 1:103–12, esp. 107–9; Stern, *Archaeology*, 410–11, 489, 497–99.

60. For the Persian-period favissa found at Tel Ẓafit, see Frederick Jones Bliss and R. A. Stewart Macalister, *Excavations in Palestine During the Years 1898–1900* (London: Palestine Exploration Fund, 1902), 38–43, 140–41, 146, fig. 53; pls. 70, 75; Frederick Jones Bliss, "Second Report on the Excavations

Significantly, Ephraim Stern has pointed out that no figurines have been found in the Persian-period boundaries of Yehud or Samaria, a situation that indicates to him the "purification" of worship from the practices of "pagan cults."[62] Although "Bes" vases have been found at Samaria, Stern considers these as part of the popular apotropaic cult practiced throughout the ancient Near East and not part of official worship.[63] The only other suggestive use of figurines by Yahwists in the archaeological record are several finds of Persian-period examples (including horse-and-rider and female figurines) from Lachish. Some fragments were present in the "solar shrine" complex: one in the drain in the inner sanctuary (room

---

at Tell Es-Sâfi," *PEFQSt* (1899): 317–33, esp. pls. opposite page 328; Stern, "Zafit, Tel," *NEAEHL* 4.1522–24; idem, *Archaeology*, 500. For the finds at Tel Zippor, see Stern, *Archaeology*, 492, 500, 503, 505. The two favissae in Area D of Tel 'Erani contained clay figurines, including at least one horse and rider, as well as fragments of stone statues. See Aharon Kempinski, "'Erani, Tel: Area D," *NEAEHL* 2.419–21; Stern, *Archaeology*, 505. For the finds at Maresha, see Amos Kloner, "מרשה," *Qadmoniot* 95–96 (1991): 70–85; Stern, *Archaeology*, 450. For the finds at Tel Hesi, see William M. Flinders Petrie, *Tell el-Hesy (Lachish)* (London: Alexander P. Watt, 1891); Frederick Jones Bliss, *A Mound of Many Cities: or, Tell el Hesy Excavated* (New York: Macmillan, 1894); W. J. Bennett Jr., and Jeffrey A. Blakely, *Tell el-Hesi: The Persian Period (Stratum V)* (vol. 3 of The Joint Archaeological Expedition to Tell el-Hesi; ed. Kevin G. O'Connell; Winona Lake, Ind.: Eisenbrauns, 1989), esp. 277–79; Valerie M. Fargo, "Hesi, Tell el-," *NEAEHL* 2:630–34; Stern, *Archaeology*, 411–12. For the finds at Tel Haror, see Eliezer D. Oren, "Haror, Tel," *NEAEHL* 2:580–84; Stern, *Archaeology*, 414. For the Greek figurines at Tel Sera' , see Eliezer D. Oren, "Ziglag: A Biblical City on the Edge of the Negev," *BA* 45 (1982): 155–66, esp. 158–59; idem, "Sera', Tel," *NEAEHL* 4:1329–35; Stern, *Archaeology*, 414. At Tel Halif, over five hundred fragments of Persian-era figurines (probably from favissae) were reused as fill in later construction projects. See http://www.cobb.msstate.edu/dig/LRP-1999-01/ (accessed Sept 19, 2004). See also Joe D. Seger, "Halif, Tel," *NEAEHL* 2:553–59.

61. In the Sinai, one kilometer west of Raphia, figurines were found in a small two-room building, the cultic nature of which is indicated by the finds in one of the courtyards, which included a plastered basin and two favissae of animal bones, ash, and charcoal. The associated pottery indicates that the structure was in use from the seventh through third centuries. See Eliezer D. Oren, "Northern Sinai," *NEAEHL* 4:1386–96, esp. 1393.

62. Ephraim Stern, "What Happened to the Cult Figurines? Israelite Religion Purified After the Exile," *BAR* 15.4 (July/August 1989): 22–29, 53–54; and see also idem, "Religion in Palestine in the Assyrian and Persian Periods," in *The Crisis of Israelite Religion: Transformation of Religious Tradition in Exilic and Post-Exilic Times* (ed. Bob Becking and Marjo C. A. Korpel; OtSt 42; Leiden: Brill, 1999), 245–55, esp. 254–55; idem, *Archaeology*, 488; and idem, "The Religious Revolution in Persian-Period Judah," in Lipschits and Oeming, *Judah and the Judeans in the Persian Period*, 199–205, esp. 201. This claim is dependent on Stern's redating of the bronze figurine of Osiris found in a pit at Gibeon, which he had previously dated to the fifth through fourth centuries B.C.E. on the basis of typology (idem, *Material Culture*, 160). Stern now considers the object to be from the late Iron Age (*Archaeology*, 498). See James B. Pritchard, *Winery, Defences, and Soundings at Gibeon* (Museum Monographs; Philadelphia: The University Museum, University of Pennsylvania, 1964), 21, fig 50:1; idem, "Gibeon," *NEAHL* 2.511–14.

63. Ephraim Stern, "Bes Vases from Palestine and Syria," *IEJ* 26 (1976): 183–87; pls. 32–33; idem, *Material Culture*, 131; idem, *Archaeology*, 507–10.

102), one with the altars in room 105, and one in room 106.[64] Others were found along with the small limestone altars in Cave 515[65] or scattered close to the surface soil in locus 522 (area in Grid Square A.22).[66] In the most recent excavations, the fragments of two additional figurines were found as surface finds and tentatively dated to the Persian period.[67] As with the incense altars, it is possible that some or all of these items were used by the non-Yahwists in the city.

With the possible exception of Lachish, there is no evidence for the use of figurines by Yahwists from the archaeological record. As such, the archaeological evidence for the use of figurines differs considerably from that of incense, the use of which by Yahwistic communities in Yehud and the Diaspora is more clear.

3.5 The Religious Use of Figurines by Yahwists in the Biblical Texts

The biblical evidence for the use of figurines during this time also differs from the evidence for the use of incense. Like many scholars in the fields of archaeology and biblical studies, I understand these objects to be smaller versions of cult images representing Asherah or other gods and goddesses, referred to in the biblical texts as אשרים, מסכה, פסל, סמל, and עצבים.[68] In contrast to the Persian-period biblical texts about incense, there is no positive notice about the use of cultic figurines and idols in the religious practices of Israel and Judah (and it follows that the use of the smaller images would also be proscribed). Unlike incense altars, whose use in Jerusalem is commended in Chronicles and whose use outside Jerusalem is commended by Malachi, the biblical texts from this period never speak favorably about the use of images in the public cult no matter the geographic context. In the book of Chronicles, for example, the use of such objects is always condemned, and their removal from the cult is always praised. For instance, the use of idols is included in the catalogue of the sins for the various condemned

---

64. Tufnell, *Lachish III*, 142–44. For these and the following figurines from Lachish, see also Stern, *Material Culture*, 158–59; idem, *Archaeology*, 500.

65. Tufnell, *Lachish III*, 221 and see also 378; pl. 33.4.

66. Tufnell, *Lachish III*, 224–25, and see also 378; pl. 33.3, 5–14, 16–20. For other figurines, see Aharoni, *Lachish V*, 4, pls. 18:3; 33:6.

67. Raz Kletter, "Iron Age and Post-Iron Age Artefacts. Section B: Clay Figurines," in Ussishkin, *Renewed Archaeological Excavations at Lachish*, 2058–83, esp. 2066; fig. 28.40:8.

68. For a history of the scholarly identification of plaque and pillar figurines with the "Asherim" and "Astarte" of biblical texts, see Raz Kletter, *The Judean Pillar-Figurines and the Archaeology of Asherah* (BAR International Series 636; Oxford: Tempus Reparatum, 1996), 16–27, 73–81. See also Judith M. Hadley, "Yahweh and 'His Asherah': Archaeological and Textual Evidence for the Cult of the Goddess," in *Ein Gott allein? JHWH-Verehrung und biblischer Monotheismus im Kontext der israelitischen und altorientalischen Religionsgeschichte* (ed. Walter Dietrich and Martin A. Klopfenstein; OBO 139; Freiburg: Universitätsverlag, 1994), 235–68. It is possible, however, that such objects depict not the goddess but the human supplicant.

kings. According to the text, during the reign of Joash, Judah "abandoned the house of YHWH . . . and served the Asherim (האשרים) and the idols (העצבים)" (2 Chr 24:18); Ahaz made "cast images (מסכות) for the Baals" (2 Chr 28:2); and Manasseh made Asheroth (אשרות; 2 Chr 33:3) and put a "carved image of the idol (פסל הסמל) that he had made" in the temple (2 Chr 33:7, 15 = 2 Kgs 21:7). Likewise, the destruction of idols is one of the tasks of the good kings. Along with removing the incense altars from Judah, Asa "broke down the memorial stones and hewed down the Asherim" (האשרים; 2 Chr 14:2). Asa also removed his mother as queen mother because she made "for Asherah an abominable image" (לאשרה מפלצת). The king subsequently cut down and burned the image (2 Chr 15:16 = 1 Kgs 15:13). Jehoshaphat removed the Asherim (אשרים) from Judah (2 Chr 17:6), and, in the reforms of Josiah, the king purged Jerusalem and Judah of "the Asherim (האשרים) and the idols (הפסלים) and the cast images (המסכות)" (2 Chr 34:3, and see also 34:4 and 7). Finally, after Hezekiah's Passover, the people went to the cities of Judah and "broke down the memorial stones, [and] hewed down the Asherim" (אשרים; 2 Chr 31:1).

Outside the book of Chronicles, there is only one reference to the use of images in the Persian period, namely, in the prayer of penitence in Neh 9. In this prayer, the people's survival after they made and worshipped a molten image of a calf (מסכה) is recounted as a sign of God's great mercy (Neh 9:18).[69]

Of course, it may be that such negative references to cultic images in Nehemiah and Chronicles indicate that they were in use during the Persian period (similar to my interpretation of the presentation of incense altars outside Jerusalem in Chronicles). Yet the biblical evidence for images in the public cult is still different from that for the use of incense in two ways: first, although Chronicles finds the use of incense acceptable as long as it is offered by ordained personnel in the central cult, there is no acceptable use of images in the text. Second, according to Mal 1:11, the use of incense outside Jerusalem is commended, indicating that the standard of use reflected in Chronicles was not adhered to by the entire community. Yet, whether within Jerusalem or outside the boundaries of Yehud, the use of images is never commended in the biblical texts. The contrasting attitudes toward incense and images in Nehemiah nicely summarize the biblical representation of these items in religious practice: incense is a crucial element of cultic accoutrements for the Jerusalem temple, but the molten figurine of a calf is a sinful device that could justifiably call down the wrath of God. This textual situation can be positively related to the archaeological evidence in which no sure sign of Yahwistic communities using the smaller figurines in their worship has yet been uncovered.

---

69. Later texts that speak (negatively) of the use of figurines in worship include Zech 13:2 where YHWH declares that in the future "I will cut off the names of the idols (העצבים) from the land." See also Zech 10:2, which claims that "The teraphim (תרפים) utter nonsense."

3.6 Conclusion

The archaeological and biblical evidence for the use of incense and figurines reveals that centrality and geography influenced more than just the practice of animal sacrifice. The use of figurines in worship seems to have been excluded in all Yahwistic worship, yet the nonsacrificial practice of Yahwistic religion is still archeologically and textually visible outside the city. Stern's thesis about the "purification" of the cult in Yehud and Samaria during this period, based on the lack of figurines found in these provinces, is striking, but to it could be added the evidence for the use of incense so that one is not left with the impression that the practice of religion left no artifactual trace outside Jerusalem. Granted, the book of Chronicles would like to circumscribe the boundaries of the use of incense as narrowly as the sacrifice of animals, but this project seems to have had opposition. The incense burners found at Tel en-Naṣbeh and Gezer, as well as those at Lachish, may point to the use of incense among Yahwists outside Jerusalem. In addition, since Stern includes the province of Samaria in his argument, it is significant to note the finds of incense burners in the city of Samaria and Shechem.[70] The texts from Elephantine and Mal 1:11 point to the use of incense by Yahwists farther afield in the greater Diaspora. Thus, the archaeological and textual evidence reveal both the cultic hegemony of Jerusalem and the practice of religion outside the city walls. The geography of religious practice is nuanced such that, while figurines did not seem to be used by Yahwists regardless of locale (with the possible exception of Lachish), animal sacrifice was largely confined to Jerusalem, and incense had no geographic limitation.

---

70. As noted previously in this chapter. For Samaria, see Reisner, *Harvard Excavations at Samaria*, 1.333; 2.pl. 80:a–c; Crowfoot et al., *The Objects from Samaria*, 466, 468, fig. 119.2; Stern, *Material Culture*, 184; idem, *Archaeology*, 513; Shea, "The Small Cuboid Incense-Burner," 84–85. For Shechem, see Stern, "Achaemenian Tombs from Shechem," 90–111, pls. 13–15; idem, *Archaeology*, 510–11.

CHAPTER 4

JERUSALEM AS A PILGRIMAGE CENTER
IN THE PERSIAN PERIOD

Another traceable aspect of centralized religious practice of the Persian period is that of pilgrimage to Jerusalem. Although such pilgrimage was not widespread until the Hasmonean period and later, it is possible to see its earlier manifestations in the biblical texts from the Persian period, including the prophets, the historical narratives (i.e., Ezra, Nehemiah and Chronicles), and Psalms 120–134.[1] As with the other practices examined in this monograph, pilgrimage does not have a consistent profile throughout the biblical texts from the Persian period, and the different genres maintain different emphases when describing the practice. The prophets emphasize eschatological pilgrimage and include both the Diaspora and the foreign nations as participants. In other texts, however, these eschatological aspects and openness to foreigners are barely discernible, if at all. The book of Chronicles, for example, recounts pilgrimage as a past event (with on-going relevance) and emphasizes the participation not of the nations but of the twelve tribes. In Ezra and Nehemiah, pilgrimage is both a present-day occurrence and a motif for the accounts of the community's returns from Babylon. Finally, Psalms 120–134 speak little of the ethnic categories of the participants but incor-

---

1. For a study of pilgrimage in the Hasmonean period and later, see Shmuel Safrai, *Die Wallfahrt im Zeitalter des Zweiten Tempels* (trans. Dafna Mach; Forschungen zum jüdisch-christlichen Dialog 3; Neukirchen-Vluyn: Neukirchener Verlag, 1981); Daniel Sperber, "Social Legislation in Jerusalem during the Latter Part of the Second Temple Period," *JSJ* 6 (1975): 86–95. Note that, according to Safrai, there is no good textual evidence for Persian-period pilgrimage, and the few biblical examples are only exceptions that prove the rule: "Vereinzelte Fälle von Wallfahrt aus der Diaspora gab es wohl schon immer, aber es lässt nachweisen, dass es sich um keinen verbreiteten Brauch handelte" ("There are various cases of pilgrimage from the Diaspora, but this only proves that there was no kind of widespread need." Ibid., 8, n. 45). The present study is an attempt to investigate the textual evidence that Safrai discounts. For a study of pilgrimage traditions in the bible that seem to date to an earlier time, see Arthur L. Merrill, "Pilgrimage in the Old Testament: A Study in Cult and Tradition," *Ecumenical Institute for Advanced Theological Studies: Yearbook* (1973–74): 45–62 and the additional monographs that he cites.

porate several themes that relate to and encourage pilgrimage to Jerusalem. This chapter discusses the evidence for each genre in turn. Given the scant remains of Persian-period Jerusalem uncovered in excavation, the question remains how the textual evidence for the practice can be reconciled with the archaeological evidence. The final part of this chapter briefly presents two models for understanding the practice of pilgrimage to Jerusalem in the Persian period based on these two types of evidence.

For the purposes of this study, I define pilgrimage as travel outside one's sphere of daily activity to a site designated as holy by the community in order to worship or communicate with the divine.[2] In ancient Israel and Greece, pilgrimage seems to have been a frequent event. For instance, Exod 23:17; 34:23 and Deut 16:16 command every male to appear before YHWH three times a year (although it seems likely that this was not fully enacted by all Yahwists), and journeys to a central cult site also could be made on other occasions such the birth of a child (Lev 12:6–8). In ancient Greece, the festival at Olympia was celebrated once every four years, the festivals at Nemea and Isthmia were celebrated every two years, and spectators and participants could attend festivals at various other sites.[3] With the possible frequency of ancient pilgrimage (at least as a desideratum), there was not the same emphasis on the penitential hardship requiring a long or arduous journey as is found in Christian pilgrimage in the Late Antique and Middle Ages, or in Muslim practice.[4] Further, not specifying a particular geographical distance in the definition of pilgrimage, only that the worshipper must leave the confines

---

2. Others who discuss pilgrimage in the ancient world give similar definitions. Matthew Dillon, focusing on ancient Greece, defines pilgrimage as "paying a visit to a sacred site outside the boundaries of one's own physical environment" (*Pilgrims and Pilgrimage in Ancient Greece* [London: Routledge, 1997], xviii). In his work on ancient Israel, Mark S. Smith considers the "major features of pilgrimage" to include a "sacred journey and arrival to the temple, with the prayers and sacrifices which ensue" (*The Pilgrimage Pattern in Exodus* [with contributions by Elizabeth M. Bloch-Smith; JSOTSupp 239; Sheffield: Sheffield Academic Press, 1997], 16).

3. Dillon, *Pilgrims and Pilgrimage*, 99.

4. The condition of hardship is not included in the definitions of pilgrimage given by Dillon and M. S. Smith in the context of ancient communities (see above). For its inclusion in pilgrimage (based on parallels with Muslim pilgrimage), see William G. Johnsson's article, "The Pilgrimage Motif in the Book of Hebrews," *JBL* 97 (1978): 239–51, where he borrows his definition from H. B. Partin's dissertation, "The Muslim Pilgrimage: Journey to the Center" (Ph.D. diss., University of Chicago, 1967), 145–52. Partin recognizes four aspects of pilgrimage: separation from home and usual activity, a sacred place as a destination, a fixed purpose (purification or forgiveness of sins, of which attainment is associated with arrival at the destination), and hardship (so that failure is a possibility). In the Christian tradition, hardship in pilgrimage is part of the penitential process that can allow a purging of sin. In their description and analysis of St. Patrick's Purgatory (a pilgrimage site in Ireland), Victor Turner and Edith Turner write, "in the 'economy of salvation' in pre-Reformation theology, living souls require penitence as the dead require purgatory." See their classic work, *Image and Pilgrimage in Christian Culture* (New York: Columbia University Press, 1978), 113.

of his or her daily world, allows both those coming from within the province of Yehud and those traveling from farther away to be designated pilgrims.[5]

4.1 PILGRIMAGE TO JERUSALEM IN THE BIBLICAL TEXTS

Although pilgrimage in the Hebrew Bible is sometimes designated by the terms חגג or חג ("to make a pilgrimage," and "feast, pilgrim-feast," so BDB), journeys to a sacred place are also designated by other terms of travel. There is nothing specifically cultic or ritualistic about these travel terms, since most appear frequently in the Hebrew Bible and can encompass secular meanings; nevertheless, some have a particular use as designators of journeys to holy sites. In this aspect, Hebrew is similar to Greek, where pilgrimage is designated with terms such as "those going" and "those coming."[6] For instance, בוא ("to go in, enter") describes the journey to the place where YHWH or other gods are worshipped,[7] sometimes in the explicit context of a חג (Deut 31:11; Isa 30:29; 2 Chr 30:5). In addition, the *hiphil* form of בוא designates the bringing of offerings and sacrifices to YHWH.[8] The root הלך can designate the journey to a sacred area, including Deut 14:25 in the context of instructions for people who live far from the holy place, and 1 Kgs 3:4 when the king went to worship and sacrifice at Gibeon.[9] עלה is the verb used to designate travel in the pilgrimage legislation of Exod 34:23–24: "no one

---

5. This definition differs from more modern conceptions of pilgrimage that predominantly focus on once-in-a-lifetime treks involving a great distance. The radical break from regular social conditions that such long and arduous treks may involve has been examined by scholars such as Van Gennup and Victor and Edith Turner. See Victor W. Turner, "The Center Out There: Pilgrim's Goal," *HR* 12 (1973): 191–230; idem, *The Ritual Process: Structure and Anti-Structure* (Chicago: Aldine, 1969); idem, "Pilgrimage and Communitas," *Studia Missionalia* 23 (1974): 305–27; and Turner and Turner, *Image and Pilgrimage*. Given that ancient pilgrimage often occurred more than once in a person's lifetime, and given that people from the local communities could worship together at the cult, such radical breaks do not seem as relevant to the ancient world.

6. Other terms for pilgrimage in Greek texts include "the watchers" (θεαται), "those attending a panegyris" (πανηγυρίζοντες), and those who wish "to go, to sacrifice, to seek an oracle and to watch." See Dillon, *Pilgrims and Pilgrimage*, xv–xvi.

7. The verb בוא describes the journey to worship YHWH in Jerusalem (Isa 27:13; 30:29; 2 Kgs 12:10), to worship other gods in their sacred precincts (Judg 9:46; 1 Sam 5:5; 2 Kgs 10:21 [3x]; Ezek 20:29; Hos 9:10), or to where a prophet resides (1 Kgs 14:3, 5; 2 Kgs 4:42; Ezek 20:1, 3; and see also Ezek 14:4, 7).

8. So Gen 4:3, 4; Num 15:25; Mal 1:13 (2x). It also designates the bringing of offerings and sacrifices to the priests (Lev 2:2; 5:11, 12; 2 Kgs 4:42; 12:5 [2x]) or into the temple (2 Chr 31:10; 34:9), and to YHWH's storehouse (Mal 3:10).

9. Other examples of this term used to describe a journey to a place of worship and/or sacrifice or divine inquiry are found in Gen 25:22 (Rebekeh); Exod 3:18, 19 (YHWH wanting the Israelites to take a three-day journey into the wilderness); Deut 26:2 (the nation); Judg 11:37, 40 (Jephthah's daughter and her companions); Qoh 4:17; Ps 55:15; Isa 30:29; and Jer 3:6. Related examples from outside the Hebrew Bible include the letter from Mari when Kiru, the daughter of Zimri-Lim, asked her father

shall covet your land when you go up (בעלתך) to appear before YHWH your God three times in the year," and it describes the journey of Elkanah and his family to worship at Shiloh (1 Sam 1:3, 7, 24). The prophets also use it in their visions of future worship in Jerusalem: according to Mic 4:2//Isa 2:3, many nations will say, "Come, let us go up (ונעלה) to the mountain of YHWH."[10]

Having covered some preliminary remarks about the definition and vocabulary of pilgrimage, this study turns to examine biblical texts from the Persian period to see the varying descriptions and constructions of pilgrimage during this time.

4.1.1 Pilgrimage in Haggai, Zechariah, and Trito-Isaiah

Zech 6:9–12 recounts exiles coming (באו) to Jerusalem from Babylon bearing silver and gold. For the prophet, this act initiates future pilgrimage: immediately following this account is a prophecy that this pilgrimage will be repeated both by the Diaspora and by Gentile nations ("Those who are far off shall come [יבאו] build the temple of YHWH" [Zech 6:15]). In addition, YHWH will bring (הבאתי) people from the east and west to live in Jerusalem (Zech 8:7–8). Others will come at their own initiative, with Jews, "strong nations," and "the inhabitants of many cities" issuing their own call to pilgrimage: "Come, let us go (נלכה הלוך) to entreat the favor of YHWH, and to seek YHWH of hosts; I myself am going (אלכה)" (Zech 8:21). Further, the prophet declares that in days to come, "ten men from nations of every language shall take hold of a Jew (יהודי) . . . saying, 'Let us go (נלכה) with you, for we have heard that God is with you'" (Zech 8:23).[11] The emphasis on the nations participating with the chosen community is also evident

---

permission to leave her situation to "go" (lu-ul-li-ka-am-ma) to the gods of her father and sacrifice (ARM X 113.20–22, quoted by Bernard Frank Batto, *Studies on Women at Mari* [The Johns Hopkins Near Eastern Studies; Baltimore and London: The Johns Hopkins University Press, 1974], 128).

10. The prophecy in Isa 2:3//Mic 4:2 lacks a reference to the pilgrim's return home, a situation that I would explain by the passage's emphasis on the cult site and the journey to it as well as the eschatological overtones. For other uses of עלה in what I consider pilgrimage contexts, see Jer 31:6 and the account when Moses and Joshua "went up (ויעל) into the mountain of God" (Exod 24:13, 15, 18).

11. For more on Jerusalem as the "epicenter" of Yahwism in Zech 8, see Carol L. Meyers and Eric M. Meyers, "Jerusalem and Zion After the Exile: The Evidence of First Zechariah," in *"Sha'arei Talmon": Studies in the Bible, Qumram, and the Ancient Near East Presented to Shemaryahu Talmon* (ed. Michael Fishbane and Emanuel Tov; Winona Lake, Ind.: Eisenbrauns, 1992), 121–35, esp. 131.

Return to Jerusalem is also part of the later prophecies of Third Zechariah. In chapter 10, YHWH promises to bring back the people scattered among the nations (הושבותים in v. 6 of the Leningrad Codex; השיבותים in v. 10). They will return (ושבו, v. 9), and YHWH will bring them back (אביאם, v. 10) to the land of Gilead and to Lebanon (Zech 10:6–12). Note also Zech 14:16–19 where the nations will go to Jerusalem annually to keep the festival of Booths. For more on this passage, see Walter Harrelson, "The Celebration of the Feast of Booths according to Zech xiv 16–21," in *Religions in Antiquity: Essays in Memory of Erwin Ramsdell Goodenough* (ed. Jacob Neusner; SHR 14; Leiden: Brill, 1968), 88–96.

in Zech 2:15, where the prophet declares that "many nations shall join themselves (ונלוו) to YHWH on that day, and shall be my people; I will dwell in your midst."

Haggai and Third Isaiah also prophesy such future and/or eschatological pilgrimage, although it is primarily the nations and their wealth that are in view instead of the nations with the Diaspora. In Haggai, YHWH promises to shake the heaven, the earth, the sea, the dry land, and all the nations, "so that the treasure of the nations shall come (ובאו), and I will fill this house with splendor . . ." (Hag 2:6–8).[12] In Third Isaiah, foreigners who keep the Sabbath and the covenant will be brought (*hiphil* of בוא) to YHWH's holy mountain to offer burnt offerings and sacrifices (Isa 56:6–7). The text also includes the promise that "nations shall bring (להביא) you their wealth . . . to beautify the place of my sanctuary" (Isa 60:9, 13; cf. 60:6–16). Taken together with the texts in Zechariah, these texts emphasize both the future expectation of pilgrimage and the inclusion of foreigners (and their wealth) with the nation in worshipping YHWH in Jerusalem.

4.1.2 PILGRIMAGE IN EZRA[13]

The book of Ezra records two pilgrimage celebrations, the festival of Booths in Ezra 3:1–4 and the festival of Passover and Unleavened Bread in Ezra 6:19–22. These festivals are themselves bracketed by two accounts of the community's return from Babylon, one led by Zerubbabel and Jeshua in Ezra 1–2 and another led by Ezra in Ezra 7–8. Although many argue that these returns (or Ezra 1 at least) are deliberately modeled on the exodus from Egypt, they are better interpreted by the imagery of pilgrimage. The returns in Ezra emphasize Jerusalem as the destination of the journey (and not the larger geographic region of the promised land), they are explicitly cultic (with priests, sacrifice, and cultic vessels specifically highlighted), and they involve several journeys of the nation (not one constitutive trip made by the people together). In the four accounts, then, the book of Ezra highlights pilgrimage both as a practice and as a narrative motif for the community's return to the land.

Besides the most basic feature of journey, the motif of gift giving is probably the most frequently adduced parallel between the exodus and the returns in Ezra (Ezra 1:4, 6 and Exod 3:21–22; 11:2; 12:35–36).[14] Nonetheless, there are

---

12. For more on the eschatological sense of this text, see John A. Kessler, "The Shaking of the Nations: An Eschatological View," *JETS* 30 (1987): 159–66.

13. An earlier version of this section was presented to the Chronicles-Ezra-Nehemiah Section of the Society of Biblical Literature in November, 2000, under the title "The Returns as Pilgrimage in Ezra," and later published as "Pilgrimage Imagery in the Returns in Ezra," *JBL* 123 (2004): 57–74 (used with permission).

14. The connection is made by, among others, Jacob M. Myers, *Ezra Nehemiah* (AB 14; Garden City, N.Y.: Doubleday, 1965), 9 and Mark Throntveit, *Ezra-Nehemiah* (Interpretation; Louisville, Ky.: John Knox, 1992), 16. For an account of this motif in the Exodus narratives themselves, see G. W. Coats,

some major discontinuities between the two accounts in the details of this motif, namely, the ethnicity of the gift givers, their source of compunction, the content of the gifts, and the rhetorical point of the motif. In terms of ethnicity, those who gave gifts to the returnees (כל־הנשאר ["all the rest/those who remained"], Ezra 1:4, 6) can be understood to include both Jews (v. 4)[15] and Gentiles (v. 6).[16] A similar ethnic mix of gift givers is found in the second return in Ezra 7:15–16 where gifts from the king and "the whole province of Babylonia" are brought along with those of "people and the priests . . . for the house of their God in Jerusalem." The designation of Yahwists along with Gentiles as those who gave gifts to returnees contrasts with the exodus narratives, in which only the Egyptians gave items of value.[17]

The accounts in Exodus and Ezra differ also in the rhetorical point of the gift giving. While the original purpose of the account in Exodus might have been etiological, perhaps related to a seasonal children's game or carnival holiday,[18] its immediate purpose in the present narrative is indicated by the editor's summarizing trope of the event: "Thus the Israelites will plunder (*piel* of נצל) the Egyptians."[19] As emphasis, the trope is said in prospect by God in Exod 3:22 ("will plunder") and in retrospect by the narrator in Exod 12:36 ("plundered"). A sense of mistreatment is absent in the Ezra narrative: whereas the gifts are given at the

---

"Despoiling the Egyptians," *VT* 18 (1968): 450–57; Sara Japhet, "The Temple in the Restoration Period: Reality and Ideology," *Union Seminary Quarterly Review* 44 (1991): 195–252, esp. 213–14; and Julian Morgenstern, "The Despoiling of the Egyptians," *JBL* 68 (1949): 1–28. For more on the second exodus theme, see Klaus Koch, "Ezra and the Origins of Judaism," *JSS* 19 (1974): 173–97.

15. Here I am reading "אנשי מקמו" ("the men of his place") in Ezra 1:4 not as the subject of the verb ינשאוהו but rather as an explanatory gloss of the awkward and confusing preceding phrase (גר־שם כל־הנשאר מכל־המקמות אשר הוא; "and all who remained, from all of the places where he sojourns"). This reading is supported by the smoother and shorter reading of 1 Esd 2:6, which describes the givers simply as "οι περικυκλω αυτων." This reading is also followed by H. G. M. Williamson, "The Composition of Ezra i–iv," *JTS* n.s. 34 (1983): 1–30, esp. 9–11.

16. Those who maintain that the givers were both Jews (Ezra 1:4) and Gentiles (Ezra 1:6) include Myers, *Ezra Nehemiah*, 8–9; and H. G. M. Williamson, *Ezra, Nehemiah* (WBC 16, Waco, Tex.: Word Books, 1985), 5, 14–16. Those who read these two verses as indicating Gentiles include D. J. A. Clines, *Ezra, Nehemiah, Esther* (NCBC; Grand Rapids, Mich.; Eerdmans, 1984), 38–39; and Ralph W. Klein, "The Books of Ezra & Nehemiah," in *The New Interpreter's Bible* (vol. 3; Nashville, Ky.: Abingdon, 1999): 661–851, esp. 678–79.

17. Although C. F. Keil also includes Jews as part of those who gave gifts to the returnees, he does so by including Jews and Gentiles as part of the סביבתיהם in Ezra 1:6. See his commentary, *The Books of Ezra, Nehemiah, and Esther* (trans. Sophia Taylor; Biblical Commentary on the Old Testament 3; Edinburgh: T&T Clark, 1879; repr., Grand Rapids, Mich.: Eerdmans, 1983), 25.

18. So J. B. Segal, *The Hebrew Passover* (Oxford: Oxford University Press, 1963), 148–49, 260; and William H. C. Propp, *Exodus 1–18* (AB 2; New York: Doubleday, 1998), 208, 412–13.

19. The *piel* form of נצל points to some measure of ill treatment: in addition to the two uses in the Exodus accounts, it appears in 2 Chr 20:25 in the context of taking booty after a military victory.

command of Cyrus (whose spirit has been "stirred" by God), there is no sense that the givers have been exploited; indeed, the explicit purpose of the gifts is "to assist" (*piel* of נשא; Ezra 1:4) and "to support" (literally "they strengthened their hands," חזקו בידיהם; Ezra 1:6).

Exodus and Ezra also differ in the source of compunction for the gifts. The Egyptians give their goods as a result of the personal entreaties of the Israelites: ". . . each woman shall ask her neighbor . . . for silver vessels . . ." (Exod 3:22, and see also 11:2 and 12:35), and there is no notice that Pharaoh was involved in the process. In marked contrast, the gift giving in Ezra 1 is at the direct command of Cyrus: "Thus says King Cyrus of Persia . . . those who remain behind . . . shall assist him [i.e., the returnees] . . . with silver . . ." (Ezra 1:2, 4). When the command is fulfilled, Cyrus himself "brought out" the cultic vessels and had them given to the returnees (Ezra 1:7–8). Thus God's command that the Israelites "ask" the Egyptians for items is replaced by Cyrus' command that those in Babylon "assist" the returnees. Indeed, in place of the antagonism between Israel and Pharaoh, the Persian political power is obliging in the extreme. In Ezra 1–2, Cyrus is neither absent nor antagonistic: the giving of gifts occurs with the explicit direction and participation (under the guidance of God) of the political ruler.

Finally, the gifts also differ in content. According to Exod 3:22 and 12:35, the gifts consisted of "vessels of silver, and vessels of gold, and clothing," but the Ezra narratives omit the clothing and add some additional items (". . . silver and gold and goods and beasts . . . besides freewill offerings for the house of God . . ." in Ezra 1:4, and ". . . silver vessels, with gold, with goods, with beasts, and with valuable gifts, besides all that was freely offered" in Ezra 1:6).[20]

These small differences in the accounts in Exodus and Ezra point to the larger differences between an exodus and a pilgrimage. Both journeys involve travel, but this travel has different emphases. In an exodus, an oppressed group leaves a place of bondage as a single group and enters into a land of freedom (a promised land). It is a political journey, sometimes with religious aspects, that emphasizes the leave-taking part of the journey. When the destination of the exodus group is named in the biblical accounts, it is not a specific cultic location but rather the larger land area in which they will dwell. YHWH informs Moses from the burning bush that the destination is "the place/land of the Canaanites, the Hittites, the Amorites, the Perizzites, the Hivites, and the Jebusites" (Exod 3:8, 17);[21] the

---

20. There is an additional notice that King Cyrus sent the basins, bowls, and vessels taken from the Jerusalem temple by Nebuchadnezzar (Ezra 1:7–11).

21. In Exod 3:7, the Sam and LXX add "and the Girgashite" after "the Perizzite." See K. G. O'Connell, "The List of Seven Peoples in Canaan: A Fresh Analysis," in *The Answers Lie Below: Essays in Honor of Lawrence Edmond Toombs* (ed. H. O. Thompson; Lanham, Md.: University Press of America, 1984), 221–41.

destination is also given as the "land of the Canaanites" (so Exod 13:11; 34:11), or the land that YHWH "swore to Abraham, Isaac, and Jacob" (Exod 33:1).[22] This emphasis on leaving and the lack of a specific cult site as the goal is distinguished from a pilgrimage, which, in my usage, emphasizes a specific sacred destination (pilgrims leave their daily world to go to a holy place) and activity (to worship). Pilgrims usually also return to their homes again, although this is not always emphasized in textual accounts, which tend to be more concerned with the cultic destination (for instance, there is no mention of the return trip in the pilgrimage legislation in Exod 23:17; 34:23; and Deut 16:16, only the instruction that all the males are to appear before YHWH three times a year). Throughout the accounts in Ezra, these pilgrimage emphases are seen in the repeated designation of the holy destination and the stated religious purpose of the journeys.

The different journeys also have different sociological consequences.[23] The exodus was a one-time event involving the entire community and was the defining moment in the constitutive life of the community and their God ("I am YHWH your God, who brought you out of the land of Egypt . . ." Deut 5:6; cf. Neh 9:9–11). In contrast, the journey out of Babylon was never viewed as a single event (several journeys from Babylon are mentioned in the Ezra-Nehemiah material), and there is no sense that those who participated in the first return, recorded in Ezra 1, were granted more status in the community. Indeed, the account of the return emphasizes several times that this journey was voluntary, with no aspersion cast on those who did not come along. After listing those who arose to go on the journey as the heads of the families of Judah and Benjamin and the priests and the Levites, a significant aside specifies the travelers more closely as "all the people whose spirit was stirred by God" (Ezra 1:5). Given that the text provides no psychological or spiritual portrait of those who remained behind (claiming only that the spirits of those who went were stirred by God), one cannot assume that only the returnees were obedient to God (contra Josephus and C. F. Keil).[24]

---

22. My interpretation of Exodus' destination is different from that given by Mark S. Smith (*The Pilgrimage Pattern in Exodus* [with contributions by Elizabeth M. Bloch-Smith; JSOTSupp 239; Sheffield: Sheffield Academic Press, 1997], 16), who claims that, in the priestly redaction of the text, the destination of the journey is "the mountain of God": "It may be suggested tentatively that the priestly redaction may have interpreted the Exodus passages as the people's pilgrimage to the mountain," in contrast to the book of Numbers, which "might be regarded as depicting a pilgrimage journey from the mountain to the sanctuary-land, but not in a manner precisely parallel to Exodus," pp. 286–87).

23. The distinctions that I draw between the two journeys differ somewhat from Eugene H. Merrill's analysis of the motifs of exodus and pilgrimage in the prophetic literature, where he identifies the two elements of pilgrimage to be a "gathering from throughout the earth (not merely from a single place of bondage) and the emphasis on Zion and the temple" ("Pilgrimage and Procession: Motifs of Israel's Return," in *Israel's Apostasy and Restoration: Essays in Honor of Roland K. Harrison* [ed. Avraham Gileadi; Grand Rapids, Mich.: Baker Book House, 1988], 261–72, esp. 262).

24. See the *Antiquities* 11.1.3 where Josephus claims that those who stayed behind in Babylon were "not willing to leave their possessions." See also Keil, *Ezra, Nehemiah, and Esther,* 25.

Obedience to God in Ezra 1 has to do with a correct response to this divine stirring in the individual rather than a return en masse. The lack of a list naming the returnees over against those who continued to reside in Babylon also points to the nonconstitutive nature of this first journey out of Babylon.[25]

In sum, although both a pilgrimage and an exodus involve a journey, the two journeys have different emphases and sociological functions. The acknowledgment that the return from Babylon was accomplished in a series of journeys, rather than a single constitutive one, distinguishes it from an exodus. This serial nature of the returns in Ezra, along with the emphasis on the destination as Jerusalem, combine with a thick cultic component in the narratives to emphasize their identity as pilgrimage. This cultic component, as I discuss in the next few paragraphs, is seen in the emphasis throughout the two accounts on worship, cultic personnel, and the use of pilgrimage vocabulary for the journey.

---

25. Ezra 1–2 does not distinguish the returnees from those who remained or those who came later. The compendium of names in Ezra 2 may seem to function as such a list: "Now these were the people of the province who came from the captive exiles . . . they went (√שוב) to Jerusalem and Judah, all to their own towns. They came (√בוא) with Zerubbabel, Jeshua, Nehemiah . . ." (Ezra 2:1–2; note that the more original reading of the list in Ezra 2:1–67 is better preserved in the two witnesses of Neh 7:6–69 and 1 Esd. See Ralph Walter Klein, "Old Readings in I Esdras: The List of Returnees from Babylon [Ezra 2 // Nehemiah 7]," *HTR* 62 [1969]: 99–107). But this compendium is actually a list of those who settled in Judah rather than those who returned in this one trip. This is in contrast to the list of returnees in Ezra 8, entitled "these are the heads of the fathers' houses, and this is the genealogy of them that went up with me from Babylon," which is indeed a list of those who made the journey with Ezra. Yet there is not the same potential ideological weight as the list in Ezra 2 because they are not part of the premier group. In context, the list in Ezra 2 is simply a list of returnees, not a list of the first returnees who came out of Babylon and constitute the new Israel. This would be the only way to explain the surprising absence of Sheshbazzar in the list. Further, the inconsistencies of the list point to the fact that it represents several different sources. The names are first listed by family names (Ezra 2:3–18), then by place names (vv. 19–28), then by family names again (vv. 29–32), then by place names again (vv. 33–34), and finally by the family of Senaah (v. 35; this is the ordering of Kurt Galling, "The Gōlā-List According to Ezra 2//Nehemiah 7," *JBL* 70 [1951]: 149–58, esp. 152. A revision of the article is found in "Die Liste der aus dem Exil Heimgekehrten," in *Studien zur Geschichte Israels im persischen Zeitalter* [Tübingen: J. C. B. Mohr (Paul Siebeck), 1964], 89–108). See also Wilhelm Rudolph, *Esra und Nehemia* [HAT 20; Tübingen: J. C. B. Mohr (Paul Siebeck), 1949], 7–28). Although others divide differently, the visible seams show that the list is certainly not smooth. This list may have been cobbled together from different registers during 539–538 to 515 (so Rudolph, *Esra und Nehemia*, 7–28), or from a collection of general names from this period (so Lester L. Grabbe, *Ezra-Nehemiah* [Old Testament Readings; London: Routledge, 1998], 13). It may also have been originally generated (in any of its forms) for the purpose of taxation, or as a list of the "fathers' houses" of the civic temple community (so Joel Weinberg, *The Citizen-Temple Community* [trans. Daniel L. Smith-Christopher; JSOTSupp 151; Sheffield: Sheffield Academic Press, 1992], 49–61). In addition, since it is from the group that stayed behind in Babylon that subsequent heroes such as Ezra and Nehemiah arose, it is plausible that the author would prefer not to glorify the first returnees in order not to reflect poorly on those who initially stayed behind in Babylon (this point is also made by Throntveit, *Ezra-Nehemiah*, 16).

As befits a pilgrimage, Ezra 1–2 emphasizes the destination as a holy place. Unlike the exodus, where the travelers went to "the land," Ezra 1–2 specifies the destination three times as Jerusalem ("Whosoever of YHWH's people . . . let him go up to Jerusalem," Ezra 1:3–4; "All these Sheshbazzar brought up . . . to Jerusalem," Ezra 1:11; "As soon as they came to the house of YHWH in Jerusalem . . .," Ezra 2:68).[26] Likewise, Ezra 7–8 also emphasizes the sacred destination of the travelers, naming Jerusalem as the destination five separate times (Ezra 7:7, 8, 9, 13; 8:31, and see also 8:32 where the entire party traveling with Ezra stayed in the city for three days).

The purpose of the journey to Jerusalem in Ezra 1–2 and 7–8 is specifically religious, namely, to worship. In Ezra 1–2, worship had to be preceded by rebuilding the temple. According to Cyrus' edict, YHWH charged the emperor "to build him a house at Jerusalem" (Ezra 1:2). Accordingly, Cyrus permitted YHWH's people to go up to the city "and rebuild the house of YHWH" (Ezra 1:3).[27] When YHWH stirred up the spirits of the people, it was so that they would "go up to build the house of YHWH in Jerusalem" (Ezra 1:5). The cultic purpose of Ezra's journey is also manifest in the frequent mention of cultic personnel.[28] Although the group originally set out with priests, Levites, temple singers, gatekeepers, and temple servants (הנתינים; Ezra 7:7), these religious functionaries apparently were not enough and Ezra subsequently sent a special delegation to Iddo at Casiphia to ask for "ministers" (משרתים) for the house of God (Ezra 8:17). The delegation was a success, and several families of Levites and 220 temple servants joined the group (Ezra 8:20).

The items that both sets of travelers carried with them also attest to the goal of worship. In Ezra 1–2, they take silver, gold, goods, animals, and "freewill offerings" specifically designated "for the house of God in Jerusalem" (Ezra 1:4, 6). To

---

26. In a related way, the chapters emphasize the presence of YHWH in Jerusalem. Chapters 1–2 refer both to YHWH's location ("he is the God who is in Jerusalem;" Ezra 1:3) and to the building of God's "house" (Ezra 1:2, 3, 4, 5, 2:68 [2x]). Although Ezra 1–2 emphasize that YHWH has the geographical flexibility to influence the decisions of Cyrus in Persia (Ezra 1:1) and that he is "the God of heaven" (Ezra 1:2), it concomitantly emphasizes YHWH's unique presence in Jerusalem. In Ezra 7–8 the designation of the temple as "the house" of YHWH occurs twelve times (Ezra 7:16; 17, 19, 20, 23, 24, 27; 8:17, 25, 30, 33, 36), with the added description that this house is "in Jerusalem" four times (Ezra 7:16, 17, 27; 8:30; and see also the expression in Ezra 7:15: "the God of Israel, whose dwelling is in Jerusalem").

27. Here I disagree with Kurt Galling, "Von Naboned zu Darius," *ZDPV* 70 (1954): 4–32, esp. 11–13, who reconstructs two original edicts (one for rebuilding, one for return), which are here consolidated. In contrast to the memorandum in Ezra 6:3–5, the edict in Ezra 1 holds both activities (to go up and to build) as inseparable.

28. So Koch, "Ezra and the Origins of Judaism," 185: "The main part of the edict of ten verses concerns the house or dwelling of the God who is in Jerusalem, and the equipment for its worship. Therefore the purpose of the march is not the Law and its validity, but the establishment of a permanent and effective worship . . . ."

these offerings Cyrus adds the gold and silver temple vessels that Nebuchadnezzer had seized, which the returnees take as if by proxy (Ezra 1:7–11).[29] In Ezra 7–8, the group also takes along gifts from their community and the king to be used in the temple: "silver and gold" from the king and his counselors (Ezra 7:15), "silver and gold" from Babylonia, and "freewill offerings" from the people and the priests (Ezra 7:16), which are to be used to buy sacrificial animals and grain and drink offerings to be "offered on the altar" of YHWH in Jerusalem (Ezra 7:17). The group also brings along "vessels . . . for the service of the house of your God" (Ezra 7:19). The king designates that additional funds for "whatever else is required for the house of your God" can be acquired from the royal treasury (Ezra 7:20) and instructs the treasurers in the province Beyond the River to give silver, wheat, wine, oil, and salt "for the house of the God of heaven" (Ezra 7:21–23). Similar to the list of vessels in Ezra 1, the record of Ezra's journey also lists an inventory of gold and silver vessels given to them by the king, the political establishment, and the people of Israel (Ezra 8:26–27), which Ezra pronounces "holy" along with the priests who carried them (Ezra 8:28).

Both accounts also employ the vocabulary of pilgrimage. The predominant verb used to describe the return in Ezra 1–2 is עלה.[30] The term appears in Cyrus' edict (Ezra 1:3), in anticipation of the journey (Ezra 1:5), and, as העלה, is used twice in a summary of the event (once applied to the vessels and once to the people; Ezra 1:11).[31] The account also uses בוא (Ezra 2:2, 68). Similarly, the author records that Ezra "went up (עליו) from Babylonia" (Ezra 7:6), and the other members of the group also "went up (עליו)" to Jerusalem (Ezra 7:7). Ezra "gathered leaders from Israel to go up (לעלות)" with him (Ezra 7:28) and records, "These are the family heads and the genealogies of those who went up (העלים) with me from Babylonia" (Ezra 8:1). Significantly, the account also refers to "the journey up from Babylon" (המעלה מבבל; Ezra 7:9), using a rare term that in its plural form is also found in the superscription to the "songs of ascents" (שיר המעלות; Pss 120–134). Less frequently, the term בוא also is used (Ezra 7:8, 9; 8:32, 35).

---

29. The list of vessels is difficult, both in terms of vocabulary and arithmetic: some of the terms appear nowhere else in the MT, and, although the total number of vessels is given in Ezra 1:11 as 5,400, this number conflicts with the enumerated inventory in Ezra 1:9–11.

30. The term used for the settlement of the people in the land in Ezra 2:1 is שוב.

31. Williamson, "The Composition of Ezra i–iv," 14–15, has drawn attention to the possible exodus parallels that Ezra 1:11 may indicate with the use of העלה, a use that, according to Williamson, "echoes the descriptions of the Exodus." See also the article by J. Wijngaards that Williamson cites, "הוציא and העלה: A Twofold Approach to the Exodus," *VT* 15 (1965): 91–102, in which the author notes that the formula העלה + object (Israel) + "from Egypt" is used forty-one times throughout the Hebrew Bible to refer to the exodus, and that there are several instances where the formula also includes the phrase "to the land" (either אל־הארץ or אל־הארץ טובה or similar variations; Gen 50:24; Exod 3:8, 17; cf. Exod 33:1; ibid., 98–99; note also "אל־המקום הרע הזה" in Num 20:5). Ezra 1:11b does indeed include the

In addition to emphasizing the holy destination and purpose and using the vocabulary of pilgrimage, Ezra 1 contains a call to pilgrimage. Cyrus' call to go up to Jerusalem, sent throughout the land via a herald (Ezra 1:1), has no parallel in the exodus material. It is more closely aligned with the calls to pilgrimage in texts such as 1 Sam 11:14 ("Come, let us go up to Gilgal") and Isa 2:3 ("Come, let us go up to the mountain of YHWH"; note the parallel use of the jussive in Ezra 1:3). In addition, there are several parallels between the call in Ezra 1 and 2 Chr 30 where Hezekiah's call to the Passover festival in Jerusalem is recorded: "Children of Israel, turn back to YHWH . . . and enter into his sanctuary" (2 Chr 30:5, 6, 8). The two calls were issued in both an oral and a written form, and sent throughout the land (Ezra 1:1; 2 Chr 30:1, 5).[32]

Like all pilgrims (and in contrast to those in the exodus who leave the place where they are currently living to dwell in another place), the travelers in Ezra 1–2 return home. Instead of returning to Babylon, however, the people return to what could be called their true home, namely, their ancestral towns in Yehud. The text uses the term "town" with a possessive three times to specify the ultimate destination of the travelers after their trip to Jerusalem (איש לעירו, Ezra 2:1; בעריהם, Ezra 2:70 [2x]).

Finally, as befits a pilgrimage, Ezra's journey ends with sacrifice. His coterie arrived in Jerusalem, remained for three days, handed over the gold, silver and vessels on the fourth day, and then sacrificed ("At that time those who returned

---

first three elements of the formula (with the replacement of "from Egypt" with מבבל), and thus the exodus imagery seems operational. However, there are two differences in the notice of the traveler's destination: instead of being marked with אל-, it is marked with ל, and instead of being designated "the land," it is the specific site of Jerusalem (the verse reads העלות הגולה מבבל לירושלם). It may be that these differences should be considered only minor variations on the exodus formula, but, given that העלה also can describe the presenting of gifts at the altar on the occasion of a pilgrimage feast (1 Kgs 12:32), it may also be that Ezra 1:11 includes not only exodus imagery but pilgrimage imagery as well.

32. For the oral and written form of the calls, compare the following texts: "Hezekiah sent word to all Israel and Judah, and wrote (כתב) letters also to Ephraim and Manasseh that they should come to the house of YHWH . . ." (2 Chr 30:1); "Cyrus . . . sent a proclamation [literally, 'he made a voice pass'] throughout all his kingdom, and also in a written edict (במכתב) . . ." (Ezra 1:1). For the sending out of the calls throughout the land, note that Cyrus' edict was sent via a herald "throughout all his kingdom" (Ezra 1:1) and Hezekiah's call went "from Beer-Sheba to Dan" (2 Chr 30:5). Even if the later author/ editor of Ezra expanded the original audience intended by the proclamation from a more localized community, as Williamson argues in "The Composition of Ezra i–iv," 9, the parallel between other calls to pilgrimage in the Hebrew Bible remains. When Williamson excludes 2 Chr 30:5–9 as comparable to Cyrus' edict, his objection is on content and lack of imperatival form, and he concludes that "the Chronicler has merely put a Levitical sermon into the mouths of the king's messengers." I would suggest that, at least on the basis of their shared purpose (to call a group of people to go to Jerusalem) and in the account of how such an account would be published (in an oral and written form), 2 Chr 30:5–9 remains a valid parallel to Ezra 1:1.

from captivity, the returned exiles, offered burnt offerings to the God of Israel . . ." Ezra 8:32–35).

Thus the returns in Ezra are heavily weighed with pilgrimage imagery. The people, along with their cultic vessels and cultic personnel, went up to Jerusalem to rebuild the temple and worship. In both instances the journeys were voluntary and partial. Only some of the community went to Jerusalem, and no aspersion is cast on those who stayed behind. This explicit acknowledgement that the return was accomplished in a series of journeys (rather than in a single one participated in by the entire community) distinguishes it from the exodus.

Recognizing the motif of pilgrimage in the returns in Ezra gives the text literary coherence and more fully comprehends the historical experience. As a book, Ezra would still fall into two major cycles (Ezra 1–6 and 7–10), but instead of each cycle beginning with a "second exodus" (thus raising the problem of having Ezra's return be a second "second exodus"), the cycles each begin with a pilgrimage to Jerusalem. Seeing a series of returns instead of a single major one also corresponds to a more accurate historical picture in which the return occurred as a series of settlement waves back to Yehud.

In addition to pilgrimage appearing in the book of Ezra as a narrative trope for the returns from Babylon, the text recounts specific pilgrimage feasts celebrated in Jerusalem. Immediately after the conclusion of the first group's return from Babylon and resettlement in their towns (Ezra 2:70), the narrative recounts the departure of the "sons of Israel" from these towns to go and celebrate the festival of Booths in Jerusalem (Ezra 3:1–4). As Bezalel Porten points out, the account of this festival is itself closely linked to the preceding journey to Jerusalem via repetition of vocabulary such as בנה√ and עלה√ ("Let him go up . . . and build," Ezra 1:3 and "they built the altar . . . and offered . . ." Ezra 3:3).[33] Next follows notices about the institution of offerings throughout the year (Ezra 3:5–6), the temple dedication service (Ezra 3:10–13) and, just before the account of the second return in Ezra 7–8, the celebration of the pilgrimage feasts of Passover and Unleavened Bread (Ezra 6:19–22).[34] It is significant that here, in addition to the inclusion of another pilgrimage feast, this feast is the venue at which the bound-

---

33. "Those who 'go up' 'go up to build' the Temple and they begin by 'building' an altar 'to raise up' upon it offerings." Bezalel Porten, "Theme and Structure of Ezra 1–6: From Literature to History," *Transeu* 23 (2003): 27–44, esp. 35. Porten lists additional links such as "the importance of the 'written' word" in both accounts as well as the authority of Cyrus.

34. For more on the centrality of the Passover festival in Ezra, see Bob Becking, "Continuity and Community: The Belief System of the Book of Ezra," in *The Crisis of Israelite Religion: Transformations of Religious Tradition in Exilic and Post-Exilic Times* (ed. Bob Becking and Marjo C. A. Korpel; Oudtestamentische Studiën 42; Leiden: Brill, 1999): 256–75, where the author claims that the whole of Ezra 3–6 is most correctly understood under the title of "the abolition of the non-celebration of the Passover festival" (ibid., 270). See also Joseph Fleishman, "An Echo of Optimism in Ezra 6:19–22," *HUCA* 69 (1998): 15–29.

aries of the community is expanded to include those who had returned from exile (השבים מהגולה), and also "all who had joined them (כל הנבדל) and separated themselves from the pollutions of the nations of the land to seek YHWH, the God of Israel" (Ezra 6:21). In retelling the story of this festival, the text gives a definition of the community that includes not only those who had been exiled to Babylon and had returned but also those who joined with the returnees to worship.[35]

In sum, the book of Ezra employs pilgrimage as a narrative motif to signify the return from Babylon and also records pilgrimage celebrations in Jerusalem by the community. The serial nature of the returns recorded in Ezra and the emphasis on the destination as Jerusalem combine with a thick cultic component in the narratives to emphasize their identity as pilgrimage. Through this imagery, the community is portrayed as a worshipping community and one that is open to its Diasporic components: Jews in Babylon or other places can all include themselves in the community by making pilgrimage to Jerusalem. In the narrative account of a pilgrimage festival in Ezra 6, worship is held up by the author as the true litmus test for inclusion in the community, and thus the pilgrimage festivals together with the pilgrimage-like returns link the narrative as well as the nation.

4.1.3 PILGRIMAGE IN NEHEMIAH

The book of Nehemiah adds another pilgrimage festival to those recounted in Ezra. According to Neh 8:13–18, the festival of Booths was kept again in Jerusalem. During the celebration "the assembly of those who had returned from the captivity" made booths, "kept the festival seven days," and concluded with a solemn assembly on the eighth day. Just as in Ezra 3, the location for the celebration in Neh 8 is Jerusalem: the text specifies that the people gathered branches and made booths for themselves "each on the roofs of their houses, and in their courts and in the courts of the house of God, and in the square at the Water Gate and in the square at the Gate of Ephraim" (Neh 8:16). Although some have argued that these several locations indicate that the festival was celebrated both within Jerusalem and at locations outside the city,[36] the text allows the interpretation that it was kept by the community that gathered together in Jerusalem. According to Neh 8:17–18, Ezra read the law to the celebrants, a detail that assumes that the

---

35. See Christiane Karrer, *Ringen um die Verfassung Judas: Eine Studie zu den theologisch-politischen Vorstellungen im Esra-Nehemia-Buch* (BZAW 308; Berlin: de Gruyter, 2001), 108–10.

36. Michael Fishbane, *Biblical Interpretation in Ancient Israel* (Oxford: Oxford University Press, 1985), 111; J. L. Rubenstein, "History of Sukkot During the Second Temple and Rabbinic Periods: Studies in the Continuity and Change of a Festival" (Ph.D. diss., Columbia University, 1992), 79–80; W. R. Scott, "The Booths of Ancient Israel's Autumn Festival" (Ph.D. diss., The Johns Hopkins University, 1993), 116–17, 120.

whole community was together in one large place. Further, as Michael Duggan points out, the *hiphil* of בוא in Neh 8:15 and 16 ("'Go ... and bring branches ... to make booths' ... So the people went out and brought them ...") suggests that the branches were brought to a central location.[37] Finally, because most of the locations named for the booths are in Jerusalem (the courts of the house of God, and the squares at the Water Gate and at the Gate of Ephraim), it is probable that the other two locations (the roofs of their houses, and in their courts) also were in Jerusalem (that is, the residents of the city constructed the booths around their houses, and visitors made use of the city's public spaces).[38] Although the festival ordinances in Exod 23:14–19 and 34:18–26 (and see also Lev 23:39–43) instruct the people to celebrate the festivals "before" YHWH, a centralized sanctuary is not specified. Keeping with the ordinance in Deut 16:16, the authors of Ezra and Nehemiah confine the festivals of both Passover and Booths to the one place that YHWH has chosen for worship: in the holy city the returned community reinstitutes the centralized pilgrimages.

4.1.4. PILGRIMAGE IN CHRONICLES

Ending strategically with Cyrus' declaration ("Let him go up!"; 2 Chr 36:23), the book of Chronicles enjoins the permanent relocation of Yahwists to Jerusalem. Yet pilgrimage to the city is also encouraged throughout the book, most obviously by making it an explicit and commendatory part of the reigns of Hezekiah and Josiah.[39] Similar to the prophets, the author specifically includes the people of both Israel and Judah in pilgrimage festivals, and, in one account, the nations as well. According to the text, word of Hezekiah's Passover festival in Jerusalem went to "all Israel and Judah," as well as Ephraim and Manasseh (2 Chr 30:1). Although those accepting consisted of only "a few" from Asher, Manasseh, and Zebulun, those who attended included Judahites and celebrants from Ephraim and Issachar, along with resident aliens (הגרים) from Israel and Judah (2 Chr 30:11–12, 18, 25). The combined crowd consisted of "many people" (2 Chr 30:13), and the large numbers required that 2,000 bulls and 17,000 sheep be offered, and for the

---

37. Michael W. Duggan, *The Covenant Renewal in Ezra-Nehemiah (Neh 7:72b–10:40): An Exegetical, Literary, and Theological Study* (SBLDiss 164; Atlanta: Society of Biblical Literature, 2001), 132.

38. This is the interpretation also adopted by Williamson (*Ezra-Nehemiah*, 296): "The residents of Jerusalem evidently erected their booths on or beside their own houses, while those who travelled in from the countryside found various open spaces they could use—in the temple courts, by the Water Gate ... or by the Gate of Ephraim."

39. For further discussion about the link with Hezekiah and Josiah (and, ultimately, the link of these two kings with David and Solomon) via the retellings of their Passover celebrations, see Simon J. De Vries, "Festival Ideology in Chronicles," in *Problems in Biblical Theology: Essays in Honor of Rolf Knierim* (ed. Henry T. C. Sun and Keith L. Eades with James M. Robinson and Garth I. Moller; Grand Rapids, Mich.: Eerdmans, 1997), 104–23.

priests to sanctify themselves "in great numbers" (2 Chr 30:24). In the account of Josiah's Passover festival, pilgrims are also mentioned coming from both Israel and Judah, although there is no specific notice that the participants included foreigners (2 Chr 35:18). The large number of animals sacrificed (over 41,000) points to the author's desire to highlight worship at the Jerusalem temple.

The Chronicler also includes an additional religious practice related to pilgrimage, namely, the turning of the body toward the temple when praying in a different locale.[40] Like pilgrimage, the practice emphasizes the singularity of Jerusalem for worship, and also explicitly includes the possibility of participation by foreigners. When the book of Chronicles reiterates Solomon's prayer at the dedication of the temple, the author retains the thrice-repeated instructions to pray toward the city. First, Solomon prays that when a "foreigner (הנכרי) . . . [who] comes (ובא) from a distant land . . . and prays toward this house (אל־הבית הזה)," YHWH will hear (1 Kgs 8:41–43 = 2 Chr 6:32–33). Then the king asks that when YHWH's people go out in battle and they "pray to YHWH, toward the city (העיר אל־יהוה דרך) that you have chosen and the house that I have built for your name . . ." (1 Kgs 8:44–45 = 2 Chr 6:34–35), YHWH will hear their prayer.[41] Finally, when YHWH's people are carried off into captivity, Solomon prays that when they pray "to you toward their land (אליך דרך ארצם)," YHWH will forgive them (1 Kgs 8:46–50 = 2 Chr 6:36–39).[42] The directions for the physical orientation of the worshipper include both Jews and Gentiles: foreigners in the land, warriors who have left the city, and the people who have been deported. Thus, Solomon's directives for the physical manifestation of Jerusalem in worship are ethnically inclusive.

Although the historical narratives from the Persian period emphasize the holy city through pilgrimage (and, in the case of Chronicles, in the direction of prayer as well), the texts differ somewhat regarding the ethnic identity of the participants. In Nehemiah, pilgrimage to Jerusalem includes the restored community only, but the boundaries are more open in Chronicles and Ezra with the inclusion of the whole nation (Chronicles) and the returnees and those who joined the worshipping community (Ezra). There is a difference in the time frame of the practice as well: the prophets generally construe pilgrimage to Jerusalem primarily in the future, but the historical texts highlight its significance in the present life of the community via the presentation of pilgrimage in the community's history.

---

40. This practice is also recorded in Dan 6:11 and, with the architecture of their temple oriented towards Jerusalem, the worshippers at Elephantine also showed homage to Jerusalem in their posture of worship.

41. In 2 Chr 6:34 the divine name is replaced with אליך. In major witnesses of the LXX for 1 Kgs 8:44, the divine name is replaced with "εν ονοματι."

42. The term אליך is missing in the phrase in 2 Chr 6:38.

4.1.5 PILGRIMAGE IN PSALMS 120–134

Additional evidence for pilgrimage to Jerusalem during the Persian period comes from Psalms 120–134.[43] This cluster of texts, all with the superscription שיר למעלות (שיר המעלות in Ps 121), incorporates several themes that indicate and encourage pilgrimage to Jerusalem. With the exception of some rabbinic and patristic interpretations, the collection is usually understood to indicate pilgrimage to Jerusalem.[44] Although some have understood the texts as a sort of cultic-liturgical manual used in chronological order by pilgrims at the various stages of their departure, worship in the temple, and return,[45] this theory is dif-

---

43. Although there are other psalms related to pilgrimage in the Psalter, the evidence that Pss 120–134 were deliberately edited during the Persian period make them a particularly compelling corpus. For a discussion of Pss 42–49, 84–88, 107–112 as well as 120–137 as groups of pilgrimage psalms (*Wallfahrtspsalmengruppen*), see Matthias Millard, *Die Komposition des Psalters: Ein formgeschichtlicher Ansatz* (FAT 9; Tübingen: J. C. B. Mohr [Paul Siebeck], 1994). For a discussion of Pss 120–134 different than my approach, see Alastair G. Hunter, "The Psalms of Ascents: A Late Festival Recovered?" in *Proceedings of the Twelfth World Congress of Jewish Studies: Jerusalem, July 29–August 5, 1997, Division A, The Bible and its World* (ed. Ron Margolin; Jerusalem: World Union of Jewish Studies, 1999), 173*–87*.

44. Some early Christian commentators such as Origen of Alexandria and Augustine of Hippo understood the title to refer to the allegorical "ascent" that the believer made to God or Christ (noted in Loren D. Crow, *The Songs of Ascents [Psalms 120–134]: Their Place in Israelite History and Religion* [SBLDS 148; Atlanta: Scholars Press, 1996], 4–9). Jewish tractates Middoth and Sukkah interpret the superscription as a liturgical rubric, specifying where or how these psalms were to be sung. Tractate m. Mid 2.5 claims that "fifteen steps led up from within [the Court of the Women] to the Court of the Israelites, corresponding to the fifteen Songs of Ascents in the Psalms, and upon them the levites used to sing." (This and all following quotes from Mishnaic texts are from Herbert Danby, *The Mishnah: Translated from the Hebrew with Introduction and Brief Explanatory Notes* [Oxford: Oxford University Press, 1933]). Likewise, m. Sukkah 5.4 states that "countless levites [played] on harps, lyres, cymbals and trumpets and instruments of music, on the fifteen steps leading down from the Court of the Israelites to the Court of the Women, corresponding to the Fifteen Songs of Ascents in the Psalms" (Danby, *The Mishnah*, 180). According to Ibn Ezra, the superscription indicates the name of the tune to which the text was sung (noted in Cuthbert C. Keet, *A Study of the Psalms of Ascents: A Critical and Exegetical Commentary Upon Psalms CXX to CXXXIV* [London: The Mitre Press, 1969], 4–5).

In a few modern assessments, the superscription has been interpreted as a generic classification. Wilhelm Gesenius argues that המעלות is a technical term for step rhythm (*anadiplosis*) in which the closing word of a verse is repeated at the beginning of the next verse (for example, the use of the term "peace" in Ps 120:6–7; see also 121:1–2, 3–4, 4–5). See Gesenius, *Thesaurus Philologicus Criticus Linguae Hebrae et Chaldae Veteris Testamenti* (2nd ed.; Leipzig: Fr. Chr. Wil. Vogelius, 1839), 2:1031–32 (noted in Crow, *Songs of Ascents*, 15). Additionally, Mitchell Dahood (*Psalms* [AB 16–17A; Garden City: Doubleday, 1965–1970], 3:194–95) posits that the title refers to the praising nature of the texts and is best translated "song of extolments," based on his reading of 11QPs[a] Zion, 14.

45. Klaus Seybold, *Die Wallfahrtspsalmen: Studien zur Entstehungsgeschichte von Psalm 120–134* (BTS 3; Neukirchen-Vluyn: Neukirchener Verlag, 1978), and Marina Mannati, "Les Psaumes Graduels constituent-ils un genre littéraire distinct à l'intérieur du psautier biblique?" *Sem* 29 (1979): 85–100.

ficult to apply to the entire collection. Ps 134 is indeed a blessing and might have been used for pilgrims while they were in the temple, yet it is more difficult to consider Ps 128 as the words of greeting that the inhabitants of Zion gave to the newly arrived pilgrims. The connection to pilgrimage in Pss 120–134 is best made not by locating the texts at specific liturgical moments but by locating the several themes that relate to pilgrimage throughout the ancient world.[46] After a brief discussion about the date of the collection, I will highlight four aspects of pilgrimage in the collection: the call to the shrine, an emphasis on YHWH's geographic connection to Jerusalem, the desire for agricultural and biological fertility, and the pursuit of justice.

Because these texts are not generally employed in reconstructions of life in the Persian period, a brief word about their date is in order. With Loren Crow and Matthias Millard, I date the collection to this period on the basis of linguistic evidence that suggests an LBH redaction,[47] including the phrase למען לא (Ps 125:3),[48] the use of the particle ש instead of אשר (Pss 122:3, 4; 123:2; 129:6, 7; 133:2, 3),[49] the plural

---

46. In his analysis of Pss 120–134, Millard (*Die Komposition des Psalters*, 208–12) likewise emphasizes the themes of pilgrimage within the collection rather then construing it as a pilgrimage liturgy.

47. Millard, *Die Komposition des Psalters*; and Crow, *Songs of Ascents*. The standard work on this topic is by Avi Hurvitz, בין לשון ללשון: לתולדות לשון המקרא בימי בית שני (Jerusalem: Bialik Institute, 1972). See also Ursula Schattner-Reiser, "L'hébreu postexilique," in *La Palestine à l'époque perse* (ed. Ernest-Marie Laperrousaz and André Lemaire; Etudes annexes de la Bible de Jérusalem; Paris: Cerf, 1994), 189–224.

48. This indicator of negative purpose occurs only in exilic/post-exilic texts (Ezek 14:11; 19:9; 25:10; 26:20; Zech 12:7; Ps 119:11, 80), with several semantic equivalents used in earlier texts: פן (Exod 23:33; Judg 7:2); לבלתי (Josh 23:6; Deut 17:12); למען אשר לא (Deut 20:18); and אשר לא (Gen 11:7). It also occurs in later texts outside the Hebrew Bible (Ben Sira 38:8; 45:26). The expression thus fulfills the three criteria of Hurvitz's list for dating linguistic elements, namely, biblical distribution, linguistic contrast, and extra-biblical sources. See Avi Hurvitz, "Continuity and Innovation in Biblical Hebrew – The Case of 'Semantic Change' in Post-Biblical Hebrew," in *Studies in Ancient Hebrew Semantics* (ed. T. Muraoka; Abr-Nahrain Supp 4; Louvain: Peeters, 1995), 1–10. See also on this particular phrase, Mark F. Rooker, *Biblical Hebrew in Transition* (JSOTSupp 90; Sheffield: Sheffield Academic Press, 1990), 172–73. Rooker notes that Hurvitz has suggested that the phrase may appear in an Aramaic text from the seventh century: עם לבשי שמוני למען לאחרה לתהגנם אדעתי (Nerab 2:7–8). Although this text is similar, the parallel is not exact.

49. I understand this to be a feature of LBH, but it may also indicate a northern provenance. According to Eduard Yechezkel Kutscher (*A History of the Hebrew Language* [Jerusalem: Magnes Press, 1984], §45), this feature is "common in the vernacular of Northern Palestine," although present in biblical texts "that are supposed to reflect LBH, e.g., Ecclesiastes." As F. W. Dobbs-Allsopp points out ("Linguistic Evidence for the Date of Lamentations," *JANES* 26 [1998], 17), although the particle occurs 136 times in the Hebrew Bible, it is used in probable northern texts only six times (including Judg 6:17; 7:12; 8:26; 2 Kgs 6:11). Although the particle may not indicate lateness by itself, it can be a sign of lateness, especially when present with other grammatical and linguistic features that point to a late date. See the article by C. L. Seow concerning Persian-era texts, "Linguistic Evidence and the Dating of Qohelet," *JBL* 115 (1996): 643–66, esp. 660–61.

and definite form of הצדיקים (Ps 125:3),[50] the noun הסליחה ("forgiveness," in Ps 130:4),[51] and the plene spelling of דויד (Ps 122:5).[52] Several Aramaisms in the collection also may point to a late date, including the ending of צרתה in Ps 120:1 (the Aramaic emphatic state) and the Aramaic style of the term שנא ("sleep"), with א substituted for ה in Ps 127:2.[53] Of course, all Aramaisms are not necessarily late since they may reflect Old Aramaic, but a large quantity of Aramaisms may suggest a later date (i.e., during the time when Aramaic became the lingua franca).[54] In like manner, putative northernisms in the corpus (such as the use of ש in place of אשר) may alternatively be considered late markers because southern Hebrew was probably influenced by northern Hebrew from the exilic period on.[55] Finally, Crow has recognized six repeated formulae that occur throughout the collection

---

50. The term exhibits the LBH preference for plural forms of terms that appear in the singular form in earlier texts. Robert Polzin points out this pattern in *Late Biblical Hebrew: Toward an Historical Typology of Biblical Hebrew Prose* (HSM 12; Missoula: Scholars Press, 1976), 42–43. As an example he cites גבורי חילים in 1 Chr 7:5 in contrast to גבורי החיל in Josh 1:14. For more examples, see Dobbs-Allsopp, "Linguistic Evidence," 14–15. In addition, the term appears with the definite article, a situation paralleled only in Qoh 8:14 and 9:1, as well as Gen 18:24, 28 (the term appears as הצדיקם in the two Genesis texts).

51. The term occurs in this form only in Ps 130:4 and two other late texts, Dan 9:9 (הסלחות) and Neh 9:17 (סליחות). The adjective "forgiving" (סלח) appears in Ps 86:5.

52. This is an orthographic preference of LBH texts. In the corpus of Samuel–Kings, the name "David" is written 668 times with defective orthography (דוד) and only three times with plene orthography (דויד). The plene orthography is consistently used in Chronicles, Ezra, and Nehemiah where the name occurs 271 times, all in the plene form (although note that Qoh 1:1 represents the personal name as דוד). In addition, the plene form is consistently used in 1QIsaᵃ and 5Q51. See Rooker, *Biblical Hebrew*, 68–71; David N. Freedman, "The Spelling of the Name 'David' in the Hebrew Bible," *HAR* 7 (1983): 89–102; and Francis I. Anderson and A. Dean Forbes, *Spelling in the Hebrew Bible* (Rome: Biblical Institute Press, 1986), 4–9.

53. Paul Joüon, *A Grammar of Biblical Hebrew* (trans. T. Muraoka; Subsidia Biblica 14.I–II; Rome: Pontificio Instituto Biblico, 1991), I §7b. The other option is taking the verb as a third א root, as with Dahood ("prosperity, peace," in Dahood, *Psalms*, 3:223–24 where he notes the parallels Syriac *šaynā'* ["prosperity"], and Ethiopic *sene'* ["peace"]; cf. idem, "The aleph in Psalm CXXVII 2," *Or* 44 [1975]: 103–5). J. A. Emerton likewise posits a third א root, with the meaning of "to be, or become high," in "The Meaning of *šēnā'* in Psalm CXXVII 2," *VT* 24 (1974): 15–31, especially 27 where he gives the text from b.Šabb. 10B, "let no man exalt (ישנה) [show special favor to] one son above his other children." As Crow points out, this meaning is outside the theme of the psalm (Crow, *Songs of Ascents*, 67–69).

54. For the analysis of Aramaisms with regard to dating texts, see A. Hurvitz, "The Chronological Significance of 'Aramaisms' in Biblical Hebrew," *IEJ* 18 (1968): 234–40.

55. So Gary A. Rendsburg (*Linguistic Evidence for the Northern Origin of Selected Psalms* [SBLMS 43; Atlanta: Scholars Press, 1990], 87–93, 103–4), although he does argue that there are northern elements in Pss 132 and 133, specifically the divine epithet אביר יעקב (Ps 132:2, 5), the feminine singular nominal ending on שנת (Ps 132:4), and a feminine singular noun with a plural ending (עדתי in Ps 132:12). In addition, Rendsburg's identification of northern elements in Ps 133 include נעים (Ps 133:1), מדותיו (Ps 133:2), a reduplicatory plural form, הררי (Ps 133:3), and the use of ש (Ps 133:2, 3). For a response to Rendsburg's work, see C. L. Seow's review in *JBL* 112 (1993): 334–37.

that seem to indicate a post-exilic redaction that provides cohesiveness and an emphasis on Jerusalem.[56] Of course, identifying LBH linguistic features in this collection does not necessarily indicate that the origin of the entire collection is equally late.[57] Given this mix of linguistic features, it seems that Pss 120–134 (or parts of the texts) predate the later redaction when a constellation of LBH features was incorporated into some of them. It appears that in the Persian period these different texts were gathered, edited, and grouped together via repeated formulae and a matching superscription.

The Persian-period edition of the collection contains four aspects that can be related to pilgrimage. The first is the formulaic call to make a pilgrimage, consisting of the designation of the shrine and a verb of travel in the cohortative and/or imperative plural form.[58] Such a call is scattered throughout the collection. The first verse of Ps 122 reads, "I rejoiced when they said to me, 'We will go to the house of YHWH! (בית יהוה נלך)."[59] Similarly, Ps 132:7 reads, "let us enter (נבואה) into [God's] dwellings, let us worship toward the footstool of [his] feet."

The second aspect of pilgrimage is the emphasis on the geographic connection between Jerusalem and YHWH, seen in several ways but primarily by claiming simply that YHWH lives in the city. Ps 132 relates David's quest to provide a dwelling place for YHWH in Zion (vv. 1–5) and YHWH's own election of the city as a dwelling (vv. 13–14). The city is directly called the place where YHWH dwells: it is the deity's "place" (מקום ליהוה, v. 5), YHWH's "dwelling place"

---

56. The repeated formulae are: עשה שמים וארץ (121:2; 124:8; 134:3); מעתה ועד־עולם (121:8; 125:2; 131:3); יאמר־נא ישראל (124:1; 129:1); שלום על־ישראל (125:5; 128:6; 133:3, according to 11QPsa); מציון יברכך יהוה (128:5; 134:3); יחל ישראל אל־יהוה (130:7; 131:3). Crow notes that all of these phrases occur at least twice in the collection and several appear rarely or never in the rest of the Hebrew Bible. See Crow, *Songs of Ascents*, 129–58.

57. Possible indicators of antiquity (or archaistic style) include phrases similar to Ugaritic expressions such as מעתה ועד־עולם ("for now and forever" in Pss 121:8; 125:2; 131:3; see Aqhat 19.154 (repeated in Aqhat 19.161–62): 'nt.brh.p'lm.h 'nt.pdr[.dr] ("Be a fugitive now and evermore / Now and to all gen[erations]"), *CML*, 119. Similarly, עשה שמים וארץ ("maker of heaven and earth," in Pss 121:2; 124:8; 134:3) may be related to an Ugaritic expression. So Norman C. Habel, "'Yahweh, Maker of Heaven and Earth': A Study in Tradition Criticism," *JBL* 91 (1972): 321–37, followed (with revisions) by Crow, *Songs of Ascents*, 42, 137–38.

58. Outside the Psalter, other calls to go on pilgrimage are found in 1 Sam 11:14 when Samuel says to the people, "Come, let us go to Gilgal (לכו ונלכה הגלגל) and we will renew there the kingship"; Isa 2:3 when the prophet sees a future time in which "many people will come and say, 'Come, let us go to the mountain of YHWH' (לכו ונעלה אל־הר־יהוה)"; and Jer 31:6 where sentinels call in Ephraim, "Arise, let us go to Zion (קומו ונעלה ציון), to YHWH our God." A related "call to worship" in the collection of Pss 120–134 closes the collection: "Behold, bless YHWH, all you servants of YHWH, who stand in the house of YHWH by night" (Ps 134:1).

59. The joy that the psalmist experienced upon hearing the call in Ps 122:1 (שמחתי) echoes the festival legislation in Deut 16:14 where the people are commanded to "rejoice" (ושמחת) during the festival of Succoth.

(משכן, vv. 5, 7), "resting place" (מנוח, vv. 8, 14), and "habitation" (מושב, v. 13). The terms usually occur with a possessive suffix to indicate YHWH's possession or ownership of the place.[60] This theme is also picked up in Ps 122, a text that begins and ends by referring to Jerusalem as "the house of YHWH" (בית יהוה, v. 1; אלהינו בית יהוה, v. 9), and "house of YHWH" also occurs in Ps 134:1 in connection with the Zion sanctuary.

The emanation of YHWH's blessing "from Zion" (Pss 128:5 and 134:3) also ties YHWH's presence to the city geographically. A similar thought is expressed in Ps 133:3, which claims that on the mountains of Zion YHWH ordained his blessing (שם צוה יהוה את־הברכה).

This geographic connection of YHWH with Jerusalem is further emphasized in Ps 122 with the assertion that YHWH built the city. Verse 3 is a crux, and, although the 'athnāch is marked under the second word, BHS divides the verse after the third term: ירושלם הבנויה כעיר שחברה־לה יחדו. Some scholars adopt the syntax of 3a recommended by the editors of the BHS: "Jerusalem built as a city, especially firmly walled about!" (Hans-Joachim Kraus),[61] and "Jerusalem, wieder aufgebaut wie eine Stadt, die in sich fest geschlossen ist [wo man zusammenk-ommt]" (Klaus Seybold).[62] With Rick Marrs, I would propose a different reading of 122:3a and suggest that the term הבנויה may have been misread from an origi-nal בונה יה (note that the divine name יה also appears in Ps 122:4a and 130:3a).[63] Verse 3a could be restored thus: ירושלם בונה יה "Jerusalem—her builder [is] Yah," maintaining the 'athnāch of the Leningrad codex and YHWH's special relation to the city.[64]

For all the stress that the collection places on YHWH's relation to Zion, such geographic specificity does not preclude YHWH's protection and care of those outside the city walls. Amidst the alignment of YHWH with Jerusalem in the texts is a thread that disseminates the presence of the Lord. YHWH, who is enthroned in the heavens (Ps 123:1), is able to hear cries from the depths (Ps 130:1).[65] YHWH's presence is ubiquitous (the shade at one's right hand in Ps 121:5 and the keeper of one's going out and coming in according to Ps 121:8).

---

60. 3ms in vv. 7 and 13 (with the preposition לו in v. 13), 2ms in v. 8, and 1cs in v. 14 (significantly, in a direct quote by YHWH).

61. Hans-Joachim Kraus, *Psalms 60–150* (trans. Hilton C. Oswald; Minneapolis: Augsburg, 1989), 431.

62. Seybold, *Wallfahrtspsalmen*, 88.

63. Rick Marrs, "The Šyry-Hmʿlwt (Psalms 120–134): A Philological and Stylistic Analysis" (Ph.D. diss., Johns Hopkins, 1982), 44 n. 3.

64. See also Ps 147:2 where YHWH is the builder (בנה) of Jerusalem.

65. Although the references to Meshech and Kedar in Ps 120 may be only symbolic (so Erhard S. Gerstenberger, *Psalms, Part 2, and Lamentations* [The Forms of Old Testament Literature 15; Grand Rapids: Eerdmans, 2001], 320), the text nevertheless declares that YHWH is able to hear those who are residing as aliens in foreign territories.

Thus, the emphasis on YHWH's presence in Jerusalem is not static or a confining concept; YHWH transcends this connection and can be present outside the city. Still, this placement of YHWH within Jerusalem—a placement that nevertheless does not bind the divine presence to a single locale—is, of course, quite relevant to those who are on the pilgrim way and still outside the holy precincts.

In addition to the call to the shrine and an emphasis on YHWH's geographic relation to Jerusalem, the third aspect of pilgrimage in Pss 120–134 is the pursuit of justice. In the ancient world, pilgrimages were sometimes undertaken as a way to pursue justice, since centralizing the legal system to the environs of a main cult center was not unusual.[66] There is evidence for this in association with Inanna and her temple and the temple of Šamaš in Larsa,[67] in Babylonia during the Persian period,[68] as well as in Jerusalem (Deut 17:8–9 and 2 Chr 19:8–11; see also Isa 2:3–4).[69] This same theme of justice appears in Pss 120–134 as a reason for

---

66. For the bringing of legal cases to Babylonian temples and local shrines, see Karel van der Toorn, *Family Religion in Babylonia, Syria, and Israel: Continuity and Change in the Forms of Religious Life* (Studies in the History and Culture of the Ancient Near East 7; Leiden: Brill, 1996), 35–36.

67. In a neo-Sumerian hymn to Inanna, the goddess and her house are associated with justice: "(The assembled people) come to her with . . ., they bring their matters before her,/ Then she knows the matter, she recognizes evil,/ She renders an evil judgement to the evil, she destroys the wicked, /She looks favorably upon the just, she determines a good fate for them." Translated by Daniel Reisman in his article, "Iddin-Dagan's Sacred Marriage Hymn," *JCS* 25 (1973): 185–202, specifically lines 116–19. See also the text quoted by van der Toorn in *Family Religion*, n. 176: "The men have acted as though there were no lawsuit or judge. If you are truly my father, send them to Larsa that they might investigate their matter in the temple of Šamaš; and if they have suffered injustice they will receive compensation by the verdict of Šamaš."

68. See Muhammed A. Dandamayev, "State and Temple in Babylonia in the First Millennium B.C.," in *State and Temple Economy in the Ancient Near East: Proceedings of the International Conference Organized by the Katholieke Universiteit Leuven from the 10th to the 14th of April 1978* (ed. Edward Lipiński; Orientalia Lovaniensia Analecta 6; Leuven: Departement Oriëntalistiek, 1979), 589–96, esp. 590–91 where he points out that, although the influence of the royal and temple courts vacillated in this period, the temple courts still operated.

69. The text records that in earlier times, difficult legal cases were brought "before God" (Exod 22:8; cf. 18:15–16; 33:7), i.e., Moses or local judges. With the program of centralization, the cases were then brought to Jerusalem where they would be decided by the levitical priests and the current judge (Deut 17:8–9). In the account of Jehoshaphat's reforms in 2 Chr 19, the king appointed a seat in Jerusalem for the Levites, priests, and heads of families of Israel for the judging of cases that came from the towns. Notice also that Isaiah of Jerusalem associated Jerusalem with justice in his picture of the time when people from all nations would desire to go to Jerusalem ("Come, let us go to the mountain of YHWH") so that they might be taught by YHWH. Further, in his prophecies he claims that "the law will go out from Zion, and the oracle of YHWH from Jerusalem. He will judge over the nations and adjudicate between many peoples" (Isa 2:3–4).

The tradition continued into the days of Josephus. In *Ant.* 4.218, Josephus represents Deut 17:8–9 as follows: "But if the judges do not understand how they should give judgment about the things that have been laid before them—and many such things happen to people—let them send the case up untouched to the holy city, and when the chief priest and the prophet and the senate have come together, let them

pilgrimage. In Ps 122:5 the causal כי[70] highlights the journey of "the tribes," who went up to Jerusalem and praised YHWH because "the thrones of justice (למשפט כסאות), the thrones of (כסאות) the house of David" were set up in Jerusalem. The question remains as to whether this image would make sense in Persian-era Yehud. Would pilgrims have come to Jerusalem to stand before these "thrones of justice"? Some commentators such as Keet and Crow claim that Ps 122:5 refers to a distant memory.[71] Yet the city still functions as a place for justice: Ezra returns to Jerusalem to teach the statutes and the judgments (משפט) "in Israel" (Ezra 7:10),[72] and, in Zech 8:16, YHWH instructs Jerusalem to "render true and peace-producing judgments (אמת ומשפט שלום שפטו) in your gates." Additionally, the term כסא was still a live metaphor to describe political power during the Persian era (Neh 3:7; Hag 2:22; and Zech 6:13).[73] Thus there is evidence that the terminology of thrones was still alive and that Jerusalem continued to function as a place for justice during the Persian period.

The final theme of pilgrimage in the collection is the emphasis on fertility, something prayed for at temples throughout the ancient world. At Delphi, Kreousa is asked whether her journey to the holy site concerns "crops or children,"[74] and such matters are related to cult centers throughout the literature of the ancient Near East, including the Hebrew Bible.[75] In ways appropriate for pil-

---

give judgment as to what seems fit" (translated by Sarah Pearce, "Josephus as Interpreter of Biblical Law: The Representation of the High Court of Deut. 17:8–12 according to Jewish Antiquities 4.218," *JJS* 46 [1995]:30–42, esp. 32). Although the precise identity of the high court and its relation to the Mosaic model of justice is a matter of debate, it is significant that Josephus's model assumes that Jerusalem was still the center of justice.

70. Those who understand the כי as causal include Dahood, *Psalms* 3:206, and Crow, *Songs of Ascents*, 44–45. Others, such as Leslie C. Allen, (*Psalms 101–150* [WBC 21; Waco, Tex.: Word Books, 1983], 156 n. 5a), understand it as emphatic.

71. Keet claims that the psalmist remembers pre-exilic Jerusalem "as a centre of justice" (Keet, *Psalms of Ascents*, 36). Similarly, Crow considers the reference to the Davidic throne and "tribes of Yah" to have a "nostalgic flavor" (Crow, *Songs of Ascents*, 47). According to Herbert Donner ("Psalm 122," in *Text and Context: Old Testament and Semitic Studies for F. C. Fensham* [ed. W. Claassen; JSOTSupp 48; Sheffield: Sheffield Academic Press, 1988], 86–89), Ps 122:5 refers to memorial places in the Temple area, where pilgrims would be guided by "local guides [who] showed them all objects of interest in Jerusalem," including the place where "thrones for judgment [were] placed . . . in former times." In contrast to these scholars, I suggest that, because the reference to visiting Jerusalem on account of the "thrones of justice" does not specify that this refers only to past memories, it is best not to overinterpret the text.

72. In Ezekiel's vision of the new temple, priests serve as judges in disputes (Ezek 44:24).

73. The editors of BHS note that the second occurrence of "throne" in Zech 6:13 might be changed to "right hand," citing the LXX (ἐκ δεξιων αὐτου). As the lectio difficilor, the Leningrad Codex is to be preferred.

74. Quoted in Dillon, *Pilgrims and Pilgrimage*, 87.

75. In Aqhat, Dan'il pursued biological fertility by going and sleeping in a temple, after which the gods gave him a son (KTU 1.17.1.1–1.17.2.46). Other examples of visitations to a temple to cure

grimage texts, the theme of fertility is asserted in Psalms 126, 127, and 128. In the first text, it is the fecundity of the land that is primarily in view with the request that YHWH enact prosperity in the land just as YHWH had done previously. This petition is articulated via strategic repetition: the text begins with a historical remembrance "When YHWH restored the fortunes of Zion . . ." (את־שיבת ציון בשוב יהוה),[76] then, after conveying what the effects of this "restoration" were ("our mouth was filled with laughter . . ."),[77] the text uses a similar phrase to demand that the restoration continue: "Restore, YHWH, our fortunes" (יהוה את־שבותנו שובה). Although some have argued that the phrase שיבות . . . שוב refers to the specific return from captivity in Babylonia,[78] and although the phrase can designate the return of property,[79] it is also used to denote agricultural abundance and

---

infertility include the Hittite tradition in which male impotence is cured when a man sacrifices to a goddess and sleeps on the clothes worn during the sacrificial offering on a bed before the sacrificial altar. During his sleep, the goddess and the man have intercourse, and his dilemma is solved (*KUB* 7.5 [with joins] col. iv, 1–10; *CTH* 406). In addition, a Sumerian hymn to Nisaba claims that the goddess grants sons and that no house or city can be built without her doing. The hymn is in Adam Falkenstein and Wolfram von Soden, *Sumerische und akkadische Hymnen und Gebete* (Zürich: Artemis, 1953), 65–67. For other examples of the divine cure of infertility and sickness within a sanctuary in the ancient world, see C. A. Meir, *Ancient Incubation and Modern Psychotherapy* (trans. Monica Curtis; Evanston: Northwestern University Press, 1967) and Susan Ackerman, "The Deception of Isaac, Jacob's Dream at Bethel and Incubation on an Animal Skin," in *Priesthood and Cult in Ancient Israel* (ed. Gary A. Anderson and Saul M. Olyan; JSSOTSupp 125; Sheffield: JSOT Press, 1991), 92–120.

In the Hebrew Bible, note that Hannah, once she was at the Shiloh temple, prayed to YHWH that she be given a son (1 Sam 1:9–18). For the connection of agricultural fertility with the temple, see Zech 14:17, which records the belief that the amount of the autumn rains will depend on whether or not the nations make a pilgrimage to Jerusalem. Note also Ezek 47 in which the prophet is shown a river that flows out from the temple, desalinizing the Dead Sea and making fish abundant (Ezek 47:9).

76. I translate this in the simple past, although it could also reflect the recurring past in the indicative mood ("whenever YHWH restored the fortunes . . ."). See Ernst Ludwig Dietrich, שוב שבות: *Die endzeitliche Wiederherstellung bei den Propheten* (BZAW 40; Giessen; Alfred Töpelmann, 1925).

77. The text also compares the community to חלמים after YHWH "restored" their "fortunes." The translation of the term is difficult. Ancient versions understood the root of חלם as "be healed"—so LXX ὡς παρακεκλημένοι ("like those comforted"; cf. the Vulgate translation, *consolati*), Targum דאיתסיים היך מרעיא ("like sick ones who become healthy"). See John Strugnell, "A Note on Ps. CXXVI.1," *JTS* NS 7 (1956): 239–43. Although the sense of healing is conceivable in a text that highlights reversal (sorrow changes to joy, tears become laughter), the term is translated by most today as "dreamers." Thus Charles Augustus Briggs and Emilie Grace Briggs, *A Critical and Exegetical Commentary on the Book of Psalms* (ICC 13.2; Edinburgh: T&T Clark, 1907), 455; Walter Beyerlin, *We Are Like Dreamers: Studies in Psalm 126* (trans. Dinah Livingstone; Edinburgh: T&T Clark, 1982); Scott R. A. Starbuck, "Like Dreamers Lying in Wait, We Lament: A New Reading of Psalm 126," *Koinonia* 1.2 (1989): 128–49. I would repeat the comment of Crow: "Perhaps the most that can be said is that in some way the word serves to indicate the joy felt by the community at God's restoration of fertility at some point in the past" (Crow, *Songs of Ascents*, 62).

78. Kraus, *Psalms 60–150*, 449; Beyerlin, *Dreamers*, 8–10.

79. A line from the Sefire texts records how the territory of Tal'ayim came to belong to another through the agency of the gods, but "now, however, (the) gods have brought about the return (שיבת

fertility in texts such as Amos 9:14, Ps 85:2, and Jer 32:44.[80] Although the resto-ration of refugees may be a satisfying (re)application of the psalm, agricultural prosperity and restoration certainly pertain to this text, which compares YHWH's coming restoration to the wadis in the desert,[81] pleads for those who plant and reap, and ends by mentioning seed bags and the carrying of sheaves.[82]

Psalm 128 also picks up this theme of agricultural fertility when it promises that walking in the way of YHWH results in eating "the fruit of the labor of your hands" (Ps 128:2). In addition, Psalms 127 and 128 understand biological fertility as a gift from YHWH. Psalm 127 links YHWH's building the house (יבנה בית) with the appearance of children, and characterizes sons as a "heritage" of YHWH (נחלת יהוה; Ps 127:3). The final verse declares that blessings (אשרי) are upon the man whose "quiver" (אשפתו) is full of sons (Ps 127:5). The theme of biological fertility continues in Ps 128:3, "Your wife will be like a fruitful vine (גפן) within the 'private parts' of your house."[83]

By accentuating themes that are commonly associated with pilgrimage (fer-tility, justice, and the relation of the deity with the pilgrimage site), Pss 120–134 are well suited as pilgrimage texts. Although it is impossible to recover whether

---

(השבו אלהן) of my [father's ho]use [and] my father's [house has grown great] and Tal'ayim has returned (ושבת) to [PN] . . . and to his offspring forever" (Stele III.24–25). For a translation and photographs, see Joseph A. Fitzmyer, *The Aramaic Inscriptions of Sefire* (rev. ed.; BO 19/A; Rome: Pontifical Biblical Institute, 1995), 140–41, 160–61, pls. XIII, XVII. Note also the Mesha Stele lines 8–9 in which Kemosh restored property (ו[יש]בה כמש). For this reading, see Patrick D. Miller, Jr., "A Note on the Meša' Inscription," *Or* 38 (1969): 461–64.

80. In Amos 9:14, YHWH's promise to "restore the fortunes (ושבתי את־שבות)" of Israel occurs within a picture of a coming time when "the mountains will drip sweet wine," and when the Israelites will rebuild their cities, plant vineyards and gardens, and consume the produce. Likewise, Ps 85:2 draws a parallel between the time when YHWH "restored the fortunes of Jacob (שבת שבות יעקב)" and when "YHWH was favorable to [the] land." The text closes with a view to the future full of agricultural richness: "YHWH will give us what is good, and our land will yield its increase" (Ps 85:13). In Jer 32:44, YHWH promises that, when he restores the people's fortunes (אשיב את־שבותם), fields will be bought throughout the land.

81. On the use of this motif to denote fertility, see Nelson Glueck, *Rivers in the Desert: A History of the Negev* (New York: Farrar, Straus and Cudahy, 1959), 92–94.

82. Crow likewise argues that Ps 126 relates to agricultural fertility, claiming that the text was used in a time of agricultural failure when the people hoped for renewed agricultural prosperity (Crow, *Songs of Ascents*, 61–66). See also Sigmund Mowinckel, (*The Psalms in Israel's Worship* [trans. D. R. Ap-Thomas; Oxford: Basil Blackwell, 1962], 1.223), who claims that "in Ps. 126 it is most natural to take the mention of sowing and reaping as referring to real life, and not merely as a metaphor for 'salvation' in general, the hoped-for restoration."

83. This translation, which intends to convey the double entendre of the term ירכתים (corners and inner thigh), comes from Crow, *Songs of Ascents*, 71–73. In his work, Crow cites Daniel Grossberg (*Centripetal and Centrifugal Structures in Biblical Poetry* [SBLMS 39; Atlanta: Scholars Press, 1989], 43–44) who relates "in the innermost parts of your house" to the concept of fruitfulness.

they were recited at specific moments on the way, they are appropriate companions on the journey.

4.2 PILGRIMAGE AND THE SCANT ARCHAEOLOGICAL REMAINS OF JERUSALEM

The presence of accounts of pilgrimage or pilgrimage motifs in Persian-period biblical texts brings one to ask about the archaeological evidence for the possibility of regular visits to Jerusalem during this time. As noted previously, settlement in the city was fairly scant throughout the period. Is it possible that such a meager site could be the focus of a pilgrimage cult?

There are two possible ways to interpret the texts along with the archaeological evidence. The first is that they reflect the wishes of the authors that Jerusalem be restored as the center of worship. Matthias Millard has suggested that Psalms such as 120–134 can be understood as propaganda for going on pilgrimage to Jerusalem during the Persian era as well as serving as a substitute for the practice.[84] Similarly, Crow argues that Pss 120–134 were redacted in the Persian period in order to "convince Israelites from outlying areas to make pilgrimage to Jerusalem."[85] One could also argue that the presentation of the pilgrimage festivals in Ezra, Nehemiah, and Chronicles have to do with the author's desire to draw parallels between the temple worship of the post-exilic community and that of earlier periods with the goal to increase the temple's influence and authority among all the communities of Yahwists.[86] Thus, the texts reflect a small Jerusalem that intends to grow both in influence as well as size.

The second way to interpret the evidence is to disassociate the significance of a cult center from the size of its surrounding city, so that a small Jerusalem could nevertheless be the destination of a fairly large pilgrimage cult. It is true that some ancient cultic centers were within thriving cities, including the cult of Jupiter in

---

84. "Der Psalter ist also einerseits in persischer Zeit Ersatz für die Wallfahrt, doch andererseits wirkt er mit der Umspielung der Wallfahrtsthemen wie ein Propangandabuch der Wallfahrt." Millard, *Komposition des Psalters*, 209.

85. According to Crow, at the earliest level the texts were individual psalms reflecting a non-Jerusalemite context and concerned with the family and farming life (Crow, *Songs of Ascents*, 154–57, 187).

86. According to Blenkinsopp, the festivals of Booths and Passover in Ezra and Nehemiah (Ezra 3:1–4; 6:19–22; Neh 8:13–18) parallels the Chronicler's accounts of the same festivals during the time of Solomon, Hezekiah, and Josiah (2 Chr 5–7; 30; 35:1–19), accounts that themselves refer back to Samuel and Joshua (Blenkinsopp, *Ezra-Nehemiah*, 290). For the stylized depiction of the pilgrimage festivals in Chronicles, see, among others, Herbert Haag, "Das Mazzenfest des Hiskia," in *Wort und Geschichte: Festschrift für Karl Elliger zum 70. Geburtstag* (ed. Hartmut Gese and Hans Peter Rüger; AOAT; Neukirchen-Vluyn: Neukirchener, 1973): 87–94; De Vries, "Festival Ideology," 104–24; and M. Patrick Graham, "Setting the Heart to Seek God: Worship in 2 Chronicles 30:1–31:1," in *Worship and the Hebrew Bible: Essays in Honour of John T. Willis* (ed. M. Patrick Graham, Rick R. Marrs, and Steven L. McKenzie; JSOTSupp 284; Sheffield: Sheffield Academic Press, 1999): 124–41, esp. 130–33.

Rome and the Akropolis in Athens, which had been the site of cult and habitation since 1600 B.C.E.[87] Other cult centers, however, were in uninhabited areas with few full-time residents connected to the sanctuary and whose influence and catchment area (the geographic and demographic extent of appeal) exceeds the limits of one population center. Cultic sites such as the oracular shrine at Delphi, the cult of Zeus at Olympia, and the shrine to Fortuna at Prinesti are examples of sacred areas that were remote from population sites that nevertheless were frequently visited. Thus, a religious area can still be a popular pilgrimage site even if there is little evidence of related settlement, and the theme of pilgrimage in the texts does not have to correlate to a design to build up the population of the sacred site.

4.3 CONCLUSION

Pilgrimage is present throughout the various genres of biblical texts from the Persian period, and accounts of the practice reveals different concerns and emphases. In the prophets, pilgrimage is future-oriented and involves the community as well as the nations and their enriching wealth. In the historical narratives, pilgrimage is presented as a contemporary practice of the community (or, in the case of Chronicles, a practice from the past that has contemporary relevance), and the nations cease to be noticeably involved. In the book of Ezra pilgrimage is especially significant in that it even shapes the accounts of the returns. The divergences between the prophets and the historical narratives are barely detectable in Pss 120–134, however, because the collection does not describe the practice of pilgrimage as much as it reflects the concerns that pilgrims manifest.

The biblical emphasis on Jerusalem in light of the archaeological evidence for a small city is thus open to two models of interpretation, wish or reality. If it is wish, the emphasis on pilgrimage in the Persian period is a means to encourage the faithful to visit regularly and perhaps even settle in the holy center. If it is reality, the faithful have manifested their religious geography by their regular journeys to the city (but not their domicile there). In both of these interpretations, Jerusalem still has claims for being the geographic center of the Yahwistic religion of this period, although its visitors are greater or lesser in number depending on the chosen model.

---

87. Louise Bruit Zaidman and Pauline Schmitt Pantel, *Religion in the Ancient Greek City* (trans. Paul Cartledge; New York: Cambridge University Press, 1992), 97–100. Other cult sites were close to cities, such as the sanctuary at Perachora facing Corinth and the sanctuary at Heraion that served Argive. For the relation of the cult center to city (and the role of the cult center in forming cities and articulating the territory of emerging cities), see the classic treatment by François de Polignac, *Cults, Territory, and the Origins of the Greek City-State* (trans. Janet Lloyd; Chicago: University of Chicago Press, 1995).

CHAPTER 5
CENTRALITY THROUGH ECONOMICS: PAYING TAXES
AND TITHES IN JERUSALEM

The centrality of the temple can also be examined from an economic perspective. The regular sending or bringing of taxes and/or tithes to Jerusalem
reflects and/or compels a posture of obligation toward the city, and the following section looks at the evidence for such economic activity. As with the other
chapters, I try to distinguish the practices of the population of Yehud and the
Diaspora to see some of the geographic reach of financial obligation toward the
temple. Also, as with the other chapters, I distinguish the varying economic scenarios depicted in the separate biblical books—although there is a general picture
of Jerusalem as the recipient of offerings from Yehud, the texts represent various
aspects of this picture quite differently and indicate different perspectives on the
additional support of the Persian imperium, the nations, and the Diaspora. For
example, the book of Haggai makes no mention of regularized tithes but includes
only the strongly worded mandate that the local community must contribute to
the rebuilding of the temple and a prophecy in which the nations make rich contributions to the temple in the future. In Ezra, however, the dominant funder of
both the temple building and its ongoing maintenance is the Persian imperium.
Nehemiah presents a different picture in which the temple is sustained primarily
by the regular offerings of the people. Mention of offerings from Diaspora communities is made only in Zechariah, Trito-Isaiah, and Ezra. After examining the
biblical texts, I briefly review some of the pertinent archaeological findings such
as inscriptions, the $yh(w)d$ jar-handles and coins. Such evidence partially shows
the ways and extent to which the temple's centrality was enacted in the economic
realm.

5.1 THE PAYMENT OF TITHES IN JERUSALEM
ACCORDING TO THE BIBLICAL TEXTS

Paying offerings to the temple of YHWH was of course not a Persian-period
innovation but constituted the means by which the non-land-owning Jerusalem

cult had traditionally generated its income.[1] According to texts such as Exod 35:29; Deut 12:6, 11; 14:22–26; Lev 27:30–33; and Num 5:9, the people were to offer gifts to the cult and its clergy, and the texts use the vocabulary of tithe (מעשר), contribution (תרומה), and votive offering (נדבה), among others.[2] In addition, later texts from the Apocrypha and extra-biblical materials claim that the Diaspora regularly brought or sent their offerings and/or tithes to Jerusalem.[3]

---

1. Although Joseph Blenkinsopp argues that the temple may have accumulated some amount of donated property ("Did the Second Jerusalemite Temple Possess Land?" *Transeu* 21 [2001]: 61–68), this would not have been enough to support the cult entirely (see Neh 10:33–40; 13:10–14).

2. The tithe (מעשר) is traditionally understood as a mandatory gift of one-tenth of one's goods to the temple for the use of the clergy (Num 18:21, 26; Deut 12:17–18; 26:12; but cf. Deut 14:22–29). For some of the standard treatments on tithing, see Otto Eissfeldt, *Erstlinge und Zehnten im Alten Testament. Ein Beitrag zur Geschichte des Israelitisch-Jüdischen Kultus* (BWANT 22; Leipzig: J. C. Hinrich, 1917); and H. Jagersma, "The Tithes in the Old Testament," in *Remembering All the Way . . .: A Collection of Old Testament Studies Published on the Occasion of the Fortieth Anniversary of the Oudtestamentisch Werkgezelschap in Nederland* (OTS 21; Leiden: Brill, 1981), 116–28. See also Lester L. Grabbe, *Judaic Religion in the Second Temple Period: Belief and Practice from the Exile to Yavneh* (London: Routledge, 2000), 137–38.

For a discussion of the etymology of תרומה see Gary A. Anderson, *Sacrifices and Offerings in Ancient Israel: Studies in their Social and Political Importance* (HSM 41; Atlanta: Scholars Press, 1987), 137–44; and G. R. Driver, "Three Technical Terms in the Pentateuch," *JSS* 1 (1956): 97–105.

The term "offering" (מנחה) can designate sacrifices in general (e.g., Gen 4:4–5; 1 Kgs 18:29, 36), or specifically a grain offering (the latter designation is especially prevalent in P). It can also have a secular sense, designating gifts (Gen 32:19–21) or the tribute brought by nations (2 Sam 8:2; Ps 72:10; 2 Chr 9:24). For a discussion, see Anderson, *Sacrifices and Offerings*, 27–34.

For a discussion of the translation of נדבה as "votive offering," signifying a gift by a Yahwist to the temple, see Joseph Blenkinsopp, *Ezra-Nehemiah: A Commentary* (OTL; Philadelphia: Westminster Press, 1988), 76.

The traditions and laws regarding such offerings are difficult to reconstruct based on the limited and sometimes contradictory biblical texts. For a later tradition involving two tithes (the first given to the priests, the second brought to Jerusalem), see Tob 1:6–8.

3. According to Josephus, an annual tax for the temple was collected from all Jews over the age of twenty whether they lived in Judah or the Diaspora. He also writes that funds were sent by Diaspora Jews for the Jerusalem sanctuary both during and prior to the Hasmonean period: "all the Jews throughout the habitable world . . . had been contributing to [the Jerusalem temple] for a very long time" (*Ant.* 16.162–163; 16.166–173; 18. 312). Philo writes of funds collected by the Jewish community in Rome and sent to Jerusalem (*Legat.* 23.156) as well as funds collected in Egypt for the sanctuary (*Spec.* I.14.78). See also Tob 1:6–8 and Bar 1:5–7, 10. Some of these examples are from Magen Broshi, "The Role of the Temple in the Herodium Economy," *JJS* 38 (1987): 31–37. In addition, two inscriptions (ca. 250–175 and 150–50 B.C.E.) tell of offerings from "the Israelites on Delos" to Mt. Gerizim: "The Israelites on Delos who make offerings (απαρχομενοι) to hallowed Argarizein [that is, Har Garizim, or Mount Garizim]." The two inscriptions were found within one hundred meters of the synagogue on the island. See Philippe Bruneau, "'Les Israélites de Délos' et la juiverie délienne," *BCH* 106 (1982): 465–504; A. T. Kraabel, "New Evidence of the Samaritan Diaspora has been Found on Delos," *BA* (March 1984): 44–46.

5.1.1 TITHES IN HAGGAI

Within the book of Haggai there is no mention of taxes or regularized tithes for the temple, but the text does emphasize that the local community must put its financial and physical resources toward the building of the temple. The word of YHWH that came to the prophet instructed the people to "Go up to the hills and bring wood and build the house!" (Hag 1:8). Subsequently, under the inspiration of God, the governor Zerubbabel and the high priest Joshua, together with "all the remnant of the people," "came and worked on the house of YHWH" (Hag 1:14). Although there is no evidence in the text for additional offerings, the book clearly attributes the rebuilt temple to the resources of the local community.

The text also promises that additional financial resources for the temple will come from the nations. Although the new temple does not compare favorably to the "former glory" of the first temple, YHWH promises to shake the heavens, the earth, the sea, the dry land, and all the nations, "so that the treasure of the nations shall come, and I will fill this house with splendor . . . The latter splendor of this house shall be greater than the former . . . says YHWH of hosts" (Hag 2:6–9).

5.1.2 TITHES IN ZECHARIAH 1–8

In the book of Zechariah, financial support for the temple from outside Yehud comes not from the nations but rather from the Diaspora. In Zech 6:10–11 YHWH instructs the prophet to "collect (לקוח) [silver and gold][4] from the exiles—from Heldai, Tobijah, and Jedaiah—who have arrived this day from Babylon . . . take the silver and gold and make a crown. . . ." Additional offerings from the Diaspora are prophesied in Zech 6:15: "Those who are far off (רחוקים) shall come and help to build the temple of YHWH."[5]

In addition, the text may hint at the temple's role as an "interface" for the people's payment of Persian taxes. Joachim Schaper argues that the connection of "היוצר" with the temple in Zech 11:13 (". . . I took the thirty shekels of silver and cast them to היוצר in the house of YHWH") may indicate that the temple melted down the people's offerings into ingots and thus facilitated their tax payments to the central authorities.[6] In Schaper's view, the יוצר was an official, responsible to the Persian king, who oversaw the collection of imperial taxes at the temple.

---

4. The terms "silver and gold" are lacking in v. 10 but present in v. 11.

5. Although the nationality of these רחוקים is not explicit, members of the Diaspora seem most likely. For more on the Diaspora identity of the רחוקים, see David L. Petersen, *Haggai and Zechariah 1–8*, 79–80.

6. Joachim Schaper, "The Jerusalem Temple as an Instrument of the Achaemenid Fiscal Administration," *VT* 45 (1995): 528–39, esp. 537, and idem, "The Temple Treasury Committee in the Times of Nehemiah and Ezra," *VT* 47 (1997): 200–206.

Additional extra-biblical evidence for this theory is mentioned briefly in the section of this chapter that reviews the archaeological evidence.

5.1.3 Tithes in Trito-Isaiah

Combining aspects of Zechariah and Haggai, the Jerusalem temple is the future destination for the wealth of both the Diaspora and the nations in Trito-Isaiah. The text emphasizes that the wealth of nations will come to Jerusalem, and some of these goods are specifically designated as temple offerings: YHWH pronounces that the animals of Kedar and Nebaioth "shall be acceptable offerings on my altar" (Isa 60:7),[7] and the trees of Lebanon will be used for the sanctuary (Isa 60:13;[8] see also Isa 61:6 and 66:12). The Diaspora (בניך) will also bring silver and gold as gifts to YHWH (Isa 60:9). There is no mention of funding from additional sources except as an analogy for the future ingathering of the people: according to Isa 66:19–20, survivors will go to the nations and "bring all your kindred from all the nations as an offering to YHWH . . . to[9] my holy mountain Jerusalem . . . just as the Israelites bring an offering (את־המנחה) in a clean vessel [to] the house of YHWH."

5.1.4 Tithes in Malachi

As opposed to the emphasis on financial gifts to fund the temple from outside of Yehud in the books of Haggai, Zechariah, and Trito-Isaiah, the book of Malachi refers solely to the offerings of the local temple adherents. According to Mal 1:7–8 and 13, the offerings currently brought to the altar are polluted, yet the prophet declares that "the offerings of (מנחת) Judah and Jerusalem will be pleasing to YHWH" once the Levites are purified (Mal 3:3–4). The text also complains that the tithes currently being brought to the Jerusalem cult are too few and impure: the people "rob" YHWH by not giving their full "tithes and offerings" (המעשר והתרומה; Mal 3:8), and YHWH demands that they "Bring to me all the tithes (כל־המעשר) into the storehouse that there might be meat in my house" (Mal 3:10). Although the people of Judah and Jerusalem are not giving enough to the temple for the regular offerings, the prophet does not expect funding from another additional source.

---

7. Reading with the smoother version of 1QIsaᵃ (so Blenkinsopp, *Isaiah*, 56–66, 206). Even if one prefers the version in the Leningrad Codex, the sense of using the animals for burnt sacrifice still seems to be in play.

8. As Odil Hannes Steck notes ("Jesaja 60,13 – Bauholz oder Tempelgarten?" *BN* 30 [1985]: 29–34), this verse likely has a double reference—it looks forward to the restoration of the Temple as well as the transformation of Jerusalem into an edenic garden of God.

9. Reading אל (with 1QIsaᵃ) instead of על.

Although the prophetic texts name the same sources of funding for the temple, each text presents a distinct combination of these sources. In addition, the time frame for these donations can differ. In Haggai, the temple is funded by the local community and the nations in the future; in Zechariah, the funders consist of the those who have recently returned from exile, and these offerings will be enriched by future gifts from the Diaspora; Trito-Isaiah emphasizes the future gifts of the Diaspora as well as the nations; and Malachi encourages the local community alone to support the temple in the present day.

5.1.5 Tithes in Ezra

The book of Ezra presents a markedly different vision of the temple's funding. Although the returnees and the Diaspora make contributions, the source of the funding for temple building and maintenance most emphasized is the Persian imperium. Gifts from the Diaspora are mentioned twice in the book: once when Cyrus instructs the "people of his place" who were not returning to Jerusalem to give the returnees gifts of silver, gold, goods, and livestock along with a freewill offering (הנדבה) for the temple (Ezra 1:4, 6), and once when Artaxerxes instructs Ezra and his party to convey to Jerusalem "all the silver and gold that you shall find in the whole province of Babylonia, and with the freewill offerings (התנדבות) of the people and the priests . . ." (Ezra 7:16). Upon arrival, these items (presumably along with the "contribution" of the returnees) were weighed out in the temple and handed over to a group of priests and Levites (Ezra 8:33). The book of Ezra also mentions the temple offerings of the returnees. Upon arrival in the city, "some of the chiefs of the clans" gave a freewill offering (התנדבו) to construct the house of God, donating to the "treasury of the work" 6,100 drachmas of gold, 5,000 minas of silver, and 100 priestly robes (Ezra 2:68–69), and, following their first celebration of the festival of Tabernacles in Jerusalem, the returnees gave the regular offerings for the new moons and sacred times as well as freewill offerings to YHWH (נדבה ליהוה; Ezra 3:5).

Overwhelmingly, however, the source of funding for the temple and its upkeep in Ezra comes from the Persian imperium in the form of gifts and redirected revenue. Besides refurbishing the temple with the vessels removed by earlier conquers (Ezra 1:7–11), Cyrus also grants authorization for money, food, drink, and oil to be paid to the various workers and suppliers of the temple (Ezra 3:7). According to Ezra 6:4, the cost of rebuilding the temple was to be paid from the royal treasury, and Ezra 6:8 further stipulates that the funds are to come "from the royal revenue, the taxes of the province of Beyond the River." Darius also instructs that animals for burnt offerings as well as wheat, salt, wine, and oil, as required by the priests in Jerusalem, be given to the temple, and presumably this was to come from the redirected tribute as well (Ezra 6:9). When Ezra went to Jerusalem he took in his hand a letter from King Artaxerxes stipulating that he was "sent by the king . . . to convey the silver and gold which the king and his counselors have freely offered (התנדבו) to the God of Israel . . . With this money, then, you shall with all diligence buy bulls, rams . . . and you shall offer them . . ." (Ezra 7:15–17). The letter also specified that "whatever else is required" for the temple that Ezra is to supply, he can "provide out of the king's treasury" (Ezra 7:20). In addition, the king decreed that the treasurers in the province Beyond the River must fulfill requests from Ezra, up to one hundred talents of silver, one hundred kor of wheat, one hundred bath of wine, one hundred bath of oil, and salt without limit (Ezra 7:21–22). The king's generosity also extended directly to the temple personnel such that he disallowed their payment of tribute and taxes (מנדה בלו והלך; Ezra 7:24).[10] Ezra also gave to the chief priests the silver, gold, the vessels, the "contribution" (תרומת) to the temple from the king, the Persian officials, and Israel (Ezra 8:25), and later declared that the silver and gold is a "freewill offering" (נדבה) to God (Ezra 8:28; cf. 8:36). Finally, in his prayer of penitence, Ezra says that God "has disposed the king of Persia favorably toward us, to furnish us with sustenance and to raise again the House of our God, repairing its ruins and giving us a hold in Judah and Jerusalem" (Ezra 9:9).

Although the text may present an imperium generous to the temple building and ongoing maintenance, it also indicates a sizable tax burden upon the people. According to the Aramaic correspondence in Ezra 4, the people in Jerusalem had traditionally paid "tribute, poll-tax and land-tax" (מנדה־בלו והלך) to fund the royal revenue (Ezra 4:13, 20). Within the narrative of Ezra, these funds are significant enough that building Jerusalem's walls seem inevitably linked to the possibility that the city dwellers will try to avoid paying them: "if this city is rebuilt and the walls completed, they will not pay tribute, poll-tax, or land-tax . . ." (Ezra 4:13). Even if this scenario seems historically untenable, the narrative relates an anxiety about high tax assessments.[11]

---

10. See the frequently adduced text where Darius criticizes Gadatas for charging tribute to the "sacred gardeners of Apollo" at Magnesia, in Russell Meiggs and David M. Lewis, *A Selection of Greek Historical Inscriptions to the End of the Fifth Century B.C.* (rev. ed.; New York: Oxford University Press, 1992), 20–22. For an overview of the discussion regarding the text's authenticity, see Lester L. Grabbe, *Yehud: A History of the Persian Province of Judah* (vol. 1 of A History of the Jews and Judaism in the Second Temple Period; Library of Second Temple Studies 47; London: T&T Clark, 2004), 116–17.

Although Joel Weinberg applies this tax exemption in Ezra 7:24 to the entire Citizen-Temple community in Yehud (not just the cultic personnel), such a position is uncommon and difficult to defend (Joel P. Weinberg, *The Citizen-Temple Community* [trans. Daniel L. Smith-Christopher; JSOTSupp 151; Sheffield: JSOT Press, 1992], 87–88). Given the other evidence for tax requirements of the people, the proscription of taxes in Ezra 7:24 more likely applies to the cultic personnel in Jerusalem. The rest of Yehud was required to pay the imperial assessment.

11. According to Hugh G. M. Williamson (*Ezra, Nehemiah* [WBC 16; Waco, Tex.: Word Books, 1985], 63), the sense of risk underlying the complaint is "absurd"; and see also the comment of Jacob M. Myers (*Ezra Nehemiah: Introduction, Translation, and Notes* [AB 14; Garden City, N.Y.: Doubleday, 1965], 38): "The alleged menace to the empire is patently fantastic."

5.1.6 TITHES IN NEHEMIAH

Although their generosity may have been offset by the costly tax bill, the Persian emperors in Ezra are munificent donors to the Jerusalem temple, dwarfing the additional gifts of the returnees and Diaspora. This picture is not continued in the book of Nehemiah. According to Neh 2:8, King Artaxerxes gives Nehemiah a letter asking that Asaph give him timber for the gates of the temple fortress, the city wall, and his own residence, but there are no other notices of imperial donations to the city or the temple.

Instead of the imperium, Nehemiah emphasizes that it is the people in Yehud who paid for the temple building and the ongoing expenses for sacrifices and clergy. Nehemiah 7:69–71 relates an account in which the governor "gave to the treasury 1,000 darics of gold, 50 basins, and 530 priestly robes,"[12] and "some of the heads of ancestral houses" made contributions "to the work," including "20,000 darics of gold and 2,200 minas of silver." In addition, "the rest of the people" gave "20,000 darics of gold, 2,000 minas of silver and 67 priestly robes." Another text tells of when, in the days of Zerubbabel and Nehemiah, "all Israel gave the daily portions for the singers and the gatekeepers, and made sacred contributions (מקדשים) for the Levites, and the Levites made sacred contributions (מקדשים) for the Aaronites" (Neh 12:47).

In chapter 10 there is an extended treatment of the people's support of the ongoing material needs of the temple cult. According to the text, Nehemiah, the priests, the Levites, the leaders of the people, and "the rest of the people," including those who "separated themselves from the people of the lands" all "made a vow to support the temple with annual tithes and offerings."[13] The offerings include one-third shekel[14] (to pay for the rows of bread, the regular grain offering, the regular burnt offering, the sabbaths, the new moons, the appointed festivals, the sacred donations, the sin offerings, and for "all the work of the house of our God," Neh 10:33–34), the wood offering (to provide fuel for the altar, Neh 10:35), and the annual offering of first fruits, the firstlings of their sons, livestock, herds,

---

12. In his commentary (*Ezra, Nehemiah*, 266–67), Williamson prefers to translate "30 priestly vestments, 500 minas of silver."

13. There is considerable discussion regarding the names and historicity of this list as well as where Neh 10 fits into the chronology of the Persian era. For a helpful summary and discussion see Williamson, *Ezra, Nehemiah*, 320–31.

14. Because a one-time charge of one-half shekel was levied on the people for the tabernacle according to Exod 30:11–16, this annual charge represents a "creation of a new prescription from a precedent in Pentateuchal law" (David J. A. Clines, "Nehemiah 10 as an Example of Early Jewish Biblical Exegesis," *JSOT* 21 [1981]: 111–17, esp. 112). For an argument that the one-half shekel offering in Exod 30:11–16 is early (that is, dating to the early monarchy or earlier), see J. Liver, "The Half-Shekel Offering in Biblical and Post-Biblical Literature," *HTR* 56 (1963): 173–98.

and flocks as well as the first of their dough, contributions, wine, and oil (Neh 10:36–38).

Within the details about the transport of these annual offerings are textual problems that indicates subsequent emendation, and such emendation reveals two layers of hope that Jerusalem would be the repository of the people's regular offerings. According to the text, the wood offering was to be brought to Jerusalem by representatives from the priests, Levites, and the people who were chosen by lot (Neh 10:35). For the offerings of first fruits, the text initially specifies that the people promised to bring them to Jerusalem, presenting them either at the temple or the temple storerooms: the people vow "to bring . . . [their offerings] . . . year by year to the house of YHWH" (Neh 10:36); "to bring [the offerings] to the house of our God, to the priests who minister in the house of our God . . ." (Neh 10:36), "and to bring . . . [the offerings] . . . to the chambers of the house of our God" (Neh 10:37). This method of transport stands in contrast to the system for the carrying of the wood offering, but the two scenarios do not necessarily contradict: the priests, Levites, and the people who were chosen by lot to bring up the wood were taking on a duty in addition to the regular portion of offerings. That is, although everyone went to the house of God to present their first fruits, some had the additional and periodic responsibility to include wood among their offerings or to bring up the wood to the temple in additional journeys.

Not so easily harmonized, however, are the following verses in which the people promise to bring their tithe to the Levites, and the Levites are to take a tithe from this and bring it to Jerusalem (Neh 10:38b–39).[15] Because the people have already agreed to bring their offerings to Jerusalem, this additional pledge is contradictory and seems to indicate textual corruption or emendation. The following verse, which asserts that both the Israelites and the Levites are to bring the gifts to the storerooms (Neh 10:40) seems to be an attempt to harmonize the discrepancy. Given the confusing directions, and the designation for priest rare in the book of Nehemiah ("son of Aaron" [בֶּן־אַהֲרֹן], Neh 10:39),[16] it is likely that vv. 38b–40 are a subsequent emendation to the text.[17]

---

15. It is not likely that one should differentiate the "tithes from our soil" that are brought to the Levites in v. 38 from the other gifts that were brought by the people to Jerusalem because the people had already promised "to bring the first fruits of our soil" yearly to the house of YHWH (Neh 10:36). Neither is it likely that the H form of בוא here should be translated as "send" (indicating that the faithful would be responsible only for dispatching their tithes to Jerusalem), because, in the context of cultic regulations, this term describes the bringing of sacrifices and offerings to the deity, the temple, or the priests (Gen 4:3, 4; Deut 12:6; Num 15:25; Lev 2:2; 5:11, 12; 2 Kgs 12:5 [2×]; Mal 1:13 [2×]).

16. Within the book of Nehemiah, the terminology for priests is usually simply הכהנים, as in Neh 10:35, 37, 38, 40; cf. Neh 7:63; 12:7, 12, 35, 44; 13:5, 30; or the singular הכהן in Neh 3:20; 7:65; 8:2, 9; 12:26; 13:4, 13, 28.

17. Although this recognition is not unique to my own work, the specific basis of such recognition and its consequences are not precisely equivalent to that of other commentators. See, among others,

This textual alteration provides a glimpse into the wishes and actualities of the transport of offerings into Jerusalem. The earlier layer of the text (Neh 10:36–38a) suggests that the people (or at least the author/editor) considered annual journeys into Jerusalem to pay their tithes possible and desirable. The subsequent layer of the text (Neh 10:38b–40) demonstrates that this scenario was not practiced and that a solution was designed. Although the need for the emendation shows that not all of Yehud was bringing their offerings to Jerusalem, both layers of the text manifest the desire that Jerusalem be the repository for offerings. A similar situation is seen more explicitly in the text of Neh 13:10–13 where, when Nehemiah realizes that the people had not contributed "the portions of the Levites," he censured the prefects for neglecting the house of God, reinstalled the Levites in their posts, "and all Judah brought the tithes of (מעשר) grain, wine, and oil into the treasuries." Both Neh 10:36–40 and 13:10–13 reflect a situation (both implicit and explicit) in which offerings for Jerusalem were mandated, these offerings were not brought, and steps were taken to rectify the situation by reasserting Jerusalem as the destination for the people's offerings.

Jerusalem's reception of regular and generous tithes in Nehemiah is also indicated by certain details of the temple's storerooms and personnel. According to the text, the amount of materials brought to the temple necessitated the appointment of administrators and the apportionment of chambers. In Neh 12:44, men were appointed over "the rooms for the stores (לאוצרות), the contributions (לתרומות), the first fruits (לראשית), and the tithes (למעשרות)," into which were gathered "the portions required by the law for the priests and the Levites at the fields of the towns (לשדי הערים)." Nehemiah 13:5 mentions a large room in the temple used to store "the grain offering, the frankincense, the vessels, and the tithes (מעשר) of grain, wine, and oil, which were given by commandment to the Levites, singers, and gatekeepers, and the contributions (תרומת) for the priests." See also Neh 13:13 where Shelemiah, Zadok, Pedaiah, and Hanan are appointed to distribute Judah's tithe of grain, wine, and oil to the Levites.

Although the book of Nehemiah briefly mentions requirements that the people pay taxes to the imperium (Neh 5:4; see also 9:37 and 5:14–19), it is much more interested in the people's support of the temple cult. In the context of a certain degree of laxity of the people, the text emphasizes that the temple must be supported by their regular and generous offerings. Because the Persian emperors

---

Wilhelm Rudolph, *Esra und Nehemia* (HAT 20; Tübingen: J. C. B. Mohr [Paul Siebeck], 1949), 179–80; Joseph Blenkinsopp, *Ezra-Nehemiah* (OTL: Philadelphia: Westminster Press, 1988), 318; Hugh G. M. Williamson, *Ezra, Nehemiah* (WBC 16, Waco, Tex.: Word Books, 1985), 338–39; Clines, "Nehemiah 10," 111–17; Georg Steins, *Die Chronik als kanonisches Abschlußphänomen: Studien zur Entstehung und Theologie von 1/2 Chronik* (BBB 93; Weinheim: Beltz Anthenäum, 1995), 169–81; Titus Reinmuth, *Der Bericht Nehemias: Zur literarischen Eigenart, traditionsgeschichtlichen Prägung und innerbiblischen Rezeption des Ich-Berichts Nehemias* (OBO 183; Göttingen: Vandenhoeck & Ruprecht, 2002), 211–19.

are not nearly as generous to the cult are they are in Ezra, the book of Nehemiah emphasizes the need for the ongoing support of the community in Yehud.

5.1.7 TITHES IN CHRONICLES

Finally, in the book of Chronicles the temple is funded by both the king of Israel and Judah as well as by the nation. With his grand endowment, King David is the major patron of the temple's building. In 1 Chr 21:22–25, he bought the site of Ornan's threshing floor as the future site of the temple for the sum of six-hundred shekels of gold, an amount much higher than the fifty shekels of silver recorded in 2 Sam 24:18–25. He also provided the workers and materials for the temple in fantastic amounts (100,000 talents of gold, one million talents of silver, and bronze and iron "beyond weighing;" 1 Chr 22:2–4, 14–16). David's generosity is emphasized in his deathbed speech when he enumerates for Solomon and "the whole assembly" his large gifts for the temple from his own funds (1 Chr 29:2–5).

As Gary Knoppers points out, David's generosity seems intended to motivate others to make their own contributions to the temple.[18] At the end of the speech on his deathbed, the king asks the people in attendance, "Who then will offer willingly, consecrating themselves today to YHWH?" (1 Chr 29:5). The answer comes in the form of a large outpouring of contributions from a variety of people: the leaders of the ancestral houses, leaders of the tribes, commanders of the thousands and of the hundreds, officers, and "whoever had precious stones" all give generously to the temple building fund (1 Chr 29:6–9).

This generous response by the people to the king's gifts is part of a larger pattern present in the book.[19] Throughout Chronicles, when kings give to the temple, the people respond with additional gifts. The gifts of war booty from David and Saul for the temple's ongoing maintenance is mentioned along with the listing of additional gifts from Samuel and Abner and Joab (1 Chr 26:26–28). There is a similar pattern in the story of Hezekiah's Passover, in which the author records the king's offering of animals for the Passover celebration (one thousand bulls and seven thousand sheep), and the additional animals given by the officials (one

---

18. David "cites his own personal donations to make an effective appeal for broader material support" (Gary N. Knoppers, *1 Chronicles 10–29: A New Translation with Introduction and Commentary* [AB 12A; New York: Doubleday, 2004], 949).

19. According to Sara Japhet (*The Ideology of the Book of Chronicles and its Place in Biblical Thought* [trans. Anna Barber; BEATAJ 9; Frankfurt am Main: Peter Lang, 1989], 416–28, esp. 417), the people's inclusion in texts such as this is part of the "democratizing trend" in the book, a pattern whereby history is retold not simply as the story of various kings but one in which the people are also an "active force." Hugh G. M. Williamson (*1 and 2 Chronicles* [New Century Bible Commentary; Grand Rapids, Mich.: Eerdmans, 1982], 374) sees the people's response in 2 Chr 31:4 as a means by which the author may have tried to encourage the contemporary audience to make their contributions to the cult.

thousand bulls and ten thousand sheep; 2 Chr 30:24). After the celebration, the king organized the cultic personnel and contributed "from his own possessions" burnt offerings for the offerings of morning, evening, Sabbath, new moon, and appointed festivals (2 Chr 31:3), then commanded the residents of Jerusalem to support the priests and Levites (2 Chr 31:4). Word of this request spread, with the result that the people throughout Israel and Judah brought into Jerusalem "the tithe of cattle and sheep, and the tithe of the dedicated things that had been consecrated to YHWH their God," and laid them in large heaps (2 Chr 31:4–10).[20] Finally, the notice of Josiah's gift of Passover offerings ("from the king's possessions") is followed by the list of additional donors: "his officials . . . [and] the chief officers of the house of God . . . [and] the chiefs of the Levites" (2 Chr 35:7–9). In all of these accounts, a royal gift to the temple is followed by additional gifts from the officials and people of Israel and Judah.

Chronicles also notes an additional time when people brought gifts to the temple in the story of Joash's temple repairs. According to 2 Chr 24:4–14, funding for the project was provided by "all the princes and all the people" and brought by them into Jerusalem.

According to the book of Chronicles, the temple is funded by the king and, usually in response to the royal initiative, by the people of Israel and Judah as well. Within the biblical narratives about the Persian period itself, this royal aspect of temple funding is seen only in Ezra, although here the kings are the Persian emperors, and the contributions of both the returnees and the Diaspora are mentioned only a few times. The other texts highlight the funding of the temple in various other ways: while Haggai, Zechariah, and Trito-Isaiah emphasize the gifts of the nations and/or the Diaspora, Malachi encourages offerings only from the local temple adherents. The same emphasis is present in Nehemiah, where it is the local community who are considered responsible for the funds for the temple building and ongoing maintenance.

5.2 The Payment of Taxes and Tithes in Jerusalem according to the Archaeological Evidence

The biblical evidence for the sending and bringing of tithes to Jerusalem and for the implementation of strategies to shore up economic support for the temple should be evaluated in conjunction with the archaeological evidence. Textual evidence such as the Elephantine papyri, the Murašû archive, imperial decrees, the

---

20. For more on 2 Chr 31:4–19 see Sara Japhet, "The Distribution of the Priestly Gifts According to a Document of the Second Temple Period," in *Texts, Temples and Traditions: A Tribute to Menahem Haran* (ed. Michael V. Fox, Victor Avigdor Hurowitz, Avi Hurvitz, Michael L. Klein, Baruch J. Schwartz, and Nili Shupak; Winona Lake, Ind.: Eisenbrauns, 1996), 3–20.

works of Strabo and Pseudo-Aristotle, and excavated objects such as jar handles and coins witness to the economic workings of the empire and its temples.

According to this evidence, temples in the Persian Empire usually had to finance their ongoing maintenance (including the upkeep and repair of the building fabric, ritual supplies such as sacrificial animals, and livelihoods for the cultic personnel) and also had to pay the taxes assessed on them by the empire.[21] Although the imperium supported some cults with special allotments, most of the relevant extra-biblical inscriptions indicate that local cults were financed only by their own properties and/or the offerings of their local adherents. That is, most temples received their financial support not from the imperium but rather from local sources. For example, in the text on the reverse side of the Demotic Chronicle, a decree from Cambyses reduces or eliminates imperial allotments of wood and animals to temples in Egypt; only the major temples of Memphis, Hermopolis, and an additional temple continued to receive funding.[22] In the Xanthos Trilingual inscription (probably dating to 337 B.C.E.), the worshippers of the god Kdwrs at Xanthos support their local cult with land and additional funds.[23] According to documents from Babylonia (including a text from the Murašû archive from 523 B.C.E. that records an obligation to pay a tithe to the god Enlil in dates), temples received tithe payments from their local adherents.[24] In addition, there is a document from Elephantine that begins with the line "This is (a list of) the names of the Jewish garrison who gave money (כסף) for YHW the God, each person [2] sh(ekels)" (TAD C3.15). Then, after listing numerous names, the

---

21. For the payments that temples made to the crown in the Persian Empire, see Muhammed A. Dandamayev, "Politische und Wirtschaftliche Geschichte," in Beiträge zur Achämenidengeschichte (ed. Gerold Walser; Wiesbaden: Franz Steiner, 1972), 15–58, esp. 52–54; idem, "The Diaspora: Babylonia in the Persian Age," in Introduction; The Persian Period (vol. 1 of The Cambridge History of Judaism; ed. W. D. Davies and Louis Finkelstein; Cambridge: Cambridge University Press, 1984), 326–42, esp. 334–35; idem, "State and Temple in Babylonia in the First Millennium B.C.," in State and Temple Economy in the Ancient Near East: Proceedings of the International Conference Organized by the Katholieke Universiteit Leuven from the 10th to the 14th of April 1978 (ed. Edward Lipiński; Orientalia Lovaniensia Analecta 6; Leuven: Departement Oriëntalistiek, 1979), 589–96, esp. 594–95; and Muhammed A. Dandamaev and Vladimir G. Lukonin, The Culture and Social Institutions of Ancient Iran (trans. Philip R. Kohl; Cambridge/New York: Cambridge University Press, 1989), 360–66; Pierre Briant, From Cyrus to Alexander: A History of the Persian Empire (trans. Peter T. Daniels; Winona Lake, Ind.: Eisenbrauns, 2002), 73–76.

22. For the text and associated literature see Grabbe, Yehud, 115. See also the support of the emperors for the sanctuary of Apollo at Claros and Aulai in Briant, From Cyrus to Alexander, 38.

23. Quoted in Grabbe, Yehud, 107–9.

24. Muhammed A. Dandamaev, "Der Tempelzehnte in Babylonien während des 6.–4. Jh. v. u. Z.," in Beiträge zur Alten Geschichte und deren Nachleben: Festschrift für Franz Altheim zum 6. 10. 1968 (ed. Ruth Stiehl and Hans Erich Stier; Berlin: De Gruyter, 1969–70), 1:82–90; Dandamaev and Lukonin, Culture and Social Institutions, 361–62; Matthew W. Stolper, "The šaknu of Nippur," JCS 40 (1988): 127–55, esp. 140.

end of the text designates specific amounts for YHW as well as Ešembethel, and Anathbethel. Although the text does not explicitly specify whether these offerings are designated for the local cult of these deities, such a reading would be the most straightforward interpretation of the text. The presence of a YHW cult at Elephantine prior to 410 B.C.E. and after 407 B.C.E. (without animal sacrifice) and the lack of references to offerings sent to Jerusalem point to the local use of the funds.[25] In addition, notice of permission for the community to reinstitute their worship did not include notice of imperial funding.

Because the Jerusalem temple did not own its own land (or at least it seems that it did not own enough land to cover all operating expenditures), its construction and ongoing maintenance as well as imperial taxes had to be paid from other sources.[26] The inscriptional evidence points to a situation of local funding for temples throughout the Persian Empire, and significant evidence for economic support by the Diaspora comes only from a later period (see footnote 3 in this chapter). Given these two factors, along with the biblical evidence that largely assumes or enjoins the regular payment of tithes to the Jerusalem temple (with the notable exception of the book of Ezra), it seems likely that the temple was supported by its local adherents. In a situation where most members of the population of Yehud were subsistence farmers living in small unwalled villages, these individual offerings were probably small, so the temple would need the support of a large number of people.[27]

In addition to the temple's accepting the tithes of its local adherents, it may be that it was also a depot for the provincial taxes. That is, some of the evidence might be interpreted to suggest that all of Yehud had to make regular payments (religious and/or secular) at the temple. From extra-biblical textual evidence, such as the Cyrus Cylinder, the Murašû documents, Strabo, and Pseudo-Aristotle, it is clear that the Achaemenid bureaucracy collected a great deal of tribute and taxes from the provinces (paid in kind and silver and, later, coinage).[28] There is some evidence that such taxes could be collected at local temples. As part of

---

25. For an argument about the unlikelihood that the money represents the people's annual shekel "tax" for the Jerusalem temple based on later traditions relating to the time of year that the tax was collected, see Shmuel Safrai, *Die Wallfahrt im Zeitalter des Zweiten Tempels* (trans. Dafna Mach; Forschungen zum jüdisch-christlichen Dialog 3; Neukirchen-Vluyn: Neukirchener Verlag, 1981), 67, n. 136.

26. For the temple's possession of land, see Blenkinsopp, "Did the Second Jerusalemite Temple Possess Land?," 61–68.

27. Oded Lipschits, "Demographic Changes in Judah between the Seventh and the Fifth Centuries B.C.E.," in Lipschits and Blenkinsopp, *Judah and the Judeans in the Neo-Babylonian Period*, 323–76, esp. 363–66; Charles E. Carter, *The Emergence of Yehud in the Persian Period: A Social and Demographic Study* (JSOTSupp 294; Sheffield: JSOT Press, 1999), 247–48.

28. For evidence of tax and tribute from the Cyrus Cylinder, the Murašû archive and other sources, see Dandamaev and Lukonin, *Culture and Social Institutions*, 177–78; Dandamaev, "The Diaspora," 335–37; Briant, *From Cyrus to Alexander*, 399–410.

his argument that the יצר in Zech 11:13 refers to a situation in which an official at the Jerusalem temple diverted temple income to the imperial coffers, Schaper notes that Nabonidus introduced the "king's chest" (*quppu ša šarri*) for the collection of secular funds at temples, and the Persian Empire probably continued this practice.[29] In addition, the possibility that the economic significance of the Jerusalem temple went beyond its religious adherents might be strengthened by the coins found within Yehud and marked with the name of the province (יהד or יהוד) dating to the fourth century B.C.E. The existence of such coins has led some to hypothesize that the city contained a mint: as the capital city, Jerusalem would be a likely place for a mint, and most of the extant coins (with provenance) were found in or near the city. The connection of the mint with the temple is indicated by the inscription of the names of priests on some of the coins.[30] If the temple was connected with a mint, its centrality in the late Persian period would be enacted via economic exchanges such as the transfer of goods for coinage.

Yet there is some evidence to suggest that the economic center (at least for part of the Persian period) may have been outside Jerusalem in nearby Ramat Raḥel. In the excavations led by Aharoni, hundreds of store-jar handles stamped

---

29. Schaper, "The Jerusalem Temple," 528–39. See also his subsequent article ("The Temple Treasury Committee," 200–206) where he argues that Ezra 8:34 and Neh 13:11 also relate to a situation in which the Jerusalem temple was both the repository of religious tithes and an "outlet of the imperial 'Inland Revenue'" where imperial taxes were collected. Also see A. Leo Oppenheim, "A Fiscal Practice of the Ancient Near East" *JNES* 6 (1947): 116–20, and Dandamaev, "State and Temple," 594.

30. Leo Mildenberg, "Yehūd-Münzen," in Helga Weippert, *Palästina in vorhellenistcher Zeit* (Handbuch der Archäologie. Vorderasien 2.1; München: C. H. Beck, 1988), 721–28, pls. 22–23; Ya'akov Meshorer, *Ancient Jewish Coinage, I: Persian Period Through Hasmonaeans* (New York: Amphora Books, 1982), 30–31; Ephraim Stern, *The Assyrian, Babylonian, and Persian Periods* (vol. 2 of *Archaeology of the Land of the Bible*; Anchor Bible Reference Library; New York: Doubleday, 2001), 567; D. Barag, "A Silver Coin of Yohanan the High Priest and the Coinage of Judaea in the Fouth Century BC," *Israel Numismatic Journal* 9 (1986–87): 4–21; A. Spaer, "Jaddua the High Priest," *Israel Numismatic Journal* 9 (1986–87): 1–3; and see also John Wilson Betlyon, "The Provincial Government of Persian Period Judea and the Yehud Coins," *JBL* 105 (1986): 633–42, esp. 633. For additional studies of Persian-period coinage in Yehud, see Ya'akov Meshorer, *Jewish Coins of the Second Temple Period* (trans. I. H. Levine; Chicago: Argonaut, 1967); Leo Mildenberg, "Yehud: A Preliminary Study of the Provincial Coinage of Judaea," in *Greek Numistics and Archaeology: Essays in Honor of Margaret Thompson* (ed. Otto Morkholm and Nancy M. Waggoner; Wetteren: NR, 1979), 183–96, pls. 222; idem, "*yěhūd* und *šmryn*: Über das Geld der persischen Provinzen Juda und Samaria im 4. Jahrhundert," in *Geschichte – Tradition – Reflexion: Festschrift für Martin Hengel zum 70. Geburtstag* (ed. Hubert Cancik, Hermann Lichtenberger, and Peter Schäfer; Tübingen: J. C. B. Mohr [Paul Siebeck], 1996), 1.119–46; idem, "On the Money Circulation in Palestine from Artaxerxes II till Ptolemy I. Preliminary Studies of the Local Coinage in the Fifth Persian Satrapy. Part 5* (Pls. I–II)," *Transeu* 7 (1994): 63–71; L. Y. Rahmani, "Silver Coins of the Fourth Century from Tel Gamma," *IEJ* 21 (1971): 158–60; Betlyon, "Provincial Government," 633–42; Stern, *Material Culture*, 224–27; Nahman Avigad, *Bullae and Seals from a Post-Exilic Judean Archive* (Qedem 4; Jerusalem: Institute of Archaeology, The Hebrew University of Jerusalem, 1976), 28–29.

with the name of the province (either יהד or יהוד, and sometimes with personal names and/or official titles as well) were found. Such handles have also been found in Persian-period stratum at other sites such as Jerusalem, Tell en-Naṣbeh, Mozah, Gezer, Jericho, and En-Gedi.[31] The number of such handles found at Ramat Raḥel and the wide variety of types may indicate that the site functioned as an administrative center, with the storage jars relating to the collection of taxes in kind.[32] The jars may have been sent to the site and used there for the upkeep of the local government and/or sent from there to the imperial center.[33] Such a scenario would mirror the decisions of the earlier Assyrians who also used the city as an administrative center when they controlled the area.

5.3 CONCLUSION

The temple's centrality, usually related to either theological constructs or ritual practices, can also be registered on an economic plane. According to the archaeological and biblical evidence, it is probable that the temple received its main source of funding from the regularized donations of a fairly large number of local adherents and possible that it was also the tax depot for the entire population of Yehud. Although the book of Ezra emphasizes generous imperial support for the temple, such support is difficult to take at face value given the evidence for the local funding of cults throughout the empire.[34] In addition, the repeated empha-

---

31. See Nahman Avigad, "A New Class of Yehud Stamps," *IEJ* 7 (1957): 146–53; Frank Moore Cross Jr., "Judean Stamps," *EI* 9 (1969): 20–27; Joseph Naveh, *The Development of the Aramaic Script* (Proceedings of the Israel Academy of Sciences and Humanities 5.1; Jerusalem: Ahva Press, 1970), 58–62; see also Avigad, *Bullae and Seals*, 21–29; Stern, *Material Culture*, 202–13; idem, *Archaeology*, 544–51.

Note that a jar handle stamped לחנונה יהוד ("of/to Ḥanuna, Yehud") was found in Babylon, and a similar example was found at Tel Harasim (in the Shephelah). They seem to relate to trade or tax payments from Yehud. See Joseph Naveh, "Gleanings of Some Pottery Inscriptions," *IEJ* 46 (1996): 44–51, esp. 44–47.

32. Yohanan Aharoni, *Excavations at Ramat Rahel: Seasons 1959 and 1960* (Serie Archeologica 2; Rome: Università degli studi, Centro di studi semitici, 1962), 5–10, 27–35, as well as the relevant plates and figures; idem, *Excavations at Ramat Rahel: Seasons 1961 and 1962* (Serie Archeologica 6; Rome: Università degli studi, Centro di studi semitici, 1964), 18–22, 42–48, 120, and relevant plates and figures; idem, "Ramat Raḥel," *NEAEHL* 4:1261–67; see also Nadav Naʾaman "An Assyrian Residence at Ramat Rahel?" *TA* 28 (2001): 260–80, esp. 274–75; and Lipschits, "Demographic Changes," 330–31.

33. According to Avigad (*Bullae and Seals*, 4, 34–35), the stamped jar-handles represent "an efficient tax-gathering apparatus using special jars." For more on the jar handles, see idem, 21–29, and Stern, *Material Culture*, 202–13.

34. For more, see Peter Ross Bedford, *Temple Restoration in Early Achaemenid Judah* (JSOJ Supp 65; Leiden: Brill, 2001), esp. 132–57 where he compares the account of temple rebuilding in Ezra with texts from the larger Persian Empire and concludes that they are undependable as historical accounts of temple funding.

sis on the need for the community to support generously the Jerusalem temple in the texts of Haggai, Zechariah, Malachi, Nehemiah, and Chronicles, both at the time of rebuilding and thereafter, relate more coherently to a situation in which the temple did not receive such generous imperial support. The texts point to a situation in which the temple establishment needed to generate and motivate the economic generosity of its local adherents toward the temple. Although offerings from the Diaspora are occasionally mentioned in the texts, such revenues do not appear to have been substantial until a later period. It seems most likely that the building and ongoing maintenance of the Jerusalem temple were primarily funded by the tithes and offerings from its adherents in Yehud.

Evidence for the temple as a depot for taxes is less clear. Although some of the tithe money would ultimately be sent to the imperium, it is hard to say whether all of Yehud had to pay their taxes at the temple. Besides Zech 11:13 there is no clear evidence for the existence of a "king's chest" at the Jerusalem temple. The יהד coins may point to the relation of the temple with a foundry late in the Persian period, but there is no necessary connection.

Chapter 6

Conclusion: The Palimpsest of
Jerusalem's Centrality

According to the geographer Chris C. Park, "Landscape is a palimpsest,"[1] and, although it does not correlate at every point, in its varying constructions during the Persian period, the geography that comprises Jerusalem fits this aphorism in numerous ways. Because the "landscape" and "palimpsest" are not synonyms (and there is more to the notion of landscape than its function as a kind of palimpsest), I want first to examine Jerusalem's relation to the first term (landscape) before discussing its relation to the second (palimpsest). Seeing Jerusalem and its temple as a landscape—that is, taking the city into account as both built area and vista—enables one to trace its influence beyond the city walls into a broader geographical frame. Indeed, the concept of centrality demands that Jerusalem be seen outside its walls, that is, the "space" of Jerusalem must be examined in households and communities away from the city itself. Examining the centrality of Jerusalem means construing the city's space as an environment connected to communities beyond its borders, a geography that reaches out and influences other entities in varying degrees of power and scope. By drawing on the pictorial traditions that the term "landscape" connotes, I wish to mark an approach to religion and religious practice that engages the setting of religion, and engages this not simply as a stage for the production of religion but as an entity that is influenced by received memories and traditions.

Seeing Jerusalem this way illuminates the practices of centrality that my study has examined, rendering visible the connection to the city and its temple that was felt, desired, and mandated by different communities. The perdurant bonds to the city felt by those living outside it are quite obviously expressed in the act of return, and, once Cyrus came to power, Yahwists in Babylon demonstrated the continuing influence of their homeland by return and resettlement. In Ezra 1, for example, the relationship of the community to the land expressed by resettle-

---

1. Chris C. Park, *Sacred Worlds: An Introduction to Geography and Religion* (London: Routledge, 1994), 198.

ment is strong and immediate: Cyrus' announcement that they may "go up" to Jerusalem is immediately followed by the notice that "they got ready to go up" (Ezra 1:3, 5). The archaeological record of resettlement also shows that the bond between exiled Yahwists was partially expressed in resettlement.

Yet return to the land is not the only way to express affinity to Jerusalem, and my study has examined various religious practices through which Yahwists mapped themselves into the landscape of the city. The returnees, along with their coreligionists who remained outside Yehud in Babylon, or in Egyptian communities such as Elephantine, expressed their relationship to the city and its temple in a variety of religious practices that still leave their textual and archaeological traces, including the protocols enacted for animal sacrifice, the use of incense and figurines, pilgrimage, and the giving of tithes.

Briefly summarized, the available evidence indicates that to a large extent the circumscription of animal sacrifice outside Jerusalem became increasingly important within the texts that now comprise the Hebrew Bible, yet contested in the archaeological evidence. Although the practice is not of great concern in Haggai and Zechariah, Trito-Isaiah contains several polemics against animal sacrifice outside Jerusalem in locales now unidentifiable ("under every green tree" in Isa 57:5, and in "gardens" in Isa 65:3). The texts of Ezra and Nehemiah mention the practice as taking place only within Jerusalem. In addition, the author/editor of Ezra emphasizes animal sacrifice by mentioning it frequently (Ezra 3:2–6; 6:16–18, 20; 8:35), and the author/editor of Nehemiah places it at the highest point of the narrative, namely, the celebration of the walls (Neh 12:43). The Chronicler emphasizes the practice partially through the unique designation that YHWH gives the temple ("a house of sacrifice" in 2 Chr 7:12). The author also expands certain accounts of sacrifice from the narratives in Kings while suppressing others. Consequently, Chronicles contains more and lengthier references to sacrifice at the temple in Jerusalem (1 Chr 21:18–22:1; 29:21; 2 Chr 30; 35:1–19) and fewer references to sacrifice outside Jerusalem (it is missing, for example, in the summaries of the reigns of Joash/Jehoash, Amaziah, Azariah/Uzziah, and Jotham) than the Kings narratives. The book of Malachi emphasizes that, although the worship of YHWH transcends the borders of Yehud (Mal 1:5, 11, 14), animal sacrifice is localized in the Jerusalem temple. According to the archaeological remains, there is no sure evidence for animal sacrifice within Yehud during this period, although it might have occurred at Bethel before the temple was rebuilt. Outside the province, animals were offered by Yahwists at Elephantine prior to 410 B.C.E., but this practice was subsequently discontinued. It seems likely that Yahwists at Gerizim sacrificed animals in their local worship, and those at other sites (such as the "house of YHW" and Lachish) may have as well.

With regard to non-sacrificial worship, the archaeological and biblical evidence shows that, although the use of figurines seems to have been generally curtailed within Yehud (and Samaria as well), the use of incense in religious worship outside Jerusalem was more contested. In Chronicles, incense in worship is acceptable only when offered by temple personnel in the temple itself; those who violate these two requisites are condemned (Uzziah and Ahaz), and those who help to maintain the requisites by destroying altars outside the temple are commended (Asa, Hezekiah, and Josiah). The author's assertions (not found in Kings) of the threat of leprosy when laypersons offer incense (2 Chr 26:16–21) and the persistent offering of incense in Jerusalem by Aaronites and Levites (2 Chr 13:11) may relate to a situation in which the protocols concerning proper geography and personnel were not being maintained. Malachi 1:11 might be indicative of what the author of Chronicles seems to disdain when he validates the use of incense outside the temple (". . . and in every place . . .") in connection with the worship of YHWH. Malachi's perspective on incense used outside the city is paralleled in the Elephantine texts where, after the community explicitly proscribes animal sacrifice, they continue to burn incense in their worship of YHWH. The finds of incense altars in Yehud (twelve at Gezer and possibly an additional one from this period at Tell en-Naṣbeh) and in other locales where Yahwists may have worshipped (including Lachish, Samaria, and Shechem) may provide additional evidence for the use of incense in Yahwistic worship outside Jerusalem. Thus, although animal sacrifice seems to have been limited by some geographical constraints, different considerations (for different communities) were in play for the use of figurines and incense. According to the available evidence, it seems that figurines were disallowed everywhere, and, although the author of Chronicles wanted to curtail its geography more strictly, incense was permitted everywhere.

As for the practice of pilgrimage to Jerusalem, the biblical texts from the Persian period initially envision it as a future-oriented practice, mostly participated in by foreigners who enrich the temple and its worship. Exiles from Babylon usher in a future of pilgrimage from the Diaspora and nations in Zech 6:9–15 (and see also Zech 8:7–8, 21–23), and both Haggai and Trito-Isaiah foresee the journeys of nations to the temple bearing rich offerings (Hag 2:6–8; Isa 56:6–7; 60:9, 13). Pilgrimage changes from a future prophecy for the Diaspora and the nations to a present practice for the Yehud community in Ezra and Nehemiah, where the texts recount the pilgrimage festivals of Booths (Ezra 3:1–4; Neh 8:13–18) and Passover and Unleavened Bread (Ezra 6:19–22). In addition, the accounts of the returns of the community from Babylon to Yehud are told using motifs of pilgrimage journeys in Ezra 1 and 7–8. The author of Chronicles includes two accounts of Passover for which pilgrims from Israel and Judah came and celebrated in Jerusalem (2 Chr 30 and 35, accounts expanded or added to the Kings material). Finally, Pss 120–134 contain several aspects relating to pilgrimage (the call to the shrine, an emphasis on both biological and agricultural fertility, and references to the pursuit of justice), and these texts, like Ezra, Nehemiah, and Chronicles, may have functioned to encourage the community to make a pilgrimage to Jerusalem.

Funding and maintenance of the temple also instantiates the practice of centrality, and, for the most part, this was envisioned as the task of the local community in Yehud. Extra-biblical sources indicate the likelihood of local support, and this is largely represented in the biblical texts where costs for the building and maintenance of the temple are paid by the local community. In Haggai, for example, the construction of the temple is attributed to the resources of the community in Yehud, although additional "treasure" is prophesied from the nations to come in the future. In Zechariah, the temple is funded by the returned exiles as well as the Diaspora. In Malachi, it is the local community alone that bring their offerings to the temple, although the prophet encourages them to bring more and better offerings. This is similar to the situation in Nehemiah, where the main benefactor of the temple is the community in Yehud, and the text includes a vow that they will give regular offerings to the temple. Likewise, in Chronicles, the temple is funded by the people, whose offerings are motivated by the strategic donations of the king. In Ezra, however, although the Diaspora and the returnees give some amount of support for the temple's rebuilding and maintenance, the cult is largely supported by the Persian kings. When compared to the other biblical and extra-biblical texts from the Persian period, Ezra's account of imperial funding for the temple is unusual and historically doubtful. The biblical texts place their greatest stress on the local community as those who support the temple with their gifts. In so doing, the community enacts its religious association to the temple through economic means.

Seen through the practices of sacrifice, incense offering, pilgrimage and tithing, Jerusalem in the Persian period was a city connected to other communities. Although these connections display greater or lesser presentations and enactments of religious centrality, the city and its temple exhibited an influence over geography far beyond its own border.

In addition to comparing Jerusalem to a landscape, I also want to employ Park's interpretation of landscape as a palimpsest. Understanding this landscape of Jerusalem as a palimpsest captures the inherited and evolving nature of Jerusalem's centrality vis-à-vis its many constructions and reconstructions.[2] The attribution of sacrality to Jerusalem, upon which the notion of the city's religious centrality in the Persian period depends, is itself dependent on preexisting traditions of YHWH's relation to the city. Like a palimpsest, new iterations of Jerusalem's centrality are written over and beside preexisting traditions and practices.

In addition, the centrality of Jerusalem, seen in religious practice, is not a static and enshrined performance but changeable in urgency and profile, able to be rewritten, with earlier versions occasionally discernable underneath the later texts. Each text represents a state of affairs (or desired state of affairs) by a single

---

2. It might be said that the comparison also gives an implicit nod to the functional priority of the textual record in this reconstruction of Jerusalem's centrality.

community at a single moment in time, even if that community is reusing older traditions.

An example of the changeable profile of the practice of centrality still detectable in the available evidence is the account of temple funding in Chronicles. In the text, the author repeatedly mirrors the generous gifts of the king to the temple with additional offerings by the lay people (1 Chr 26:26–28; 29:5–9; 2 Chr 30:24; 31:3–10; 35:7–9). This pattern is not present in Kings, where either these gifts are not recorded, or the reciprocal offerings by the laity are absent. It may be that the notices in Chronicles were shaped to foster an attitude of generosity towards the Jerusalem cult, a generosity that, for whatever reason, is not as obvious or pressing in the account in Kings.

Another detectable case of rewriting centrality operates in Neh 10, where new rulings seem to be inserted into the original text. The addition of vv. 38b–40 to the declaration in vv. 36–38a suggests that the author or editor, in the face of the people's noncompliance with their promise to pay their tithes annually in Jerusalem, instituted a new ruling to ensure that the offerings were brought to the temple. Instructing the Levites to collect and transport the offerings contradicts the earlier declaration that the people themselves would bring up their gifts (although the new ruling also enables the community to remain true to their promise to provide the temple with their gifts). This textual alteration provides a glimpse into the wishes and actualities of the transport of offerings into Jerusalem, and the preservation of both texts together evidences changes in these wishes and actualities.

The comparison with a palimpsest also indicates not merely genial evolutions but also the attempt to replace (even efface) earlier versions. Take, for example, the different funding sources and time frames for the temple that the biblical texts present (i.e., the returnees and nations in the future in Haggai, the returnees and the future Diaspora in Zechariah, the future Diaspora and the nations in Trito-Isaiah, and the present-day local community in Malachi and Nehemiah). It might be possible to reconcile these accounts and explain their differences from one another by an appeal to the separate goals of each text—goals such as motivating or reassuring their community. Yet Ezra's construal, with its generous imperium, is quite distinct from the other biblical texts. In this text, the centrality of the temple is not financially expressed in the offerings of its adherents because these are almost superfluous. Indeed, the four notices of additional support from the returnees and the Diaspora almost go unnoticed amidst the fantastic amounts of imperial silver and gold. Ezra presents a posture of financial support for the temple so distinct from the other biblical texts that no simple harmonization is possible, and the distinctive account in some ways effaces the other traditions.

The comparison with a palimpsest also hints at the conflict involved in the recording and practicing of centrality, as opposed to, say, a trajectory, with its attendant connotations of streamlined development. Certainly it is possible to see in my reconstruction of pilgrimage to Jerusalem during the Persian period a precursor to what would burgeon in the later Hasmonean period. And, in my discussion of animal sacrifice, I have noted the general trend in the biblical texts of a growing concern with the limitation of animal sacrifice to Jerusalem alone, moving from infrequent mention in Haggai and Zechariah to a major concern in Chronicles. The explicit foregoing of animal sacrifice at Elephantine after 407 B.C.E. could be read as part of this general trend.

Yet there are also contradictions (or at least changes of foci) within these seemingly straightforward developments. For instance, the more ethnically open model of pilgrimage in the books of Haggai, Zechariah, and Trito-Isaiah, where the Diaspora as well as the nations are included, does not adhere seamlessly with that in Nehemiah, where the pilgrimage feast of Booths is celebrated only by the community that returned to the land (Neh 8:17), or with that of Chronicles, where only the twelve tribes are pointedly invited to the Passover celebrations of Hezekiah (2 Chr 30:1). In addition, within the general trend of the confinement of sacrifice to Jerusalem are the brief notices (and concomitant condemnation) in texts such as Hag 2:14 and Isa 57:5 and 65:3 of sacrifice occurring at sites that seem to be outside Jerusalem.

Although these contradictory aspects might simply be small footnotes in a trajectory model of the development of these practices, the propriety of other practices such as the religious use of incense outside Jerusalem, is more obviously contested throughout the period. For the author of Chronicles, incense should be geographically confined to the Jerusalem temple, where the clerical classes alone could use it. Yet the author's attitude towards the proper geographical confinement of incense is at odds with other textual and artifactual evidence. In Mal 1:11, YHWH speaks approvingly of incense offered "among the nations," and, at Elephantine, Yahwists continued to offer incense even after they abandoned animal sacrifice as part of their worship. Further, it is possible that the limestone cuboids from Tel en-Naṣbeh, Gezer, and Lachish indicate that other Yahwists outside Jerusalem used incense in their worship.

Since the comparison with a palimpsest can imply the contradictions in the record of religious practices and the enactment of various practices at the same time, it can be a helpful heuristic device to understand aspects of the religious practices during this period. Yet the comparison is not adequate in several aspects, including its intimation that traditions about centrality are lodged in a single textual deposit that was consciously manipulated by single scribes at discrete points in time. Clearly this was not the case for the communities of Yahwists in the Persian period that enacted different versions of centrality at one and the same time. As noted above, some communities (reflected in Mal 1:11) considered the use of incense outside Jerusalem to be an acceptable practice, while others (reflected in the text of Chronicles) disagreed. In addition, the community at Elephantine practiced a different version of centrality than their coreligionists in Jerusalem. According to their textual deposit, they clearly saw themselves in relation to Jerusalem: they architecturally aligned their temple towards Jerusalem, and they waited a considerable amount of time for the temple establishment to respond to their letter. Yet by not responding to the letter from Elephantine, the Jerusalem community seems to indicate that they do not want to acknowledge the existence of the Egyptian colony and their temple. So although Elephantine enacted one version of centrality, the Jerusalem community preferred another definition of centrality at the same time.

Such contradictions enacted concurrently point to the additional problem of unpacking the varying possible interpretations of the existence of worship centers outside Jerusalem. The existence of other cultic establishments is clearly a problem for the author of Chronicles, who wants to see all Israel worship YHWH together in Jerusalem. It may be that the cult center in Samaria was originally established in conflict with Jerusalem, perhaps as a replacement for the Jerusalem temple as its contemporary excavator, Yitzhak Magen, contends.[3] Yet, given the reverent attitude toward the Jerusalem cult expressed by the community at Elephantine, several other interpretations of extra-Jerusalem sites are possible. The existence of worship areas outside Jerusalem is not always an obvious indication of rivalry because worshippers are able to maintain complex hierarchies of allegiance between their local sites of worship and significant sites further away. For example, the texts of later Jewish communities in Egypt reveal that the existence of local cult areas did not do away with pilgrimage to Jerusalem. According to *Ep. Arist.* 84–104, Jews made pilgrimages to Jerusalem even though the temple at Leontopolis was in operation,[4] and Philo relates his own pilgrimage from Alexandria to Jerusalem in addition to his other pilgrimages to the more locally situated Therapeutae.[5] In his essay on Yahwistic shrines in the Persian and Hellenistic periods, Edward F. Campbell writes, "It may seem that no injunction of the Torah was transgressed more roundly than was the one calling for the centralization of worship at one place—except of course that Jews at each of the places we have viewed doubtless felt that somehow they were honoring that injunction."[6] Given

---

3. According to Yitzhak Magen, Sanballat, as governor of Samaria, "realized that in order to establish an independent Samaritan entity he needed not only an army, a system of administration, and coinage, but a cultic site as well, a uniquely Samaritan religious and national center that would obviate the need of Samaritans to go to Jerusalem to participate in the Temple rite and that would free Samaria of its religious dependence on the province of Judea." Yitzhak Magen, Haggai Misgav, and Levana Tsfania, *Mount Gerizim Excavations: The Aramaic, Hebrew and Samaritan Inscriptions* (JSP 2; Jerusalem: Israel Antiquities Authority, 2004), 1:11.

4. This is noted by Jörg Frey, "Temple and Rival Temple – The Cases of Elephantine, Mt. Gerizim, and Leontopolis," in *Gemeinde ohne Tempel*, 171–203 esp. 194.

5. See Philo *Prov.* 2.64 and *Contempl.* 21–23, 64–89; cited by Allen Kerkeslager, "Jewish Pilgrimage and Jewish Identity in Hellenistic and Early Roman Egypt," in *Pilgrimage and Holy Space in Late Antique Egypt* (ed. David Frankfurter; Religions in the Graeco-Roman World 134; Leiden: Brill, 1998), 99–225, esp. 107.

6. Edward F. Campbell, Jr. "Jewish Shrines of the Hellenistic and Persian Periods," in *Symposia Celebrating the Seventy-Fifth Anniversary of the Founding of the American Schools of Oriental Research*

that the texts from later Jewish communities in Egypt gesture toward a complexity in parsing sacred geographies that include Jerusalem and additional cult sites, Campbell's observation that transgression can attach to honor is apt. If Campbell is correct, then interpretations of the significance of Persian-period Yahwistic sites outside Jerusalem—the temple at Elephantine, "the house of YHW," and Mt. Gerizim, for example—must always consider the possibility that such sites housed worship that was both honorable and transgressive. Although Jerusalem may have found such sites transgressive, those who worshipped at the sites may have had a different opinion. To deny the possible coexistence of transgression with honor is to prioritize the opinion of one entity in historical reconstruction, namely Jerusalem, over that of all other Yahwists in their various locales.

Like a palimpsest, centrality was reworked through time, but it was also enacted in different ways by different communities and individuals at the same time. According to the extant textual and artifactual evidence, the practice of centrality was neither entirely univocal nor consistent. In the course of tracing the various and varying practices of Jerusalem's centrality in the Persian period, the sacred geography of the city emerges as a negotiated social process, a social process that itself is constructed and made visible by practice.

(1900–1975) (ed. Frank Moore Cross; Zion Research Foundation Occasional Publications 1–2; Cambridge, Mass.: American Schools of Oriental Research, 1979), 159–67, esp. 166.

BIBLIOGRAPHY

Abou-Assaf, Ali, Pierre Bordreuil and Alan R. Millard. *La statue de Tell Fekherye et son inscription bilingue assyro-araméenne.* Etudes Assyriologiques 7. Paris: Editions Recherche sur les Civilizations, 1982.

Ackerman, Susan. "The Deception of Isaac, Jacob's Dream at Bethel and Incubation on an Animal Skin." Pages 92–120 in *Priesthood and Cult in Ancient Israel.* Edited by Gary A. Anderson and Saul M. Olyan. Journal for the Study of the Old Testament: Supplement Series 125. Sheffield: JSOT Press, 1991.

———. "A *Marzēaḥ* in Ezekiel 8:7–13?" *Harvard Theological Review* 82 (1989): 267–81.

———. *Under Every Green Tree: Popular Religion in Sixth-Century Judah.* Harvard Semitic Monographs 46. Atlanta: Scholars Press, 1992.

Ackroyd, Peter R. *Exile and Restoration: A Study of Hebrew Thought of the Sixth Century B.C.* Old Testament Library. Philadelphia: Westminster, 1968.

———. "Studies in the Book of Haggai." *Journal of Jewish Studies* 3 (1952): 1–13.

———. "The Temple Vessels – A Continuity Theme." Pages 166–81 in *Studies in the Religion of Ancient Israel.* Leiden: Brill, 1972.

Aharoni, Yohanan. *Excavations at Ramat Rahel: Seasons 1959 and 1960.* Serie Archeologica 2; Rome: Università degli studi, Centro di studi semitici, 1962.

———. *Excavations at Ramat Rahel: Seasons 1961 and 1962.* Serie Archeologica 6. Rome: Università degli studi, Centro di studi semitici, 1964.

———. "Excavations at Tel Beer-Sheba: Preliminary Report of the Fourth Season, 1972." *Tel Aviv* 1 (1974): 34–42, plate 8.

———. "Ramet Rahel." Pages 1261–67 in vol. 4 of *The New Encyclopedia of Archaeological Excavations in the Holy Land.* Edited by E. Stern. 4 vols. Jerusalem: Israel Exploration Society & Carta, 1993.

———. "מזבח הלבונה מלכיש." *Lešonénu* 35 (1971): 3–6.

———. et al. *Investigations at Lachish: The Sanctuary and the Residency (Lachish V).* Publications of the Institute of Archaeology 4. Tel Aviv: Gateway Publishers, 1975.

Ahlström, Gösta W. *The History of Ancient Palestine*. Edited by Diana Edelman. Sheffield: Sheffield Academic Press; Minneapolis: Fortress Press, 1993.

Albertz, Rainer. *A History of Israelite Religion in the Old Testament Period*. Translated by John Bowden. 2 vols. Old Testament Library. Louisville, Ky.: Westminster John Knox, 1994.

Albright, William F. *The Excavations of Tell Beit Mirsim, III. The Iron Age*. Annual of the American Schools of Oriental Research 21–22. New Haven, Conn.: American Schools of Oriental Research, 1943.

———. "The Lachish Cosmetic Burner and Esther 2:12." Pages 25–32 in *A Light unto My Path: Old Testament Studies in Honor of Jacob M. Myers*. Edited by N. Bream, Ralph D. Heim and Carey A. Moore. Gettysburg Theological Studies 4. Philadelphia: Temple University Press, 1974.

———. "Some Recent Publications." *Bulletin of the American School of Oriental Research* 132 (1953): 46–47.

Allen, Leslie C. *Psalms101–150*. Word Biblical Commentary 21. Waco, Tex.: Word Books, 1983.

Anderson, Francis I., and A. Dean Forbes. *Spelling in the Hebrew Bible*. Rome: Biblical Institute Press, 1986.

Anderson, Gary A. *Sacrifices and Offerings in Ancient Israel: Studies in Their Social and Political Importance*. Harvard Semitic Monographs 41. Atlanta: Scholars Press, 1987.

Antonini, Sabina. "Nuovi incensieri iscritti Yemeniti." *Oriens Antiquus* 27 (1988): 133–41, plates 4–6.

Ariel, Donald T., Hannah Hirschfeld and Neta Savir. "Area D1: Stratigraphic Report." Pages 33–72 in *Excavations at the City of David*. Edited by Donald T. Ariel. Qedem 40. Jerusalem: Institute of Archaeology, The Hebrew University of Jerusalem, 2000.

Arnold, Patrick M., S.J. *Gibeah: The Search for a Biblical City*. Journal for the Study of the Old Testament: Supplement Series 79. Sheffield: Sheffield Academic Press, 1990.

Avigad, Nahman. *Bullae and Seals from a Post-Exilic Judean Archive*. Translated by R. Grafman. Qedem 4. Jerusalem: Institute of Archaeology, The Hebrew University of Jerusalem, 1976.

———. "Excavations at Makmish, 1958: Preliminary Report." *Israel Exploration Journal* 10 (1960): 90–96, plates 9–12.

———. "Excavations at Makmish, 1960: Preliminary Report." *Israel Exploration Journal* 11 (1961): 97–100; pl. 25.

———. "Makmish." *Israel Exploration Journal* 8 (1958): 276.

———. "Makmish." Pages 932–34 in vol. 3 of *The New Encyclopedia of Archaeological Excavations in the Holy Land*. Edited by E. Stern. 4 vols. Jerusalem: Israel Exploration Society & Carta, 1993.

———. "A New Class of *Yehud* Stamps." *Israel Exploration Journal* 7 (1957): 146–53.

———. "Seals of Exiles." *Israel Exploration Journal* 15 (1965): 222–32.

———. "החפירות במכמיש (סקירה ראשונה)." *Bulletin of the Israel Exploration Society* 23 (1959): 48–52.

Barag, D. "A Silver Coin of Yohanan the High Priest and the Coinage of Judaea in the Fouth Century BC." *Israel Numismatic Journal* 9 (1986–87): 4–21.

Barker, Margaret. "The Evil in Zechariah." *Heythrop Journal* 19 (1978): 12–27.

Barré, Michael L. *The God-List in the Treaty Between Hannibal and Philip V of Macedonia: A Study in Light of the Ancient Near Eastern Treaty Tradition*. Johns Hopkins Near Eastern Studies. Baltimore: The Johns Hopkins University Press, 1983.

Batto, Bernard Frank. *Studies on Women at Mari*. The Johns Hopkins Near Eastern Studies. Baltimore and London: The Johns Hopkins University Press, 1974.

Beavon, K.S.O. *Central Place Theory: A Reinterpretation*. New York: Longman, 1977.

Becking, Bob. "Continuity and Community: The Belief System of the Book of Ezra." Pages 256–75 in *The Crisis of Israelite Religion: Transformations of Religious Tradition in Exilic and Post-Exilic Times*. Edited by Bob Becking and Marjo C. A. Korpel. Oudtestamentische Studiën 42. Leiden: Brill, 1999.

Bedford, Peter Ross. *Temple Restoration in Early Achaemenid Judah*. Journal for the Study of Judaism in the Persian, Hellenistic, and Roman Periods: Supplement Series 65. Leiden: Brill, 2001.

Beentjes, Panc. "Jerusalem in the Book of Chronicles." Pages 15–28 in *The Centrality of Jerusalem: Historical Perspectives*. Edited by Marcel Poorthuis and Chanda Safrai. Kampen, The Netherlands: Kok Pharos, 1996.

Bennett, W. J., Jr., and J. A. Blakely. *Tell el-Hesi: The Persian Period (Stratum V)*. Vol. 3 of *The Joint Archaeological Expedition to Tell el-Hesi*. Edited by Kevin G. O'Connell. Winona Lake, Ind.: Eisenbrauns, 1989.

Berquist, Jon L. *Judaism in Persia's Shadow: A Social and Historical Approach*. Minneapolis: Fortress, 1995.

———. "The Shifting Frontier: The Achaemenid Empire's Treatment of Western Colonies. *Journal of World-System Research* 1 (1995). [http://jwsr.ucr.edu/archive/vol1/v1_nh.php].

Betlyon, John Wilson. "The Provincial Government of Persian Period Judea and the Yehud Coins." *Journal of Biblical Literature* 105 (1986): 633–42.

Beuken, W. A. M. *Haggai—Sacharja 1–8. Studien zur Überlieferungsgeschichte der frühnachexilischen Prophetie*. Assen: Van Gorcum, 1967.

Beyerlin, Walter. *We Are Like Dreamers: Studies in Psalm 126*. Translated by Dinah Livingstone. Edinburgh: T&T Clark, 1982.

Biran, Avraham. *Biblical Dan*. Jerusalem: Israel Exploration Society; Hebrew Union College-Jewish Institute of Religion, 1994.

Blenkinsopp, Joseph. "Bethel in the Neo-Babylonian Period." Pages 93–107 in *Judah and the Judeans in the Neo-Babylonian Period*. Edited by Oded Lipschits and Joseph Blenkinsopp. Winona Lake, Ind.: Eisenbrauns, 2003.

———. "Did the Second Jerusalemite Temple Possess Land?" *Transeuphratène* 21 (2001): 61–68.

———. *Ezra-Nehemiah: A Commentary*. Old Testament Library. Philadelphia: Westminster Press, 1988.

———. *Isaiah 56–66*. Anchor Bible 19. New York: Doubleday, 2003.

———. "The Judaean Priesthood during the Neo-Babylonian and Achaemenid Periods: A Hypothetical Reconstruction." *Catholic Biblical Quarterly* 60 (1998): 25–43.

Bliss, Frederick Jones. *A Mound of Many Cities: or, Tell el Hesy Excavated*. New York: Macmillan, 1894.

———. "Second Report on the Excavations at Tell Es-Sâfi." *Palestine Exploration Fund Quarterly Statement* (1899): 317–33.

———, and R. A. Stewart Macalister. *Excavations in Palestine During the Years 1898–1900*. London: Palestine Exploration Fund, 1902.

Bowen, Richard Le Baron, Jr., and Frank P. Albright, eds. *Archaeological Discoveries in South Arabia*. American Foundation for the Study of Man 2. Baltimore: The Johns Hopkins University Press, 1958.

Brettler, Marc. "Interpretation and Prayer." Pages 17–35 in *Minhah le-Nahum: Biblical and Other Studies Presented to Nahum M. Sarna in Honour of his 70th Birthday*. Edited by Marc Brettler and Michael Fishbane. Journal for the Study of the Old Testament: Supplement Series 154. Sheffield: JSOT Press, 1993.

Briant, Pierre. *From Cyrus to Alexander: A History of the Persian Empire*. Translated by Peter T. Daniels. Winona Lake, Ind.: Eisenbrauns, 2002.

Briggs, Charles Augustus, and Emilie Grace Briggs. *A Critical and Exegetical Commentary on the Book of Psalms*. International Critical Commentary 13.2. Edinburgh: T&T Clark, 1907.

Broshi, Magen. "Megadim, Tel." Pages 1001–3 in vol. 3 of *The New Encyclopedia of Archaeological Excavations in the Holy Land*. Edited by E. Stern. 4 vols. Jerusalem: Israel Exploration Society & Carta, 1993.

———. "The Role of the Temple in the Herodium Economy." *Journal of Jewish Studies* 38 (1987): 31–37.

Browne, Laurence E. "A Jewish Sanctuary in Babylonia." *The Journal of Theological Studies* 17 (1916): 400–401.

Bruneau, Philippe. "'Les Israélites de Délos' et la juiverie délienne." *Bulletin de correspondance hellénique* 106 (1982): 465–504.

Burkert, Walter. "The Meaning and Function of the Temple in Classical Greece." Pages 27–47 in *Temple in Society*. Edited by Michael V. Fox. Winona Lake, Ind.: Eisenbrauns, 1988.

Camp, Claudia V. "Storied Space, or, Ben Sira 'Tells' a Temple." Pages 64–80 in *'Imagining' Biblical Worlds: Studies in Spatial, Social and Historical Constructs in Honor of James W. Flanagan*. Edited by David M. Gunn and Paula M. McNutt. Journal for the Study of the Old Testament: Supplement Series 359. London: Sheffield Academic Press (Continuum), 2002.

Campbell, Edward F. Jr. "Jewish Shrines of the Hellenistic and Persian Periods." Pages 159–67 in *Symposia Celebrating the Seventy-Fifth Anniversary of the Founding of the American Schools of Oriental Research (1900–1975)*. Edited by Frank Moore Cross. Zion Research Foundation Occasional Publications 1–2. Cambridge, Mass.: American Schools of Oriental Research, 1979.

Canton Thompson, Gertrude. *The Tombs and Moon Temple of Hureidha (Hadhramaut)*. Reports of the Research Committee of the Society of Antiquaries of London 13. Oxford: Oxford University Press, 1944.

Carroll, Robert P. "Madonna of Silences: Clio and the Bible." Pages 83–103 in *Can a 'History of Israel' Be Written?* Edited byLester L. Grabbe. Journal for the Study of the Old Testament: Supplement Series 245. Sheffield: Sheffield Academic Press, 1997.

———. "So What Do We Know About the Temple? The Temple in the Prophets." Pages 34–51 in *Second Temple Studies: 2. Temple Community in the Persian Period*. Edited by Tamara C. Eskenazi and Kent H. Richards. Journal for the Study of the Old Testament: Supplement Series 175. Sheffield: JSOT Press, 1994.

Carter, Charles E. *The Emergence of Yehud in the Persian Period: A Social and Demographic Study*. Journal for the Study of the Old Testament: Supplement Series 294. Sheffield: JSOT Press, 1999.

Chary, Theophane. *Aggee-Zacharie, Malachie*. Paris: Librairie Lecoffre, 1969.

Christaller, Walter. *Central Places in Southern Germany*. Translated by C. W. Baskin. Englewood Cliffs: Prentice-Hall, 1966.

Clements, Ronald E. "The Deuteronomic Law of Centralization and the Catastrophe of 587 B.C.E.." Pages 5–25 in *After the Exile: Essays in Honor of Rex Mason*. Edited by John Barton and David J. Reimer. Macon, Ga.: Mercer University Press, 1996.

Clines, David J. A. *Ezra, Nehemiah, Esther*. New Century Bible Commentary. Grand Rapids, Mich.; Eerdmans, 1984.

———. "Haggai's Temple, Constructed, Deconstructed and Reconstructed." Pages 60–87 in *Second Temple Studies: 2. Temple Community in the Persian Period*. Edited by Tamara C. Eskenazi and Kent H. Richards. Journal for the Study of the Old Testament: Supplement Series 175. Sheffield: JSOT Press, 1994.

———. "Nehemiah 10 as an Example of Early Jewish Biblical Exegesis." *Journal for the Study of the Old Testament* 21 (1981): 111–17.

Coats, G. W. "Despoiling the Egyptians." *Vetus Testamentum* 18 (1968): 450–57.

Cody, Aelred. "When is the Chosen People called a Gôy?" *Vetus Testamentum* 14 (1964): 1–6.

Cohen, Mark E. *The Cultic Calendars of the Ancient Near East*. Bethesda, Md.: CDL Press, 1993.

Collins, John J. *Between Athens and Jerusalem: Jewish Identity in the Hellenistic Diaspora*. New York: Crossroad, 1983.

Cross, Frank Moore, Jr. "Judean Stamps." *Eretz-Israel* 9 (1969): 20–27.

———. "An Ostracon from Nebī Yūnis." *Israel Exploration Journal* 14 (1964): 185–86, plate 41.h.

———. "Two Notes on Palestinian Inscriptions of the Persian Age." *Bulletin of the American Schools of Oriental Research* 193 (1969): 19–24.

Crow, Loren D. *The Songs of Ascents (Psalms 120–134): Their Place in Israelite History and Religion*. Society of Biblical Literature Dissertation Series 148. Atlanta: Scholars Press, 1996.

Crowfoot, J. W., G. M. Crowfoot and Kathleen M. Kenyon. *The Objects From Samaria*. Samaria-Sebaste; Reports of the Work of the Joint Expedition in 1931–1933 and of the British Expedition in 1935 3. London: Palestine Exploration Fund, 1957.

Dahood, Mitchell. "The *aleph* in Psalm CXXVII 2." *Orientalia* 44 (1975): 103–5.

———. *Psalms*. Anchor Bible 16–17A. Garden City: Doubleday, 1966–1970.

Danby, Herbert. *The Mishnah: Translated from the Hebrew with Introduction and Brief Explanatory Notes*. Oxford: Oxford University Press, 1933.

Dandamaev, Muhammed A. "The Diaspora: Babylonia in the Persian Age." Pages 326–42 in *Introduction; The Persian Period*. Vol. 1 of *The Cambridge History of Judaism*. Edited by W. D. Davies and Louis Finkelstein. Cambridge: Cambridge University Press, 1984.

———. "Politische und Wirtschaftliche Geschichte." Pages 15–58 in *Beiträge zur Achämenidengeschichte*. Edited by Gerold Walser. Wiesbaden: Franz Steiner, 1972.

———. "State and Temple in Babylonia in the First Millennium B.C." Pages 589–96 in *State and Temple Economy in the Ancient Near East: Proceedings of the International Conference Organized by the Katholieke Universiteit Leuven from the 10th to the 14th of April 1978*. Edited by Edward Lipiński. Orientalia Lovaniensia Analecta 6. Leuven: Departement Oriëntalistiek, 1979.

———. "Der Tempelzehnte in Babylonien während des 6.–4. Jh. v. u. Z." Pages 82–90 in vol. 1 of *Beiträge zur Alten Geschichte und deren Nachleben: Festschrift für Franz Altheim zum 6. 10. 1968*. Edited by Ruth Stiehl and Hans Erich Stier. Berlin: De Gruyter, 1969–70.

———, and Vladimir G. Lukonin. *The Culture and Social Institutions of Ancient Iran*. Translated by Philip R. Kohl. Cambridge: Cambridge University Press, 1989.

Daviau, P. M. Michèle. "Family Religion: Evidence for the Paraphernalia of the Domestic Cult." Pages 199–229 in *The World of the Aramaeans II: Studies in History and Archaeology in Honour of Paul-Eugène Dion*. Edited by P. M. Michèle Daviau, John W. Wevers and Michael Weigl. Journal for the Study of the Old Testament: Supplement Series 325. Sheffield: Sheffield Academic Press, 2001.

De Groot, Alon, and Donald T. Ariel. "Ceramic Report." Pages 91–154 in *Excavations at the City of David V*. Edited by Donald T. Ariel. Qedem 40. Jerusalem: Institute of Archaeology, The Hebrew University of Jerusalem, 2000.

De Vries, Simon J. "Festival Ideology in Chronicles." Pages 104–24 in *Problems in Biblical Theology: Essays in Honor of Rolf Knierim*. Edited by Henry T. C. Sun and Keith L. Eades with James M. Robinson and Garth I. Moller; Grand Rapids, Mich.: Eerdmans, 1997.

Delcor, M. "La vision de la femme dans l'épha de Zach., 5, 5–11 à la lumière de la littérature hittite." *Revue de l'histoire des religions* 187 (1975): 137–45.

Demsky, Aaron. "Who Came First, Ezra or Nehemiah? The Synchronistic Approach." *Hebrew Union College Annual* 65 (1994): 1–19.

Dentan, Robert C. "The Book of Malachi." Pages 1117–44 in vol. 6 of *Interpreter's Bible*. Edited by G. A. Buttrick et al. 12 vols. New York, 1951–57.

Derfler, Steven. "Area C: The Eastern Hillock." Pages 136–40 in "Excavations at Tel Michal 1978–1979." Edited by Ze'ev Herzog. *Tel Aviv* 7 (1980): 111–52, plates 29–35.

Deutsch, R., and M. Heltzer. "New Phoenician and Aramaic Inscriptions from the Sharon Plain." Pages 69–88 in *Forty New Ancient West Semitic Inscriptions*. Tel Aviv: Archaeological Center Publication, 1994.

Dever, William G. "On Listening to the Text – and the Artifacts." Pages 1–23 in *The Echoes of Many Texts: Reflections on Jewish and Christian Traditions: Essays in Honor of Lou H. Silberman*. Edited by William G. Dever and J. Edward Wright. Brown Judaic Studies 313. Atlanta: Scholars Press, 1997.

———, H. Darrell Lance, and G. Ernest Wright. *Gezer I: Preliminary Report of the 1964–66 Seasons*. Annual of the Hebrew Union College Biblical and Archaeological School in Jerusalem. Jerusalem: Keter Publishing, 1970.

Dietrich, Ernst Ludwig. שוב שבות. *Die endzeitliche Wiederherstellung bei den Propheten*. Beihefte zur Zeitschrift für die alttestamentliche Wissenschaft 40. Giessen, Alfred Töpelmann, 1925.

Dillon, Matthew. *Pilgrims and Pilgrimage in Ancient Greece*. London: Routledge, 1997.

Dobbs-Allsopp, F. W. "Linguistic Evidence for the Date of Lamentations." *Journal of the Ancient Near Eastern Society* 26 (1998): 1–36.

———. "Rethinking Historical Criticism." *Biblical Interpretation* 7 (1999): 235–71.

Donner, Herbert. "Psalm 122." Pages 86–89 in *Text and Context: Old Testament and Semitic Studies for F. C. Fensham*. Edited by W. Claassen. Journal for the Study of the Old Testament: Supplement Series 48. Sheffield: Sheffield Academic Press, 1988.

Dothan, Moshe. *Ashdod II–III: The Second and Third Seasons of Excavations, 1963, 1965*. 'Atiqot 9–10 (English Series). Jerusalem: Department of Antiquities and Museums, 1971.

———. "A Phoenician Inscription from 'Akko." *Israel Exploration Journal* 35 (1985): 81–94.

———. "A Sign of Tanit from Tel 'Akko." *Israel Exploration Journal* 24 (1974): 44–49.

———. "Tel Acco." Pages 17–24 in vol. 1 of *The New Encyclopedia of Archaeological Excavations in the Holy Land*. Edited by E. Stern. 4 vols. Jerusalem: Israel Exploration Society & Carta, 1993.

———, and David N. Freedman. *Ashdod I: The First Season of Excavations, 1962*. 'Atiqot 7 (English Series). Jerusalem: Department of Antiquities and Museums, 1967.

Driver, G. R. "Three Technical Terms in the Pentateuch." *Journal of Semitic Studies* 1 (1956): 97–105.

Duggan, Michael W. *The Covenant Renewal in Ezra-Nehemiah (Neh 7:72b–10:40): An Exegetical, Literary, and Theological Study*. Society of Biblical Literature Dissertation Series 164. Atlanta: Society of Biblical Literature, 2001.

Dupont-Sommer, A. "Aramaic Inscription on an Altar." Pages 358–59 in *Lachish III (Tell Ed-Duweir): The Iron Age*. Edited by Olga Tufnell, with contributions by Margaret A. Murray and David Diringer. Oxford: Oxford University Press, 1953.

Dyck, J. E. *The Theocratic Ideology of the Chronicler.* Biblical Interpretation Series 33. Leiden: Brill, 1998.

Eade, John and Michael J. Sallnow, "Introduction." Pages 1–29 in *Contesting The Sacred: The Anthropology of Christian Pilgrimage.* Edited by John Eade and Michael J. Sallnow. London: Routledge, 1991.

Edelman, Diana. "The Meaning of *qiṭṭēr." Vetus Testamentum* 35 (1985): 395–404.

———. "Proving Yahweh Killed his Wife (Zechariah 5:5–11)." *Biblical Interpretation* 11 (2003): 3–44.

Eissfeldt, Otto. *Erstlinge und Zehnten im Alten Testament. Ein Beitrag zur Geschichte des Israelitisch-Jüdischen Kults.* Beiträge zur Wissenschaft vom Alten und Neuen Testament 22. Leipzig: J. C. Hinrich, 1917.

Elayi, Josette. "The Phoenician Cities in the Persian Period." *Journal of the Ancient Near Eastern Society* 12 (1980): 13–28.

Elgavish, Joseph. שקמונה. Tel Aviv: Hakibbutz Hameuchad, 1994.

Eliade, Mircea. *The Myth of the Eternal Return.* Translated by Willard R. Trask. London: Routledge & Kegan Paul, 1955.

———. *Patterns in Comparative Religion.* Translated by Rosemary Sheed. New York: Sheed & Ward, 1958.

Emerton, J. A. "The Meaning of *šēnā'* in Psalm CXXVII 2." *Vetus Testamentum* 24 (1974): 15–31.

Esler, Philip F. "Ezra-Nehemiah as a Narrative of (Re-Invented) Israelite Identity." *Biblical Interpretation* 11 (2003): 413–26.

Falkenstein, Adam, and Wolfram von Soden. *Sumerische und akkadische Hymnen und Gebete.* Zürich: Artemis, 1953.

Fantalkin, Alexander, and Oren Tal. "The Persian and Hellenistic Pottery of Level I." Pages 2174–96 in *The Renewed Archaeological Excavations at Lachish (1973–1994).* Edited by David Ussishkin. 5 vols. Publications of the Institute of Archaeology 22. Tel Aviv: Emery and Claire Yass Publications in Archaeology, 2004.

———. "Redating Lachish Level I: Identifying Achaemenid Imperial Policy at the Southern Frontier of the Fifth Satrapy." Pages 167–97 in *Judah and the Judeans in the Persian Period.* Edited by Oded Lipschits and Manfred Oeming. Winona Lake, Ind.: Eisenbrauns, 2006.

Fargo, Valerie M. "Ḥesi, Tell el-." Pages 630–34 in vol. 2 of *The New Encyclopedia of Archaeological Excavations in the Holy Land.* Edited by E. Stern. 4 vols. Jerusalem: Israel Exploration Society & Carta, 1993.

Fishbane, Michael. *Biblical Interpretation in Ancient Israel*. Oxford: Oxford University Press, 1985.

Fitzmyer, Joseph A. *The Aramaic Inscriptions of Sefire*. Rev. ed. Bibliotheca orientalis 19/A. Rome: Pontifical Biblical Institute, 1995.

Fleishman, Joseph. "An Echo of Optimism in Ezra 6:19–22." *Hebrew Union College Annual* 69 (1998): 15–29.

Floyd, Michael H. "The Evil in the Ephah: Reading Zechariah 5:5–11 in its Literary Context." *Catholic Biblical Quarterly* 58 (1996): 51–68.

———. "The Nature of the Narrative and the Evidence of Redaction in Haggai." *Vetus Testamentum* 45 (1995): 470–90.

Fowler, Mervyn D. "Excavated Incense Burners." *Biblical Archaeologist* 47 (1984): 183–86.

———. "Excavated Incense Burners: A Case for Identifying a Site as Sacred?" *Palestine Exploration Quarterly* 117 (1985): 25–29.

Frankel, Rafael. "Miẓpe Yammim, Mount." Pages 1061–63 in vol. 3 of *The New Encyclopedia of Archaeological Excavations in the Holy Land*. Edited by E. Stern. 4 vols. Jerusalem: Israel Exploration Society & Carta, 1993.

———. "המקדש מן התקופה הפרסית בהר מצפה־ימים." *Qadmoniot* 30.1 (1997): 46–53.

———, and Raphael Ventura. "The Mispe Yamim Bronzes." *Bulletin of the American Schools of Oriental Research* 311 (1998): 39–55.

Freedman, David N. "The Spelling of the Name 'David' in the Hebrew Bible." *Hebrew Annual Review* 7 (1983): 89–102.

Frey, Jörg. "Temple and Rival Temple - The Cases of Elephantine, Mt. Gerizim, and Leontopolis." Pages 171–203 in *Gemeinde ohne Tempel = Community without Temple: Zur Substituierung und Transformation des Jerusalemer Tempels und seines Kults im Alten Testament, antiken Judentum und frühen Christentum*. Edited by Beate Ego, Armin Lange and Peter Pilhofer. Wissenschaftliche Untersuchungen zum Neuen Testament 118. Tübingen: J. C. B. Mohr (Paul Siebeck), 1999.

Friedland, Roger, and Richard D. Hecht. "The Politics of Sacred Space: Jerusalem's Temple Mount/al-haram al sharif." Pages 24–28 in *Sacred Places and Profane Spaces: Essays in the Geographics of Judaism, Christianity, and Islam*. Edited by Jamie Scott and Paul Simpson-Housley. Contributions to the Study of Relgion 30. New York: Greenwood Press, 1991.

Fritz, Volkmar. "Die Bedeutung des Wortes ḥammān/ḥmn." Pages 41–50 in *Wort und Wirklichkeit: Studien zur Afrikanistik und Orientalistik*. Edited by Brigitta Benzing, Otto Böcher and Günter Mayer. Meisenheim am Glan: Anton Hain, 1976.

———. "The Meaning of the Word Ḥammān/ḥmn." *Folio Orientalia* 21 (1980): 103–15.

Gafni, Isaiah M. *Land, Center and Diaspora: Jewish Constructs in Late Antiquity.* Journal for the Study of the Pseudepigrapha: Supplement Series 21. Sheffield: Sheffield Academic Press, 1997.

Galling, Kurt. *Der Altar in den Kulturen des alten Orients. Eine archäologische Studie.* Berlin: Karl Curtius Verlag, 1925.

———. "The Gōlā-List According to Ezra 2//Nehemiah 7." *Journal of Biblical Literature* 70 (1951): 149–58.

———. "Die Liste der aus dem Exil Heimgekehrten." *Studien zur Geschichte Israels im persischen Zeitalter.* Tübingen: J. C. B. Mohr (Paul Siebeck), 1964.

———. "Von Naboned zu Darius." *Zeitschrift des deutschen Palästina-Vereins* 70 (1954): 4–32.

Garcia-Treto, Francisco Oscar. "Bethel: The History and Traditions of an Israelite Sanctuary." Th.D. diss., Princeton Theological Seminary, 1967.

Geertz, Clifford. *Interpretation of Cultures.* New York: Basic Books, 1973.

Gerstenberger, Erhard S. *Psalms, Part 2, and Lamentations.* The Forms of Old Testament Literature 15. Grand Rapids, Mich.: Eerdmans, 2001.

Gesenius, Wilhelm. *Thesaurus Philologicus Criticus Linguae Hebrae et Chaldae Veteris Testamenti.* 2nd ed. Leipzig: Fr. Chr. Wil. Vogelius, 1839.

Gitin, Seymour. "Incense Altars from Ekron, Israel and Judah: Context and Typology." *Eretz-Israel* 20 (1989): *52–*67.

———. "New Incense Altars from Ekron: Context, Typology and Function." *Eretz-Israel* 23 (1992): 43–49.

Glazier-McDonald, Beth. *Malachi: The Divine Messenger.* Society for Biblical Literature Dissertation Series 98. Atlanta: Scholars Press, 1987.

Glueck, Nelson. "Incense Altars." Pages 325–29, plates 1–5, figures 1–4 in *Translating & Understanding the Old Testament.* Edited by Harry Thomas Frank and William L. Reed. Nashville and New York: Abingdon, 1970.

———. *Rivers in the Desert: A History of the Negev.* New York: Farrar, Straus and Cudahy, 1959.

———. "מזבחות־קטורת." *Eretz Israel* 10 (1971): 120–25, figures 1–4.

Grabbe, Lester L. *Ezra-Nehemiah.* Old Testament Readings. London: Routledge, 1998.

———. *Judaic Religion in the Second Temple Period: Belief and Practice from the Exile to Yavneh.* London: Routledge, 2000.

———. *Yehud: A History of the Persian Province of Judah.* Vol. 1 of *A History of the Jews and Judaism in the Second Temple Period.* Library of Second Temple Studies 47. London: T&T Clark, 2004.

Graham, M. Patrick. "Setting the Heart to Seek God: Worship in 2 Chronicles 30:1–31:1." Pages 124–41 in *Worship and the Hebrew Bible: Essays in Honour of John T. Willis*. Edited by M. Patrick Graham, Rick R. Marrs and Steven L. McKenzie. Journal for the Study of the Old Testament: Supplement Series 284. Sheffield: Sheffield Academic Press, 1999.

Grossberg, Daniel. *Centripetal and Centrifugal Structures in Biblical Poetry*. Society of Biblical Literature Monograph Series 39. Atlanta: Scholars Press, 1989.

Gruen, Erich S. *Diaspora: Jews amidst Greeks and Romans*. Cambridge, Mass.: Harvard, 2002.

Gunneweg, J., and I. Perlman, "Hellenistic Braziers from Israel: Results of Pottery Analysis." *Israel Exploration Journal* 34 (1984): 232–38.

Guzzo, Maria Giulia Amadasi. "Two Phoenician Inscriptions Carved in Ivory: Again the Ur Box and the Sarepta Plaque." *Orientalia* 59 (1990): 58–66.

Haag, Herbert. "Das Mazzenfest des Hiskia." Pages 87–94 in *Wort und Geschichte: Festschrift für Karl Elliger zum 70. Geburtstag*. Edited by Hartmut Gese and Hans Peter Rüger. Alter Orient und Altes Testament. Neukirchen-Vluyn: Neukirchener, 1973.

Habel, Norman C. "'Yahweh, Maker of Heaven and Earth': A Study in Tradition Criticism." *Journal of Biblical Literature* 91 (1972): 321–37.

Hadley, Judith M. "Yahweh and 'His Asherah': Archaeological and Textual Evidence for the Cult of the Goddess." Pages 235–68 in *Ein Gott allein? JHWH-Verehrung und biblischer Monotheismus im Kontext der israelitischen und altorientalischen Religionsgeschichte*. Edited by Walter Dietrich and Martin A. Klopfenstein. Orbis biblicus et orientalis 139. Freiburg: Universitätsverlag, 1994.

Halpern, Baruch. "The Centralization Formula in Deuteronomy." *Vetus Testamentum* 31 (1981): 20–38.

Hanson, Paul D. *The Dawn of Apocalyptic: The Historical and Sociological Roots of Jewish Apocalyptic Eschatology*. Philadelphia: Fortress, 1975.

Haran, Menahem. "Altar-ed States: Incense Theory Goes up in Smoke." *Biblical Research* 11 (1995): 30–37, 48.

———. "'Incense Altars' – Are They?" Pages 237–47 in *Biblical Archaeology Today, 1990: Proceedings of the Second International Congress on Biblical Archaeology, Jerusalem, June–July 1990*. Edited by Avraham Biran and Joseph Aviram. Jerusalem: Israel Exploration Society, 1993.

———. *Temples and Temple Service in Ancient Israel: An Inquiry into Biblical Cult Phenomena and the Historical Setting of the Priestly School*. Winona Lake, Ind.: Eisenbrauns, 1985.

———. "The Uses of Incense in the Ancient Israelite Ritual." *Vetus Testamentum* 10 (1960): 113–29.

Harrelson, Walter. "The Celebration of the Feast of Booths according to Zech xiv 16–21." Pages 88–96 in *Religions in Antiquity: Essays in Memory of Erwin Ramsdell Goodenough*. Edited by Jacob Neusner. Studies in the History of Religions 14. Leiden: Brill, 1968.

Heger, Paul. *The Development of Incense Cult in Israel*. Beihefte zur Zeitschrift fur die alttestamentliche Wissenschaft 245. Berlin, New York: Walter de Gruyter, 1997.

Herzog, Ze'ev. "Michal, Tel." Pages 1036–41 in vol. 3 of *The New Encyclopedia of Archaeological Excavations in the Holy Land*. Edited by E. Stern. 4 vols. Jerusalem: Israel Exploration Society & Carta, 1993.

———, Ora Negbi and Shmuel Moshkovitz. "Excavations at Tel Michal, 1977." *Tel Aviv* 5 (1978): 99–130, plates 33–39.

Herzog, Ze'ev, George Rapp, Jr., and Ora Negbi, eds. *Excavations at Tel Michal, Israel*. Publications of the Institute of Archaeology 8. Minneapolis: The University of Minnesota Press and Tel Aviv: The Sonia and Marco Nadler Institute of Archaeology, 1989.

Hill, Andrew E. "Dating the Book of Malachi: A Linguistic Reexamination." Pages 77–89 in *The Word of the Lord Shall Go Forth*. Edited by Carol L. Meyers and M. O'Connor. Winona Lake, Ind.: Eisenbrauns, 1983.

Holladay, John S. Jr. "Religion in Israel and Judah under the Monarchy: An Explicitly Archaeological Approach." Pages 249–99 in *Ancient Israelite Religion: Essays in Honor of Frank Moore Cross*. Edited by Patrick D. Miller, Jr., Paul D. Hanson and S. Dean McBride. Philadelphia: Fortress, 1987.

Hunter, Alastair G. "The Psalms of Ascents: A Late Festival Recovered?" Pages 173*–87* in *Proceedings of the Twelfth World Congress of Jewish Studies: Jerusalem, July 29–August 5, 1997, Division A, The Bible and its World*. Edited by Ron Margolin. Jerusalem: World Union of Jewish Studies, 1999.

Hurvitz, Avi. "The Chronological Significance of 'Aramaisms' in Biblical Hebrew." *Israel Exploration Journal* 18 (1968): 234–40.

———. "Continuity and Innovation in Biblical Hebrew – The Case of 'Semantic Change' in Post-Biblical Hebrew." Pages 1–10 in *Studies in Ancient Hebrew Semantics*. Edited by T. Muraoka. Abr-Nahrain: Supplement Series 4. Louvain: Peeters, 1995.

———. בין לשון ללשון: לתולדות לשון המקרא בימי בית שני. Jerusalem: Bialik Institute, 1972.

Iliffe, J. H. "A Hoard of Bronzes from Askalon c. Fourth Century B.C." *Quarterly of the Department of Antiquities in Palestine* 5 (1935): 61–68, plates 29–34.

Jagersma, H. "The Tithes in the Old Testament." Pages 116–28 in *Remembering All the Way. . .: A Collection of Old Testament Studies Published on the Occasion of the Fortieth Anniversary of the Oudtestamentisch Werkgezelschap in Nederland*. Old Testament Studies 21. Leiden: Brill, 1981.

Jamme, A. "Deux autels à encens de l'Université de Harvard." *Bibliotheca Orientalis* 10 (1953): 94–95, plate 14.

Janzen, David. "The 'Mission' of Ezra and the Persian-Period Temple Community." *Journal of Biblical Literature* 119 (2000): 619–43.

Japhet, Sara. *I & II Chronicles: A Commentary*. Old Testament Library. Louisville, Ky.: Westminster John Knox, 1993.

──────. "Composition and Chronology in the Book of Ezra-Nehemiah." Pages 189–216 in *Second Temple Studies: 2. Temple Community in the Persian Period*. Edited by Tamara C. Eskenazi and Kent H. Richards. Journal for the Study of the Old Testament: Supplement Series 175. Sheffield: JSOT Press, 1994.

──────. "The Distribution of the Priestly Gifts According to a Document of the Second Temple Period." Pages 3–20 in *Texts, Temples and Traditions: A Tribute to Menahem Haran*. Edited by Michael V. Fox, Victor Avigdor Hurowitz, Avi Hurvitz, Michael L. Klein, Baruch J. Schwartz and Nili Shupak. Winona Lake, Ind.: Eisenbrauns, 1996.

──────. "'History' and 'Literature' in the Persian Period: The Restoration of the Temple." Pages 174–88 in *Ah Assyria . . .: Studies in Assyrian History and Ancient Near Eastern Historiography Presented to Hayim Tadmor*. Edited by M. Cogan and I. Eph'al. Scripta hierosolymitana 33. Jerusalem: Magnes, 1991.

──────. *The Ideology of the Book of Chronicles and Its Place in Biblical Thought*. Translated by Anna Barber. Beiträge zur Erforschung des Alten Testaments und des antiken Judentum 9. Frankfurt am Main: Peter Lang, 1989.

──────. "The Temple in the Restoration Period: Reality and Ideology." *Union Seminary Quarterly Review* 44 (1991): 195–252.

Joannès, F., and A. Lemaire. "Trois tablettes cunéiformes à onomastique ouest-sémitique (collection Sh. Moussaïeff (Pls. I–II)." *Transeuphratène* 19 (1999): 17–34.

Johnsson, William G. "The Pilgrimage Motif in the Book of Hebrews." *Journal of Biblical Literature* 97 (1978): 239–51.

Joong, Ho Chong. "Were There Yahwistic Sanctuaries in Babylonia?" *Asia Journal of Theology* 10 (1996): 198–217.

Joüon, Paul. *A Grammar of Biblical Hebrew*. Translated by T. Muraoka. Subsidia Biblica 14.I–II. Rome: Pontificio Instituto Biblico, 1991.

Kalimi, Isaac. "Jerusalem - The Divine City: The Representation of Jerusalem in Chronicles Compared with Earlier and Later Jewish Compositions." Pages 189–205 in *The Chronicler as Theologian: Essays in Honor of Ralph W. Klein.* Edited by M. Patrick Graham, Steven L. McKenzie and Gary N. Knoppers. Journal for the Study of the Old Testament: Supplement Series 371. London; T&T Clark, 2003.

Kapelrud, Arvid S. *The Question of Authorship in the Ezra-Narrative: A Lexical Investigation.* Skrifter utgitt av det Norske Videnskaps-Akademi I Oslo 1944. Oslo: Jacob Dybwad, 1944.

Karrer, Christiane. *Ringen um die Verfassung Judas: Eine Studie zu den theologisch-politischen Vorstellungen im Esra-Nehemia-Buch.* Beihefte zur Zeitschrift für die alttestamentliche Wissenschaft 308. Berlin: Walter de Gruyter, 2001.

Keet, Cuthbert C. *A Study of the Psalms of Ascents: A Critical and Exegetical Commentary Upon Psalms CXX to CXXXIV.* London: The Mitre Press, 1969.

Keil, Carl Friedrich. *The Books of Ezra, Nehemiah, and Esther.* Translated by Sophia Taylor. Biblical Commentary on the Old Testament 3. Edinburgh: T&T Clark, 1879. Repr. ed. Grand Rapids, Mich.: Eerdmans, 1983.

———. *The Twelve Minor Prophets.* Translated by James Martin. Biblical Commentary on the Old Testament. Grand Rapids, Mich.: Eerdmans, 1949.

Kellermann, Ulrich. *Nehemia: Quellen, Überlieferung und Geschichte.* Berlin: Töpelmann, 1967.

Kelso, James Leon. "Bethel." Pages 192–94 in vol. 1 of *The New Encyclopedia of Archaeological Excavations in the Holy Land.* Edited by E. Stern. 4 vols. Jerusalem: Israel Exploration Society & Carta, 1993.

———, with chapters by William F. Albright, Lawrence A. Sinclair, Paul W. Lapp and James L. Swauger. *The Excavation of Bethel (1934–1960).* Annual of the American Schools of Oriental Research 39. Cambridge, Mass.: American Schools of Oriental Research, 1968.

Kempinski, Aharon. "'Erani, Tel: Area D." Pages 419–21 in vol. 2 of *The New Encyclopedia of Archaeological Excavations in the Holy Land.* Edited by E. Stern. 4 vols. Jerusalem: Israel Exploration Society & Carta, 1993.

Kerkeslager, Allen. "Jewish Pilgrimage and Jewish Identity in Hellenistic and Early Roman Egypt." Pages 106–7 in *Pilgrimage and Holy Space in Late Antique Egypt.* Edited by David Frankfurter. Religions in the Graeco-Roman World 134. Leiden: Brill, 1998.

Kessler, John A. "Building the Second Temple: Questions of Time, Text, and History in Haggai 1.1–15." *Journal for the Study of the Old Testament* 27 (2002): 243–56.

———. "The Shaking of the Nations: An Eschatological View." *Journal of the Evangelical Theological Society* 30 (1987): 159–66.

King, Leslie J. *Central Place Theory*. Beverly Hills: Sage Publications, 1984.

Klein, Ralph W. "The Books of Ezra & Nehemiah." Pages 661–851 of vol. 3 of *The New Interpreter's Bible*. Nashville: Abingdon, 1999.

———. "Old Readings in I Esdras: The List of Returnees from Babylon (Ezra 2 // Nehemiah 7)." *Harvard Theological Review* 62 (1969): 99–107.

Kleinig, John W. "Recent Research in Chronicles." *Currents in Research: Biblical Studies* 2 (1994): 43–76.

Kletter, Raz. "Iron Age and Post-Iron Age Artefacts. Section B: Clay Figurines." Pages 2058–83 in *The Renewed Archaeological Excavations at Lachish (1973–1994)*. Edited by David Ussishkin. 5 vols. Publications of the Institute of Archaeology 22. Tel Aviv: Emery and Claire Yass Publications in Archaeology, 2004.

———. *The Judean Pillar-Figurines and the Archaeology of Asherah*. BAR International Series 636. Oxford: Tempus Reparatum, 1996.

Kloner, Amos. "מרשה." *Qadmoniot* 95–96 (1991): 70–85.

Knoppers, Gary N. *I Chronicles 1–9: A New Translation with Introduction and Commentary*. Anchor Bible 12. New York: Doubleday, 2003.

———. *1 Chronicles 10–29: A New Translation with Introduction and Commentary*. Anchor Bible 12A. New York: Doubleday, 2004.

———. "'The City Yhwh Has Chosen': The Chronicler's Promotion of Jerusalem in Light of Recent Archaeology." Pages 307–26 in *Jerusalem in Bible and Archaeology: The First Temple Period*. Edited by Andrew G. Vaughn and Ann E. Killebrew. Society of Biblical Literature Symposium Series 18. Leiden: Brill, 2003.

———. "Revisiting the Samarian Question in the Persian Period." Pages 265–89 in *Judah and the Judeans in the Persian Period*. Edited by Oded Lipschits and Manfred Oeming. Winona Lake, Ind.: Eisenbrauns, 2006.

Knowles, Melody D. "Pilgrimage Imagery in the Returns in Ezra." *Journal of Biblical Literature* 123 (2004): 57–74.

Koch, Klaus. "Ezra and the Origins of Judaism." *Journal of Semitic Studies* 19 (1974): 173–97.

———. "Haggais unreines Volk." *Zeitschrift für die alttestamentliche Wissenschaft* 79 (1967): 52–66.

Koenen, Klaus. *Bethel: Geschichte, Kult und Theologie*. Orbis Biblicus et Orientalis 192. Freiburg: Universitätsverlag, 2003.

Kottsieper, I. "Die Religionspolitik der Achämeniden und die Juden von Elephantine." Pages 150–78 in *Religion und Religionskontakte im Zeitalter der Achämeniden*. Edited by Reinhard G. Kratz. Gütersloh: Kaiser, Gütersloher Verlagshaus, 2002.

Kraabel, A. T. "New Evidence of the Samaritan Diaspora has been Found on Delos." *Biblical Archaeologist* (March 1984): 44–46.

Kratz, Reinhard G. "The Second Temple of Jeb and of Jerusalem." Pages 247–64 in *Judah and the Judeans in the Persian Period*. Edited by Oded Lipschits and Manfred Oeming. Winona Lake, Ind.: Eisenbrauns, 2006.

Kraus, Hans-Joachim. *Psalms 60–150*. Translated by Hilton C. Oswald. Minneapolis: Augsburg, 1989.

Kutscher, Eduard Yechezkel. *A History of the Hebrew Language*. Jerusalem: Magnes Press, 1984.

Lefebvre, Henri. *The Production of Space*. Translated by D. Nicholson Smith. Oxford: Basil Blackwell, 1991.

Lemaire, André. "Histoire et administration de la Palestine à l'époque perse." Pages 11–53 in *La Palestine à l'époque perse*. Edited by Ernest-Marie Laperrousaz and André Lemaire. Paris: Editions du Cerf, 1994.

———. "New Aramaic Ostraca from Idumea and their Historical Interpretation." Pages 413–56 in *Judah and the Judeans in the Persian Period*. Edited by Oded Lipschits and Manfred Oeming. Winona Lake, Ind.: Eisenbrauns, 2006.

———. *Nouvelles inscriptions araméennes d'Idumée au Musée d'Israël*. Paris: Gabalda, 2002.

Lemke, Werner E. "The Synoptic Problem in the Chronicler's History." *Harvard Theological Review* 58 (1965): 349–63.

Levenson, Jon D. "From Temple to Synagogue: 1 Kings 8." Pages 143–66 in *Traditions in Transformation: Turning Points in Biblical Faith*. Edited by Baruch Halpern and Jon D. Levenson. Winona Lake, Ind.: Eisenbrauns, 1981.

Lincoln, Bruce. "Theses on Method." *Method & Theory in the Study of Religion* 8.3 (1996): 225–27.

Lipiński, Edward. *Studies in Aramaic Inscriptions and Onomastics*. Orientalia Lovaniensia Analecta 1. Leuven: Leuven University Press, 1975.

Lipschits, Oded. "Demographic Changes in Judah between the Seventh and the Fifth Centuries B.C.E." Pages 323–76 in *Judah and the Judeans in the Neo-Babylonian Period*. Edited by Oded Lipschits and Joseph Blenkinsopp. Winona Lake, Ind.: Eisenbrauns, 2003.

———. "The History of the Benjaminite Region under Babylonian Rule." *Tel Aviv* 26 (1999): 155–90.

Liver, J. "The Half-Shekel Offering in Biblical and Post-Biblical Literature." *Harvard Theological Review* 56 (1963): 173–98.

Macalister, R. A. Stewart. *The Excavation of Gezer*. 3 vols. London: J. Murray, 1912.

Magen, Yitzhak, Haggai Misgav and Levana Tsfania. *The Aramaic, Hebrew and Samaritan Inscriptions*. Vol. 1 of *Mount Gerizim Excavations*. Judea and Samaria Publications 2. Jerusalem: Israel Antiquities Authority, 2004.

——. "עיר מקדש – הר גריזים." *Qadmoniot* 33 (2000): 74–118.

——, L. Tsfania, and H. Misgav. "הכתובות הארמיות והעבריות מהר גריזים." *Qadmoniot* 33 (2000): 125–32.

Mannati, Marina. "Les Psaumes Graduels constituent-ils un genre littéraire distinct à l'intérieur du psautier biblique?" *Semitica* 29 (1979): 85–100.

Marenof, S. "Note Concerning the Meaning of the Word 'Ephah,' Zechariah 5:5–11." *American Journal of Semitic Languages and Literature* 48 (1931–32): 264–67.

Marinkovic, Peter. "What does Zechariah 1–8 Tell us about the Second Temple?" Pages 88–103 in *Second Temple Studies: 2. Temple Community in the Persian Period*. Edited by Tamara C. Eskenazi and Kent H. Richards. Journal for the Study of the Old Testament: Supplement Series 175. Sheffield: JSOT Press, 1994.

Marrs, Rick. "The *Šyry-Hm'lwt* (Psalms 120–134): A Philological and Stylistic Analysis." Ph.D. diss., The Johns Hopkins University, 1982.

Mason, Rex. *The Books of Haggai, Zechariah, and Malachi*. Cambridge Bible Commentary. Cambridge: Cambridge University Press, 1977.

Masson, Olivier. "Pèlerins Chypriotes en Phénicie (Sarepta et Sidon)." *Semitica* 32 (1982): 45–49, plate 7.1–2.

May, Herbert G. "'This People' and 'This Nation' in Haggai." *Vetus Testamentum* 18 (1968): 190–97.

McCarter, P. Kyle, Jr. *II Samuel*. Anchor Bible 9. Garden City, N.Y.: Doubleday, 1984.

——. "Aspects of the Religion of the Israelite Monarchy: Biblical and Epigraphic Data." Pages 137–55 in *Ancient Israelite Religion: Essays in Honor of Frank Moore Cross*. Edited by Patrick D. Miller, Jr., Paul D. Hanson and S. Dean McBride. Philadelphia: Fortress, 1987.

McCown, Chester Charlton, with contributions by James Muilenburg, Joseph Carson Wampler, Dietrich von Bothmer and Margaret Harrison. *Tell en-Naṣbeh Excavated under the Direction of the Late William Frederic Badè: Archaeological and Historical Results*. Berkeley: The Palestine Institute of Pacific School of Religion and the American Schools of Oriental Research, 1947.

Meiggs, Russell, and David M. Lewis. *A Selection of Greek Historical Inscriptions to the End of the Fifth Century B.C.* Rev. ed. Oxford: Oxford University Press, 1992.

Meir, C. A. *Ancient Incubation and Modern Psychotherapy.* Translated by Monica Curtis. Evanston: Northwestern University Press, 1967.

Merrill, Arthur L. "Pilgrimage in the Old Testament: A Study in Cult and Tradition." *Ecumenical Institute for Advanced Theological Studies: Yearbook* (1973–74): 45–62.

Merrill, Eugene H. *Haggai, Zechariah, Malachi: An Exegetical Commentary.* Chicago: Moody Press, 1994.

———. "Pilgrimage and Procession: Motifs of Israel's Return." Pages 261–72 in *Israel's Apostasy and Restoration: Essays in Honor of Roland K. Harrison.* Edited by Avraham Gileadi. Grand Rapids, Mich.: Baker Book House, 1988.

Meshel, Zeev. *Kuntillet 'Ajrud: A Religious Centre from the Time of the Judean Monarchy on the Border of Sinai.* Israel Museum Catalogue 175. Jerusalem: Israel Museum, 1978.

Meshorer, Ya'akov. *Ancient Jewish Coinage, I: Persian Period Through Hasmonaeans.* New York: Amphora Books, 1982.

———. *Jewish Coins of the Second Temple Period.* Translated by I. H. Levine. Chicago: Argonaut, 1967.

Meyers, Carol L., and Eric M. Meyers. *Haggai, Zechariah 1–8.* Anchor Bible 25B. Garden City: Doubleday, 1987.

———. "Jerusalem and Zion After the Exile: The Evidence of First Zechariah." Pages 121–35 in *"Sha'arei Talmon": Studies in the Bible, Qumram, and the Ancient Near East Presented to Shemaryahu Talmon.* Edited by Michael Fishbane and Emanuel Tov. Winona Lake, Ind.: Eisenbrauns, 1992.

Mildenberg, Leo. "On the Money Circulation in Palestine from Artaxerxes II till Ptolemy I. Preliminary Studies of the Local Coinage in the Fifth Persian Satrapy. Part 5* (Pls. I–II)." *Transeuphratène* 7 (1994): 63–71.

———. "Yehud: A Preliminary Study of the Provincial Coinage of Judaea." Pages 183–96 and plate 222 in *Greek Numistics and Archaeology: Essays in Honor of Margaret Thompson.* Edited by Otto Morkholm and Nancy M. Waggoner. Wetteren: NR, 1979.

———. "Yəhūd-Münzen." Pages 721–28 and plates 22–23 in Helga Weippert, *Palästina in vorhellenistcher Zeit.* Handbuch der Archäologie. Vorderasien 2.1. München: C. H. Beck, 1988.

———. "*yĕhūd* und *šmryn*: Über das Geld der persischen Provinzen Juda und Samaria im 4. Jahrhundert." Pages 119–46 in vol. 1 of *Geschichte – Tradition – Reflexion: Festschrift für Martin Hengel zum 70. Geburtstag.* Edited by Hubert Cancik, Hermann Lichtenberger and Peter Schäfer. Tübingen: J. C. B. Mohr (Paul Siebeck), 1996.

Millard, A. R. "The Small Cuboid Incense-Burners: A Note on Their Age." *Levant* 16 (1984): 172–73.

Millard, Matthias. *Die Komposition des Psalters: Ein formgeschichtlicher Ansatz.* Forschungen zum Alten Testament 9. Tübingen: J. C. B. Mohr (Paul Siebeck), 1994.

Miller, Patrick D. Jr. "A Note on the Meša' Inscription." *Orientalia* 38 (1969): 461–64.

Mitchell, Hinckley G., John Merlin Powis Smith and Julius A. Bewer. *A Critical and Exegetical Commentary on Haggai, Zechariah, Malachi and Jonah.* International Critical Commentary 22. New York: Scribners' Sons, 1912.

Morgenstern, Julian. "The Despoiling of the Egyptians." *Journal of Biblical Literature* 68 (1949): 1–28.

Mowinckel, Sigmund. *The Psalms in Israel's Worship.* Translated by D. R. Ap-Thomas. Oxford: Basil Blackwell, 1962.

Myers, Jacob M. *Ezra Nehemiah.* Anchor Bible 14. Garden City, N.Y.: Doubleday, 1965.

Na'aman, Nadav. "An Assyrian Residence at Ramat Rahel?" *Tel Aviv* 28 (2001): 260–80.

———. "Beth-acen, Bethel, and Early Israelite Sanctuaries." *Zeitschrift des deutschen Palästina-Vereins* 103 (1987): 13–21.

Naveh, Joseph. "The Aramaic Ostraca from Tel Arad." Pages 153–76 in *Arad Inscriptions.* Edited by Yohanan Aharoni, in cooperation with Joseph Naveh. Judean Desert Studies. Jerusalem: Israel Exploration Society, 1981.

———. *The Development of the Aramaic Script.* Proceedings of the Israel Academy of Sciences and Humanities 5.1. Jerusalem: Ahva Press, 1970.

———. "Gleanings of Some Pottery Inscriptions." *Israel Exploration Journal* 46 (1996): 44–51.

Nielsen, Kjeld. *Incense in Ancient Israel.* Vetus Testamentum Supplements 38. Leiden: Brill, 1986.

North, Francis Sparling. "Aaron's Rise in Prestige." *Zeitschrift für die alttestamentliche Wissenschaft* 66 (1954): 191–99.

Noth, Martin. *The History of Israel.* Translated by P. R. Ackroyd. New York: Harper & Row, 1968.

O'Connell, K. G. "The List of Seven Peoples in Canaan: A Fresh Analysis." Pages 221–41 in *The Answers Lie Below: Essays in Honor of Lawrence Edmond Toombs.* Edited by H. O. Thompson. Lanham, Md.: University Press of America, 1984.

Oppenheim, A. Leo. "The Eyes of the Lord." *Journal of the American Oriental Society* 88 (1968): 173–80.

———. "A Fiscal Practice of the Ancient Near East." *Journal of Near Eastern Studies* 6 (1947): 116–20.

Oren, Eliezer D. "Haror, Tel." Pages 580–84 in vol. 2 of *The New Encyclopedia of Archaeological Excavations in the Holy Land*. Edited by E. Stern. 4 vols. Jerusalem: Israel Exploration Society & Carta, 1993.

———. "Northern Sinai." Pages 1386–96 in vol. 4 of *The New Encyclopedia of Archaeological Excavations in the Holy Land*. Edited by E. Stern. 4 vols. Jerusalem: Israel Exploration Society & Carta, 1993.

———. "Sera', Tel." Pages 1329–35 in vol. 4 of *The New Encyclopedia of Archaeological Excavations in the Holy Land*. Edited by E. Stern. 4 vols. Jerusalem: Israel Exploration Society & Carta, 1993

———. "Ziglag: A Biblical City on the Edge of the Negev." *Biblical Archaeologist* 45 (1982): 155–66.

Park, Chris C. *Sacred Worlds: An Introduction to Geography and Religion*. London: Routledge, 1994.

Partin, H. B. "The Muslim Pilgrimage: Journey to the Center." Ph.D. diss., University of Chicago, 1967.

Patterson, Lee. *Negotiating the Past: The Historical Understanding of Medieval Literature*. Madison, Wis.: University of Wisconsin Press, 1987.

Pearce, Sarah. "Josephus as Interpreter of Biblical Law: The Representation of the High Court of Deut. 17:8–12 according to Jewish Antiquities 4.218." *Journal of Jewish Studies* 46 (1995): 30–42.

Petersen, David L. *Haggai & Zechariah 1–8: A Commentary*. Old Testament Library. London: SCM Press, 1985.

Petrie, W. M. Flinders. *Anthedon: Sinai*. London: British School of Egyptian Archaeology, 1937.

———. *Gerar*. London: British School of Archaeology in Egypt, 1928.

———. *Hyksos and Israelite Cities*. London: Office of School of Archaeology, University College and Bernard Quaritch, 1906.

———. *Tell el-Hesy (Lachish)*. London: Alexander P. Watt, 1891.

Phythian-Adams, W. J. "Report on the Stratification of Askalon." *Palestine Exploration Fund Quarterly Statement* (1923): 60–84.

Pilgrim, Cornelius von. "Der Tempel des Jahwe." Pages 142–45 in Stadt und Tempel von Elephantine: 25./26./27. Grabungsbericht; *Mitteilungen des Deutschen Archäologischen Instituts Abteilung Kairo* 55 (1999).

———. "Textzeugnis und archäologischer Befund: Zur Topographie Elephantines in der 27. Dynastie." Pages 485–97 in *Stationen: Beiträge zur Kultgeschichte Ägyptens: Rainer Stadelmann gewidmet*. Edited by H. Guksch and D. Polz. Mainz: von Zabern, 1998.

Pitkänen, Pekka. *Central Sanctuary and Centralization of Worship in Ancient Israel: From the Settlement to the Building of Solomon's Temple*. Piscataway, N.J.: Gorgias, 2003.

Pola, Thomas. *Das Priestertum bei Sacharja: Historische und traditionsgeschichtliche Untersuchungen zur frühnachexilischen Herrschererwartung*. Forschungen zum Alten Testament 35. Tübingen: Mohr Siebeck, 2003.

Polignac, François de. *Cults, Territory, and the Origins of the Greek City-State*. Translated by Janet Lloyd. Chicago: University of Chicago Press, 1995.

Polzin, Robert. *Late Biblical Hebrew: Toward an Historical Typology of Biblical Hebrew Prose*. Harvard Semitic Monographs 12. Missoula: Scholars Press, 1976.

Porten, Bezalel. "Settlement of Jews at Elephantine and the Arameans at Syene." Pages 451–70 in *Judah and the Judeans in the Neo-Babylonian Period*. Edited by Oded Lipschits and Joseph Blenkinsopp. Winona Lake, Ind.: Eisenbrauns, 2003.

———. "The Structure and Orientation of the Jewish Temple at Elephantine: A Revised Plan of the Jewish District." *Journal of the American Oriental Society* 81 (1961): 38–42.

———. "Theme and Structure of *Ezra* 1–6: From Literature to History." *Transeuphratène* 23 (2003): 27–44.

———, and Ada Yardeni. *Textbook of Aramaic Documents from Ancient Egypt*. Vols. 1–3. Texts and Studies for Students. Winona Lake, Ind.: Eisenbrauns, 1986–93.

Pritchard, James B. "Gibeon." Pages 511–14 in vol. 2 of *The New Encyclopedia of Archaeological Excavations in the Holy Land*. Edited by E. Stern. 4 vols. Jerusalem: Israel Exploration Society & Carta, 1993.

———. "An Incense Burner from Tell es-Sa'idiyeh, Jordan Valley." Pages 3–17 in *Studies on the Ancient Palestinian World*. Edited by J. W. Wevers and D. B. Redford. Toronto: University of Toronto Press, 1972.

———. *Recovering Sarepta, A Phoenician City*. Princeton: Princeton University Press, 1978.

———. *Tell Es-Sa'idiyeh: Excavations on the Tell, 1964–1966*. University Museum Monograph 60. Philadelphia: The University Museum, The University of Pennsylvania, 1985.

———. *Winery, Defences, and Soundings at Gibeon*. Museum Monographs. Philadelphia: The University Museum, University of Pennsylvania, 1964.

Propp, William H. C. *Exodus 1–18*. Anchor Bible 2. New York: Doubleday, 1998.

Rahmani, L. Y. "Hellenistic Brazier Fragments from Israel." *Israel Exploration Journal* 34 (1984): 224–31.

———. "Palestinian Incense Burners of the Sixth to Eighth Centuries C.E." *Israel Exploration Journal* 30 (1980): 116–22, plates 12,13.

———. "Silver Coins of the Fourth Century from Tel Gamma." *Israel Exploration Journal* 21 (1971): 158–60.

Reinmuth, Titus. *Der Bericht Nehemias: Zur literarischen Eigenart, traditionsgeschichtlichen Prägung und innerbiblischen Rezeption des Ich-Berichts Nehemias.* OBO 183. Göttingen: Vandenhoeck & Ruprecht, 2002.

Reisman, Daniel. "Iddin-Dagan's Sacred Marriage Hymn." *Journal of Cuneiform Studies* 25 (1973): 185–202.

Reisner, George Andrew, Clarence Stanley Fisher and David Gordon Lyon. *Harvard Excavations at Samaria: 1908–1910.* 2 vols. Cambridge: Harvard University Press, 1924.

Rendsburg, Gary A. *Linguistic Evidence for the Northern Origin of Selected Psalms.* Society of Biblical Literature Monograph Series 43. Atlanta: Scholars Press, 1990.

Reuter, Eleonore. *Kultzentralisation: Entstehung und Theologie von Dtn 12.* Athenäums Monografien: Theologie 87. Bonner Biblische Beiträge. Frankfurt am Main: Hain, 1993.

Rignell, Lars Gösta. *Die Nachtgeschichte des Sacharja.* Lund: Gleerups, 1950.

Rooker, Mark F. *Biblical Hebrew in Transition.* Journal for the Study of the Old Testament: Supplement Series 90. Sheffield: Sheffield Academic Press, 1990.

Rosenbaum, Jonathan. "Hezekiah's Reform and the Deuteronomistic Tradition." *Harvard Theological Review* 72 (1979): 23–43.

Rost, L. "Erwägungen zu Sacharjas 7. Nachtgesicht." *Zeitschrift für die alttestamentliche Wissenschaft* NS 17 (1940–41): 223–28.

Rothstein, J. W. *Juden und Samaritaner: Die grundlegende Scheidung von Judentum und Heidentum. Eine kritische Studie zum Buche Haggai und zur jüdischen Geschichte im ersten nachexilischen Jahrhundert.* Beiträge zur Wissenschaft vom Alten Testament 3. Leipzig: J. C. Hinrichs, 1908.

Rubenstein, J. L. "History of Sukkot During the Second Temple and Rabbinic Periods: Studies in the Continuity and Change of a Festival." Ph.D. diss., Columbia University, 1992.

Rudolph, Wilhelm. *Esra und Nehemia.* Handbuch zum Alten Testament 20; Tübingen: J. C. B. Mohr (Paul Siebeck), 1949.

Ruwe, Andreas. "Die Veränderung tempeltheologischer Konzepte in Ezechiel 8-11." Pages 3–18 in *Gemeinde ohne Tempel = Community without Temple: Zur Substituierung und Transformation des Jerusalemer Tempels und seines Kults im Alten Testament, antiken Judentum und frühen Christentum.* Edited by Beate Ego, Armin Lange and Peter Pilhofer. Wissenschaftliche Untersuchungen zum Neuen Testament 118. Tübingen: J. C. B. Mohr (Paul Siebeck), 1999.

Safrai, Shmuel. "Relations Between the Diaspora and the Land of Israel." Pages 184–215 in *The Jewish People in the First Century*. Edited by S. Safrai and M. Stern. Vol. 1 of *Compendia Rerum Iudaicarum ad Novum Testamentum*. Assen: Van Gorcum, 1974.

———. *Die Wallfahrt im Zeitalter des Zweiten Tempels*. Translated by Dafna Mach. Forschungen zum jüdisch-christlichen Dialog 3. Neukirchen-Vluyn: Neukirchener Verlag, 1981.

Sallnow, Michael J. *Pilgrims of the Andes: Regional Cults in Cusco*. Washington, D.C.: Smithsonian Institution Press, 1987.

Sarna, Nahum M. "The Chirotonic Motif on the Lachish Altar." Pages 44–46 in *Investigations at Lachish: The Sanctuary and the Residency (Lachish V)*. Edited by Aharoni, Yohanan, et al. Publications of the Institute of Archaeology 4. Tel Aviv: Gateway Publishers, 1975.

Sass, Benjamin. "Section A: Vessels, Tools, Personal Objects, Figurative Art and Varia." Pages 1983–2057 in vol. 4 of *The Renewed Archaeological Excavations at Lachish (1973–1994)*. Edited by David Ussishkin. Publications of the Institute of Archaeology 22; Tel Aviv: Emery and Claire Yass Publications in Archaeology, 2004.

Sauer, Eberhard W.,ed. *Archaeology and Ancient History: Breaking Down the Boundaries*. New York: Routledge, 2004.

Schaper, Joachim. "The Jerusalem Temple as an Instrument of the Achaemenid Fiscal Administration." *Vetus Testamentum* 45 (1995): 528–39.

———. "The Temple Treasury Committee in the Times of Nehemiah and Ezra." *Vetus Testamentum* 47 (1997): 200–206.

Schattner-Reiser, Ursula. "L'hébreu postexilique." Pages 189–224 in *La Palestine à l'époque perse*. Edited by Ernest-Marie Laperrousaz and André Lemaire. Etudes annexes de la Bible de Jérusalem. Paris: Cerf, 1994.

Schmid, Hans Heinrich. *De sogenannte Jahwist: Beobachtungen und Fragen zur Pentateuchforschung*. Zurich: Theologischer Verlag, 1976.

Scott, W. R. "The Booths of Ancient Israel's Autumn Festival." Ph.D. diss., The Johns Hopkins University, 1993.

Segal, J. B. *The Hebrew Passover*. Oxford: Oxford University Press, 1963.

Seger, Joe D. "Ḥalif, Tel." Pages 553–59 in vol. 2 of *The New Encyclopedia of Archaeological Excavations in the Holy Land*. Edited by E. Stern. 4 vols. Jerusalem: Israel Exploration Society & Carta, 1993.

Seow, C. L. "Linguistic Evidence and the Dating of Qohelet." *Journal of Biblical Literature* 115 (1996): 643–66.

———. Review of Gary A. Rendsburg, *Linguistic Evidence for the Northern Origin of Selected Psalms. Journal of Biblical Literature* 112 (1993): 334–37.

Seybold, Klaus. *Die Wallfahrtspsalmen: Studien zur Entstehungsgeschichte von Psalm 120–134*. Bible et terre sainte 3. Neukirchen-Vluyn: Neukirchener Verlag, 1978.

Shea, Michael O'Dwyer. "The Small Cuboid Incense-Burner of the Ancient Near East." *Levant* 15 (1983): 76–109.

Shiloh, Yigal. *Excavations at the City of David I*. Qedem 19. Jerusalem: Institute of Archaeology, The Hebrew University of Jerusalem, 1984.

Singer-Avitz, Lily. "Stone and Clay Objects." Pages 350–60 in *Excavations at Tel Michal, Israel*. Edited by Ze'ev Herzog, George Rapp, Jr. and Ora Negbi. Publications of the Institute of Archaeology 8. Minneapolis: The University of Minnesota Press and Tel Aviv: The Sonia and Marco Nadler Institute of Archaeology, 1989.

Sjøholt, Peter. "Christaller Revisited: Reconsidering Christaller's Analysis of Services and Central Places." *Service Industries Journal* 21.4 (Oct. 2001): 198–200.

Smith, Adam T. *The Political Landscape: Constellations of Authority in Early Complex Polities*. Berkeley: University of California, 2003.

Smith, Jonathan Z. *Map is Not Territory: Studies in the History of Religions*. Leiden: Brill, 1978.

Smith, Mark S., with contributions by Elizabeth M. Bloch-Smith. *The Pilgrimage Pattern in Exodus*. Journal for the Study of the Old Testament: Supplement Series 239. Sheffield: Sheffield Academic Press, 1997.

Smith, Morton. *Palestinian Parties and Politics that Shaped the Old Testament*. New York: Columbia University Press, 1971.

Smith, Robert J. *Ancestor Worship in Contemporary Japan*. Stanford: Stanford University Press, 1974.

Soja, Edward W. *Postmodern Geographies: The Reassertion of Space in Critical Theory*. London: Verso, 1989.

———. *Thirdspace: Journeys to Los Angeles and Other Real-and-Imagined Places*. Oxford: Basil Blackwell, 1996.

Spaer, A. "Jaddua the High Priest." *Israel Numismatic Journal* 9 (1986–87): 1–3.

Sperber, Daniel. "Social Legislation in Jerusalem during the Latter Part of the Second Temple Period." *Journal for the Study of Judaism in the Persian, Hellenistic, and Roman Periods* 6 (1975): 86–95.

Stager, Lawrence E. "Ashkelon." Pages 103–12 in vol. 1 of *The New Encyclopedia of Archaeological Excavations in the Holy Land*. Edited by E. Stern. 4 vols. Jerusalem: Israel Exploration Society & Carta, 1993.

——. "Why Were Hundreds of Dogs Buried at Ashkelon?" *Biblical Archaeology Review* 17/3 (1991): 26–42.

Starbuck, Scott R. A. "Like Dreamers Lying in Wait, We Lament: A New Reading of Psalm 126." *Koinonia* 1/2 (1989): 128–49.

Starkey, J. L. "Lachish as Illustrating Bible History." *Palestine Exploration Fund Quarterly Statement* 69 (1937): 171–79.

——, and Lankester Harding. "Beth-Pelet Cemetery." Pages 22–32 and plates in *Beth-Pelet II*. Publications of the Egyptian Research Account and British School of Archaeology in Egypt 52. London: British School of Archaeology in Egypt, 1932.

Steck, Odil Hannes. "Jesaja 60,13 – Bauholz oder Tempelgarten?" *Biblische Notizen* 30 (1985): 29–34.

Steins, Georg. *Die Chronik als kanonisches Abschlußphänomen: Studien zur Entstehung und Theologie von 1/2 Chronik*. BBB 93. Weinheim: Beltz Anthenäum, 1995.

Stendebach, Franz Josef. "Altarformen im kanaanäisch-israelitischen Raum." *Biblische Zeitschrift* NS 20 (1976): 180–96.

Stern, Ephraim. "Achaemenian Tombs from Shechem." *Levant* 12 (1980): 90–111, plates 13–15.

——. *Archaeology of the Land of the Bible. Vol 2: The Assyrian, Babylonian, and Persian Periods*. Anchor Bible Reference Library. New York: Doubleday, 2001.

——. "Bes Vases from Palestine and Syria." *Israel Exploration Journal* 26 (1976): 183–87; plates 32–33.

——. "Dor." Pages 357–68 in vol. 1 of *The New Encyclopedia of Archaeological Excavations in the Holy Land*. Edited by E. Stern. 4 vols. Jerusalem: Israel Exploration Society & Carta, 1993.

——. *Dor, Ruler of the Seas: Nineteen Years of Excavations at the Israelite-Phoenician Harbor Town on the Carmel Coast*. Translated by Joseph Shadur. Jerusalem: Israel Exploration Society, 2000.

——. "A Favissa of a Phoenician Sanctuary from Tel Dor." *Journal of Jewish Studies* 33 (1982): 35–54.

——. "Limestone Incense Altars." Pages 53–54 in *Beer-Sheba 1: Excavations at Tel Beer-Sheba, 1969–1971 Seasons*. Edited by Yohanan Aharoni. Publications of the Institute of Archaeology 2. Tel Aviv: The Tel Aviv University Institute of Archaeology, 1973.

——. *Material Culture of the Land of the Bible in the Persian Period, 538–332 B.C.* Warminster, Wiltshire: Aris & Phillips, 1982.

——. "Note on a Decorated Limestone Altar from Lachish." *'Atiqot 11*, English Series (1976): 107–9.

——. "A Phoenician-Cypriote Votive Scapula from Tel Dor: A Maritime Scene." *Israel Exploration Journal* 44 (1994): 1–12.

——. "Religion in Palestine in the Assyrian and Persian Periods." Pages 245–55 in *The Crisis of Israelite Religion: Transformation of Religious Tradition in Exilic and Post-Exilic Times.* Edited by Bob Becking and Marjo C. A. Korpel. *Oudtestamentische Studiën* 42. Leiden: Brill, 1999.

——. "The Religious Revolution in Persian-Period Judah." Pages 199–205 in *Judah and the Judeans in the Persian Period.* Edited by Oded Lipschits and Manfred Oeming. Winona Lake, Ind.: Eisenbrauns, 2006.

——. "What Happened to the Cult Figurines? Israelite Religion Purified After the Exile." *Biblical Archaeology Review* 15.4 (July/August 1989): 22–29, 53–54.

——. "Ẓafit, Tel." Pages 1522–24 in vol. 4 of *The New Encyclopedia of Archaeological Excavations in the Holy Land.* Edited by E. Stern. 4 vols. Jerusalem: Israel Exploration Society & Carta, 1993.

——, and Yitzhak Magen. "Archaeological Evidence for the First Stage of the Samaritan Temple on Mount Gerazim." *Israel Exploration Journal* 52 (2002): 49–57.

——. "השלב הראשון של המקדש השומרוני בהר גריזים: עדויות ארכיאולוגיות חדשות" *Qadmoniot* 33 (2000): 119–24.

Stolper, Matthew W. "The *šaknu* of Nippur." *Journal of Cuneiform Studies* 40 (1988): 127–55.

Strugnell, John. "A Note on Ps. CXXVI.1." *Journal of Theological Studies* NS 7 (1956): 239–43.

Swetnam, James. "Malachi 1, 11: An Interpretation." *Catholic Biblical Quarterly* 31 (1969): 200–209.

Thompson, Thomas L. *The Historicity of the Patriarchal Narratives: The Quest for the Historical Abraham.* New York: de Gruyter, 1974.

Throntveit, Mark A. *Ezra-Nehemiah. Interpretation.* Louisville, Ky.: Westminster John Knox, 1992.

Tilly, Michael. *Jerusalem – Nabel der Welt: Überlieferung und Funktionen von Heiligtumstraditionen im antiken Judentum.* Stuttgart: Kohlhammer, 2002.

Tollington, Janet E. "Readings in Haggai: From the Prophet to the Completed Book, a Changing Message in Changing Times." Pages 194–208 in *The Crisis of Israelite Religion: Transformation of Religious Tradition in Exilic and Post-Exilic Times.* Edited by Bob Becking and Marjo C.A. Korpel. Oudtestamentische Studiën 42. Leiden: Brill, 1999.

——. *Tradition and Innovation in Haggai and Zechariah 1–8.* Journal for the Study of the Old Testament: Supplement Series 150. Sheffield: JSOT Press, 1993.

Toorn, Karel van der. *Family Religion in Babylonia, Syria and Israel: Continuity and Change in the Forms of Religious Life*. Studies in the History and Culture of the Ancient Near East 7. Leiden: Brill, 1996.

———. *From Her Cradle to Her Grave: The Role of Religion in the Life of the Israelite and the Babylonian Woman*. Translated by Sara J. Denning-Bolle. The Biblical Seminar 23. Sheffield: JSOT Press, 1994.

Torrey, Charles C. *Ezra Studies*. New York: Ktav, 1970.

Trotter, James M. "Was the Second Jerusalem Temple a Primarily Persian Project?" *Scandinavian Journal of the Old Testament* 15 (2001): 276–94.

Tubb, Jonathan N., and Peter G. Dorrell. "Tell Es-Saʿidiyeh 1993: Interim Report on the Seventh Season of Excavations." *Palestine Exploration Quarterly* 126 (1994): 52–67.

Tufnell, Olga, with contributions by Margaret A. Murray and David Diringer. *Lachish III (Tell Ed-Duweir): The Iron Age*. Oxford: Oxford University Press, 1953.

Turner, Victor W. "The Center Out There: Pilgrim's Goal." *History of Religions* 12 (1973): 191–230.

———. "Pilgrimage and Communitas." *Studia Missionalia* 23 (1974): 305–27.

———. *The Ritual Process: Structure and Anti-Structure*. Chicago: Aldine, 1969.

———, and Edith Turner. *Image and Pilgrimage in Christian Culture*. New York: Columbia University Press, 1978.

Uehlinger, Christoph. "Die Frau im Efa (Sach 5,5–11): Eine Programmvision von der Abschiebung der Göttin." *Bibel und Kirche* 49 (1994): 93–103.

Ussishkin, David. "The Borders and *De Facto* Size of Jerusalem in the Persian Period." Pages 147–66 in *Judah and the Judeans in the Persian Period*. Edited by Oded Lipschits and Manfred Oeming. Winona Lake, Ind.: Eisenbrauns, 2006.

———. "Excavations at Tel Lachish – 1973–1977, Preliminary Report." *Tel Aviv* 5 (1978): 1–97, plates 1–32.

———. "Excavations at Tel Lachish – 1978–1983, Second Preliminary Report." *Tel Aviv* 10 (1983): 97–175, plates 38–40.

———. *The Renewed Archaeological Excavations at Lachish (1973–1994)*. 5 vols. Publications of the Institute of Archaeology 22. Tel Aviv: Emery and Claire Yass Publications in Archaeology, 2004.

Van Beek, Gus W. "Frankincense and Myrrh." *Biblical Archaeologist* 23 (1960): 70–95.

———. "Monuments of Axum in the Light of South Arabian Archaeology." *Journal of the American Oriental Society* 87.2 (1967): 113–22.

——. "The Reexcavation of Sites: Tell Jemmeh." Pages 575–80 in *Biblical Archae-ology Today, 1990:Proceedings of the Second International Congress on Biblical Archaeology, Jerusalem, June–July 1990*. Edited by Avraham Biran and Joseph Aviram. Jerusalem: Israel Exploration Society, 1993.

Van Seters, John. *Abraham in History and Tradition*. New Haven, Conn.: Yale University Press, 1975.

Vaughn, Andrew G. "Is Biblical Archaeology Theologically Useful Today? Yes, A Programmatic Proposal." Pages 407–30 in *Jerusalem in Bible and Archae-ology: The First Temple Period*. Edited by Andrew G. Vaughn and Ann E. Killebrew. Society of Biblical Literature Symposium Series 18. Leiden: Brill, 2003.

——. *Theology, History, and Archaeology in the Chronicler's Account of Hezekiah* (Archaeology and Biblical Studies 4; Atlanta: Scholars Press, 1999).

Wampler, Joseph Carson, with a chapter by Chester Charlton McCown. *Tell en-Naṣbeh Excavated under the Direction of the Late William Frederic Badè: The Pottery*. Berkeley: The Palestine Institute of Pacific School of Religion and the American Schools of Oriental Research, 1947.

Weinberg, Joel. *The Citizen-Temple Community*. Translated by Daniel L. Smith-Christopher. Journal for the Study of the Old Testament: Supplement Series 151. Sheffield: Sheffield Academic Press, 1992.

Weinfeld, Moshe. "Zion and Jerusalem as Religious and Political Capital: Ideology and Utopia." Pages 75–115 in *The Poet and the Historian: Essays in Literary and Historical Biblical Criticism*. Edited by Richard Elliott Friedman. Harvard Semitic Studies 26. Chico, Ca.: Scholars Press, 1983.

Weippert, Helga. *Palästina in vorhellenistischer Zeit*. Handbuch der Archäologie, Vorderasien 2.1. München: C. H. Beck, 1988.

Wellhausen, Julius. *Die kleinen Propheten: übersetzt und erklärt*. Berlin: de Gruyter, 1963.

——. *Prolegomena to the History of Ancient Israel*. Translated by J. Sutherland Black and Allan Enzies, with preface by W. Robertson Smith. New York: Meridian Books, 1957.

Whybray, R. N. *Isaiah 40–66*. New Century Bible. London: Oliphants, 1975.

Wijngaards, J. "הוציא and העלה: A Twofold Approach to the Exodus." *Vetus Testamentum* 15 (1965): 91–102.

Willi-Plein, Ina. "Warum musste der Zweite Tempel gebaut werden?" Pages 57–73 in *Gemeinde ohne Tempel = Community without Temple: Zur Substituierung und Transformation des Jerusalemer Tempels und seines Kults im Alten Testament, antiken Judentum und frühen Christentum*. Edited by Beate Ego, Armin Lange and Peter Pilhofer. Wissenschaftliche Untersuchungen zum Neuen Testament 118. Tübingen: J. C. B. Mohr (Paul Siebeck), 1999.

Williamson, Hugh G. M. *1 and 2 Chronicles*. New Century Bible. Grand Rapids, Mich.: Eerdmans, 1982.

———. "The Composition of Ezra i–iv." *Journal of Theological Studies* NS 34 (1983): 1–30.

———. *Ezra, Nehemiah*. Word Biblical Commentary 16. Waco, Tex.: Word Books, 1985.

———. "The Family in Persian Period Judah: Some Textual Reflections." Pages 469–85 in *Symbiosis, Symbolism, and the Power of the Past: Canaan, Ancient Israel, and Their Neighbors from the Late Bronze Age through Roman Palaestina. Proceedings of the Centennial Symposium W. F. Albright Institute of Archaeological Research and American Schools of Oriental Research, Jerusalem, May 29–31, 2000*. Edited by William G. Dever and Seymour Gitin. Winona Lake, Ind.: Eisenbrauns, 2003.

———. "Judah and the Jews." Pages 145–63 in *Studies in Persian History: Essays in Memory of David M. Lewis*. Edited by Maria Brosius and Amélie Kuhrt. Achaemenid History 11. Leiden: Nederlands Instituut voor het Nabije Oosten, 1998.

———. "The Temple in the Books of Chronicles." Pages 150–61 in *Studies in Persian Period History and Historiography*. Forschungen zum Alten Testament 38. Tübingen: Mohr Siebeck, 2004.

Wright, Jacob L. *Rebuilding Identity: The Nehemiah-Memoir and its Earliest Readers*. Beihefte zur Zeitschrift für die alttestamentliche Wissenschaft 348. Berlin: Walter de Gruyter.

Yadin, Yigael. "Symbols of Deities at Zinjirli, Carthage and Hazor." Pages 199–231 in *Near Eastern Archaeology in the Twentieth Century*. Edited by James A. Sanders. Garden City, N.Y.: Doubleday, 1970.

Zadok, Ran. *The Jews in Babylonia During the Chaldean and Achaemenian Periods According to the Babylonian Sources*. Studies in the History of the Jewish People and the Land of Israel Monograph Series 3. Haifa: University of Haifa, 1979.

Zaidman, Louise Bruit, and Pauline Schmitt Pantel. *Religion in the Ancient Greek City*. Translated by Paul Cartledge. New York: Cambridge University Press, 1992.

Ziegler, Liselotte. "Tonkästchen aus Uruk, Babylon und Assur." *Zeitschrift für Assyriologie* 47 (1942): 224–40.

Zimmerli, Walther. *Ezekiel 1: A Commentary on the Book of the Prophet Ezekiel, Chapters 1–24*. Translated by Ronald E. Clements. Hermeneia. Philadelphia: Fortress, 1979.

Zorn, Jeffrey Ralph. "Estimating the Population Size of Ancient Settlements: Methods, Problems, Solutions, and a Case Study." *Bulletin of the American Schools of Oriental Research* 295 (1994): 31–48.

———. "An Inner and Outer Gate Complex at Tell en-Nasbeh." *Bulletin of the American Schools of Oriental Research* 307 (1997): 53–66.

———. "Mizpeh: Newly Discovered Stratum Reveals Judah's Other Capital." *Biblical Archaeology Review* 23.5 (September/ October 1997): 28–38, 66.

———. "Naṣbeh, Tell en-." Pages 1098–1102 in vol. 3 of *The New Encyclopedia of Archaeological Excavations in the Holy Land*. Edited by E. Stern. 4 vols. Jerusalem: Israel Exploration Society & Carta, 1993.

———. "Tell en-Naṣbeh: A Reevaluation of the Architecture and Stratigraphy of the Early Bronze Age, Iron Age and Later Periods." 4 vols. Ph.D. diss., University of California at Berkeley, 1993.

———. "Tell En-Naṣbeh and the Problem of the Material Culture of the Sixth Century." Pages 413–47 in *Judah and the Judeans in the Neo-Babylonian Period*. Edited by Oded Lipschits and Joseph Blenkinsopp. Winona Lake, Ind.: Eisenbrauns, 2003.

Zwickel, Wolfgang. *Räucherkult und Räuchergeräte: Exegetische und archäologische Studien zum Räucheropfer im Alten Testament*. Orbis biblicus et orientalis 97. Freiburg: Universitätsverlag, 1990.

Index of Primary Sources

ANCIENT NEAR EASTERN, GREEK, AND JEWISH NONBIBLICAL WRITINGS

INDEX OF ANCIENT NAMES AND PLACES

Geographic Names and Regions

Index of Modern Authorities

Printed in the United States
63140LVS00006B/289-405